THE BOY WHO DREW
AUSCHWITZ

THE BOY WHO DREW AUSCHWITZ

A POWERFUL TRUE STORY OF HOPE AND SURVIVAL

THOMAS GEVE

with CHARLES INGLEFIELD

HARPER

An Imprint of HarperCollins*Publishers*

HarperCollins books may be purchased for educational, business, or sales promotional use. For information, please email the Special Markets Department at SPsales@harpercollins.com.

Originally published as *Youth in Chains* in 1958 and *Guns & Barbed Wire* in 1987.

Updated illustrated edition originally published in the United Kingdom in 2021 by HarperCollins Publishers.

FIRST U.S. EDITION

Text and drawings © Thomas Geve 2021

All original artworks by Thomas Geve, holder of the copyrights thereof, are part of Yad Vashem Art Museum collection. Photographs of the drawings © Yad Vashem Art Museum, Jerusalem

Maps by Lovell Johns © HarperCollins Publishers Ltd 2021

Photographs courtesy of the author with the following exceptions: p. 30, United States Holocaust Memorial Museum, courtesy of Ilona Penner Blech; p. 47, Bildarchiv Pisarek/akg-images; p. 266, © Paul Bodot/AFBDK Paris; p. 277, Ardean R. Miller, National Archives, Washington; p. 278, Walter Chichersky, National Archives, Washington; p. 282, Charles W. Herr, Jr., National Archives, Washington.

Library of Congress Cataloging-in-Publication Data has been applied for.

ISBN 978-0-06-306199-6

21 22 23 24 25 TC 10 9 8 7 6 5 4 3 2 1

In memory of:

Eva-Ruth
Sally
Jonathan
'Little Kurt'
'Long Kurt'
'Blond Gert'
'Saucy Gert'
Ello, a lad from Slovakia
Mendel, a lad from Bialystok
Jendroe, a lad from Bohemia
Maurice, a lad from Salonika
Leo, a Dutchman
Poldi, a Swiss
Mr Pollack, a Czech
Block doctor 7a, a Belgian
Sigi, room-elder 7a, a German
Block-elder 7a, a German
Camp hairdresser, a German

CONTENTS

FOREWORD

It was often said that survivors of the Holocaust were silent after the Second World War. True, for many it was a suffering too painful to recount, and for some it remains so to this very day. But many did want to speak. They had promised their fellow inmates, most of whom did not survive, that they would bear witness and tell the world. And so they tried, only to encounter a world unable and often unwilling to hear. Survivors of the Holocaust were not silent. They were silenced.

Thomas Geve was among those who attempted immediately after the Holocaust to explain in detail what had just happened. At first, he simply wanted to tell his father, through an album of drawings. His father had been in England during the Second World War and could never imagine what his child had been through. Then Thomas wrote down his experiences for publication, only to be disappointed. But he did not give up. For over seventy-five years he has told the story you are about to read, a story that will take you deep into the terrifying world of the Nazi concentration camp system, where children, like him, were its prey.

Thomas Geve is a remarkable documentarian. His determination to detail what happened in the death and work camps in the Nazi concentration camp world reaches back into Auschwitz itself, where he found charcoal and scraps of cement sacks – he was in the bricklaying Commando – and sketched what happened there in real time. The original sketches did not survive, but the memory of what was on those scraps of paper remained in his mind, and immediately after the war, he began to draw again. He saw that other former inmates were documenting what had happened. He had his own facts to share. Somehow, the 13-year-old in Auschwitz had the presence of mind to pay attention to the details – to check, measure, count and memorise. He had remembered the daily routine by the hour, the ration portions to the gram. Even the colours of the badges the prisoners wore were committed to his mind's eye.

It seems that Geve perceived something at his tender age that adults many years his senior took much longer to realise: the minute detail of how the concentration camp system worked is key to understanding the nature of the crime itself. Through his innate curiosity, he understood that the malfeasance was so unbelievable that it may in fact not be believed, or that details could one day be erased. He was right of course: the role of Auschwitz-Birkenau at the heart of industrialised state-sanctioned genocide resulted in over a million Jews being gassed in carefully designed facilities. It was and remains unprecedented, and deserves our attention, but it was not all that happened there. Wrapped around those killing facilities was an entire machinery of sadistic daily torture and depravation. The Nazis not only murdered their victims; they created an entire system to make them suffer. That is what Geve documented first in his drawings, then in his text.

I have observed that there is a stickiness to testimony. The facts that survivors recount in their testimonies do not drift as much as one might imagine over time. I have also observed that the sooner after events accounts were documented, the more likely they are to reveal the precise nuances of the individual's own direct experience, without the overlay of later tropes and reader expectations. Geve's testimony is a case in point. His first drawings were sketched in Auschwitz in 1944, followed in 1945 by the full set of more than eighty, many of which you will encounter in this book. He then wrote an accompanying narrative in 1947, when the memories were still vivid and not interpolated with later reflection, published in 1958 as *Youth in Chains*. Through the immediacy of Geve's account, we get close and personal details of other inmates' characters, including the friends he made and lost. We learn about the moral ambiguity within the inmate hierarchy, and the pervasiveness of sexual violence among the prisoner population, both of which are often muted in accounts that survivors gave later. We also learn of the power of friendship and the sacrifices made to help each other survive. Though it is well known that some prisoners cooperated for survival, especially in the women's sections, I have never heard testimony of a four-way food pact such as he and three of his friends created. Aspects of his story are positive in ways that are new and insightful.

Geve's arrival at Auschwitz is chillingly and correctly recounted. 'For miles, I could see no trees, just empty fields. A mist rose in the distance, doubtless hiding whatever was lurking there and waiting for us.' Geve accurately describes his arrival at Auschwitz at the little-known *Alte-Juden Rampe* – the old Jewish platform, a siding in a barren landscape out of view of the camp structures. Over 600,000 Jews arrived there, but it is rarely described in later accounts, because the image of the trains pulling directly into Birkenau surrounded by barracks, with the white-gloved Josef Mengele standing by, has become the authoritative version of arrival at Auschwitz. But Geve did not know that then. And so he told the only version he knew – the one he experienced.

Seventy-five years later there is a raw and authentic ring to Geve's descriptions only possible in the immediate aftermath. He talks about victims' groups such as the Roma and political prisoners with disarming clarity. His description of the Death March, and helping the most needy while walking with blistered and aching feet, shows his sense of community and generosity even in the direst of circumstances. Most importantly, Geve's account provides an insight into just how much inmates really did know about what was happening around them, and precisely *how* it happened. It also shows that the inmates themselves could not comprehend the magnitude of what was unfolding before their eyes. On one drawing, Geve estimates the total death toll in the gas chambers to be hundreds of thousands. It is not that he was being inaccurate; at the time he was there, the tally was not calculated for the benefit of the prisoners. How could he possibly have guessed the number of Jews, gypsies and others would be so much higher?

I am grateful to Charles Inglefield for retaining much of the original testimony. While this edition of Geve's testimony is now layered with nearly eight decades of revisions and additions, the central spine of the text is faithful to his 1947 manuscript, his 1958 publication *Youth in Chains* and his 1987 edition of *Guns and Barbed*

Wire (both of which I have reviewed). Testimony does not provide the kind of evidentiary document that, say, an original photograph or transport list provides. But it is its own kind of historical document; one that provides the human story. Testimony is an extension of the author's lived experiences, seen through the ever-changing prism of life, over time. What marks Geve out is that he has consistently chosen to be faithful to his original text and reflect his testimony through the impressions he documented at the time. To this day, he takes us back to when he first told his story; that is what makes this book so unique, so authentic.

While reading this book I would urge you to take time to linger on Geve's drawings. Rarely does testimony come in both words and pictures. These two are his testament. The simple child-like stylisation belies the complex truths they tell. I imagine him as a 15-year-old furiously drawing on tiny index cards with swastikas on the back, the war not yet over, as he set to work. Even then, he knew he was the eyes and ears of the world.

He still is.

Stephen D. Smith PhD
**Finci-Viterbi Executive Director Chair USC Shoah Foundation
UNESCO Chair on Genocide Education**

INTRODUCTION

In November 1945, I arrived in London, carrying in my suitcase an album of drawings, my silent witness to 22 months of life and survival in three concentration camps. The album was for my dear father, Erich, whom I hadn't seen for six long years of war.

A year later an enthusiastic young journalist contacted me. He got to know me and my drawings and believed in the importance of revealing them to the world. He then urged me to put my drawings into words, and so I did. Writing allowed me to add another layer of expression to the facts and scenes that I had drawn. The words brought back memories, experiences, thoughts, fears, consolations and victories, all of which had been part of life during those harsh years of war. They also allowed me to talk about the many different people I had come across. The variety of human interaction and reaction – from despair to hope, from defeatism to bravery, from cruelty to kindness – all was there and everyone was affected. Most of all, these stories gave voice to my comrades who did not get to see the day of liberation. My world was their world as well. My words would give their personalities and dreams, which had perished so unfairly and too soon, eternal life.

Back in 1946, the world wasn't ready to hear. Although the London publishers shared the journalist's interest in my story, they did not have the enthusiasm to print it. 'The boy is not a Picasso,' they said. 'And audiences are looking for more cheerful topics nowadays.' Coloured printing was also beyond most publishing budgets in Europe in those post-war years.

However, my inner calling to tell the world what had really happened in Europe during the Second World War did not vanish. Years later, in 1958, a small pocket version of my word-testimony was published for the first time. My wish to protect my privacy as well as my belief that this story was not just my own but that of my camp comrades and our whole generation brought about my decision to choose a pseudonym. Thomas Geve became my testimonial name and has remained a part of my identity to this present day.

Over the years, my written and drawn testimony has been

published in different versions and languages, as well as through various media. I became an active witness, giving talks to students and adults across Europe.

In summer 2019, yet another journalist contacted me. It was Charles Inglefield. He was gripped by the testimony and believed it should be re-published in a wider and updated version. This young man's interest and dedication more than 70 years later warmed my heart. This time, not only did London share the interest but HarperCollins also had the enthusiasm. We are honoured they became our publisher.

Seventy-five years ago, I set out merely to record the truth. It became my life's mission to pass on these facts, details and stories so that they will forever be believed and remembered. I am privileged to share with you, dear reader, this new edition of my written and drawn testimony. I truly hope that it will be an eternal reminder of our human calling to make our world a kinder place for all.

This grim chapter of our past was created by people and it is people who can create a brighter future …

Thomas Geve, 2020

PROLOGUE – AN UNKNOWN FUTURE BERLIN

1939

It was a hot, stifling summer's day. Shoppers, travellers and sightseers descended upon Potsdamer Platz. Delicatessens displayed delicious luxuries, neatly wrapped and labelled. Florists showcased roses in full bloom while people admired the latest noise-free trams making their way through the heart of the city. Berlin was abuzz with activity and invention. There was much to admire, with a new subway station, a triumph of modern engineering, and queues forming outside the government's experimental television studio.

At the big glass- and steel-topped railway terminal, a semaphore arm was raised. The green light was given and yet another train puffed westwards. It was taking one of the last transports of men, who, threatened with imprisonment, had no place in this new Germany: Jews, freethinkers, democrats and socialists. Their destination was England. But it was already crowded. Others were knocking at her door, too: Austrians, Czechs, Italians and Spaniards were all seeking refuge. Among those men on the train was a Jewish doctor. He was one of the lucky few to be admitted.

A neatly dressed boy of nine, tall for his age and with meticulously combed hair soaked in brilliantine, was standing in front of a florist's window. He was bored with waiting and passed the time watching droplets of water trickling down the inside of the shop's windowpane. Through the condensation, he recognised roses, tulips and orchids. How well they were looked after.

A young and attractive dark-haired woman wearing her Sunday-best emerged from the throng of passers-by. She stopped in front of the florist's. She was crying. The boy was abruptly jerked away from his dreamy paradise of dew-dropped flowers. He thought, *Why must people be nervous and crying? After all, it is a beautiful day.*

The boy was me, the woman my mother, Berta,[1] and the Jewish doctor on the train was my father, Erich.[2]

Potsdamer Platz was busy, but now we felt alone. We returned to my grandparents' place, our temporary home. My grandfather, Julius, and my grandmother, Hulda,[3] lived at 19 Winterfeld Strasse, a quiet middle-class street in Schöneberg, Berlin's seventh district.

'I'll be busy making arrangements for joining Dad,' sighed Mother, 'and grandparents have their own worries, so you'll have to be a good boy from now on without someone there to discipline you.'

That day I thought for the first time about what people called 'the future'. I grappled with my thoughts and tried to imagine what was to follow. It had all happened so abruptly, so unexpectedly, and far too quickly for me to understand.

PART 1

CHAPTER 1
STETTIN AND BEUTHEN
1929-39

I was born in the autumn of 1929, in Stettin on the Baltic, near the Oder in Germany.* Mother, too, had been born there, while Father hailed from Beuthen in Upper Silesia. My father had studied medicine and had served briefly in the First World War before taking over the practice of Dr Julius Goetze in Stettin. Now established as a General Practitioner with his own practice, he fell in love and married my mother, Berta, the doctor's daughter.

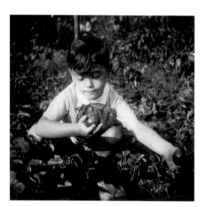

Picking the best tomatoes – Stettin, 1933.

As a toddler, strange faces seemed to have frightened me. Like most babies, my pastime was crying. The nightly wail of the siren that called out the voluntary fire brigade terrified me. For it sounded like the howling of a monster lurking in the dark, eager to snatch me away at the first opportunity.

Time passed and my early childhood became more cheerful. Auntie Ruth,[4] my mother's sister, took me on rowing trips across the Oder to our garden plot. Being in nature and sitting in a boat in the middle of the wide stream made great impressions on me. Even more so than being allowed to pick and devour the best tomatoes. There were also fun excursions to seaside resorts. I loved being around animals and plants and being surrounded by nature. But my favourite occupation was that of snail hunting: catching and collecting slimy little rolls that climbed up park walls.

* Nowadays this is Poland.

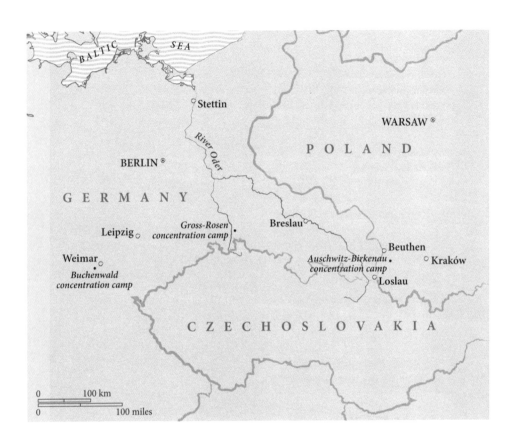

This map shows the position of the German-Polish border in the 1930s.

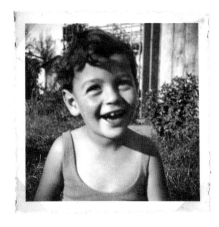

My happy early childhood – Stettin 1933

When, in 1933, Hitler came to power, these leisurely and carefree times disappeared.

My father had been a doctor and surgeon in Stettin, but lost his practice due to the discriminatory laws, and we had to return to his hometown of Beuthen, about three hundred kilometres south-east of Berlin. Mother's family, including Auntie Ruth and my grandparents, had moved to Berlin. And although I was only three then, I felt that I was constantly being left in the care of others, including my Aunt Irma[5] and our housekeeper, Magda.[6]

Beuthen was a mining town of some hundred thousand inhabitants with a strong Polish community. The German/Poland borders crossed suburbs, parks and even mining tunnels. Some of Beuthen's streets had both German and Polish tramways running through them. People there spoke Polish in what was Germany, and German in what was Poland. When I returned from walks to the suburbs to Krakauer Strasse 1, a large four-storey building where we lived, I was never quite certain which of the two countries I had actually been through.

The town's main square was even more confusing. To simple folk, it was 'The Boulevard'. To more pedantic people, it was 'Kaiser Franz Joseph Square'. But now, the new power in Beuthen decided it would become 'Adolf Hitler Square'. And it was on that square that pure and loyal Germans swore allegiance to their new god.

If I had not been told off, I might have cheerfully joined them. For I rather liked this new cult. It meant flags, shiny police horses, colourful uniforms, torchlights and music. It was also free and easily accessible, meaning that I did not have to pester Dad to take me to a Punch and Judy show or be treated to an hour beside my auntie's radio set. But I was chided for my improper enthusiasm towards this new presence in town. Instead I was given more pocket money, and, to avoid any further embarrassment to the family, an instruction to toe the family's anti-Nazi line – whatever that meant to a four-year-old boy.

So, I obeyed. While the other youngsters on the square learned of their superior origin and destiny, my role would be that of the underdog.

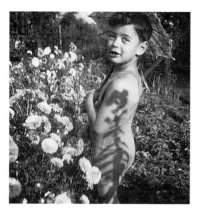

Enjoying the beauty of nature – Beuthen, 1936.

Quickly, my life became a more secluded one. In the morning I was escorted to the nearby Jewish kindergarten. The afternoons were filled with solitary play or piano lessons under the tutelage of Father's sister, Irma, a music teacher, who now lived with us.

I was supposed to have inherited much of Auntie Irma's musical ability, but my rebellious temperament soon ruled out the chance of my becoming a slave to the giant, black 'Bechstein' piano. Instead, my talents were limited to gobbling up the fragrant apples that served as props to help me learn how the musical notes split into fractions. My interest in playing a musical instrument vanished, but my love of music, songs and remembering lyrics had just been ignited.

In 1936, aged six, I started at Beuthen's Jewish school. Father, too, had once felt its cane, the punishment cellar and its strict Prussian discipline. He, likewise, had retaliated by scribbling and etching on the school's benches.

Father's teachers, already above retirement age, still taught there, and still could not afford anything more than white cheese sandwiches, which made them the subject of general ridicule. Aware of my family traditions, I tried to be a pleasant pupil, but never did more than was absolutely necessary.

We used both old textbooks and new Nazi textbooks. I remember Hitler's birthday, 20 April, being a holiday. On this day, in accordance with some paragraph in the new educational laws, we gathered to hear recitations to the glory of the fatherland. The more insightful of our teachers, however, hinted that we would have no share in that glory.

We learned that there was to be no equality. Our only weapon was pride. We wanted to compete with the new youth movements springing up across Germany. School outings turned into occasions to show off our disciplined marching, impressive singing and sporting prowess. But, one by one, these demonstrations were forbidden. Soon, we could not even retaliate to the stones being thrown at us in our schoolyard by the 'Aryan' boys outside. That would be a crime. Now we had become despised 'Jew boys'. The only playground that remained safe for us was the park at the Jewish cemetery on Piekarska Strasse. We were actually glad to have a safe place to play in.

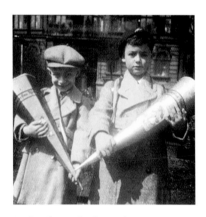

My first day at school – Beuthen, 1936.

At my father's urging, I joined a Zionist sports club, 'Bar Kochba'.* The training was strictly indoors, but the self-confidence it gave us was not so confined. There we learned about the principles of strength and heroism. Our newly acquired courage accompanied us everywhere.

One evening, a friend and I were making our way to the club and passed by the wintry synagogue square. We were greeted by a hail of snowballs. Then came the abusive insults. Behind the columns of the synagogue's arcade, we caught glimpses of black Hitler Youth† uniforms sported by lads who seemed to be about our age.

---

* Bar Kochba was a Jewish leader who was known for his physical fitness and strength and, above all, for his bravery. He led a heroic revolt against the Roman Empire (132–5 CE) and his character gave inspiration to the young Jewish boys.

† The Hitler Youth was the sole youth organisation of the Nazi Party in Germany between 1933 and 1945.

Pride momentarily gained the better of our obligation to be docile underlings, and we gave chase. Our perplexed opponents had not reckoned on the sudden fury that overtook us. I grabbed one of them, threw him onto the snow and hit him repeatedly. When he started yelling, I had to retreat. His friends were nowhere to be seen, and darkness shrouded our little adventure in secrecy. That was to be my first and last chance to hit back openly.

Soon I grew more inquisitive about the world I lived in. We boys sneaked away to visit nearby coalmines, factories and railway installations. Our young minds were thirsty for knowledge.

The glaring white blast furnaces, the endless turning wheels of the pitheads, the enormous slag dumps, the ore-filled trolleys gliding along via sagging overhead steel cables – everything was teeming with activity. Trains in particular fascinated me. The squeaking industrial rail lines and the big black locomotives that came in from afar and relieved their exhaustion by blowing off clouds of smelly steam. It was all waiting to be analysed by our young minds, inspiring us with a desire to understand life. The world was still to be discovered by us.

There was so much for us to explore, despite the restrictions that were enforced on us.

While we roamed the town, curious to discover, Beuthen's Hitler Youth were drilled, marched and taught to sing praises to the glory of their Führer. Not all of them possessed the required mental strength for this training. Some, seeing their future predestined by authoritarian rules, retreated into a state of misery. Others, with less delicate minds, worried about flat feet, corns and blisters, for these were much more realistic obstacles for inclusion in the 'master race'.

A few times a year, Beuthen's streets would come alive with processions. On Ascension Day and Easter, Catholic clerics – masters of pomp and ceremony – would swing incense on elaborately decorated floats, and carry their main attraction, the bishop, under a gold embroidered canopy. And on May Day,

Hitler's substitute for the 1 May holiday, fairs and bandstands would decorate Beuthen, and festive national costumes celebrating industrial and agricultural achievements would be on full display.

In contrast to the joyful sounds and bright colours of celebratory street scenes, increasingly, black jackboots could be heard marching to the tune of sober martial music. The Brownshirts' contrived a new kind of procession: the night-time torchlight parade. Some ended with non-believers, Jews or similarly oppressed people, being beaten up.

My freedom was curtailed. I was ordered to stay home. There I watched these 'shows' from behind drawn curtains, with Mother explaining that these events were 'not for our benefit' and that I was to 'avoid the streets and concentrate on indoor games'.

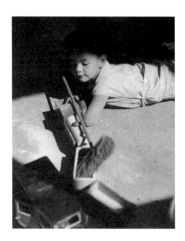

Playing with my Meccano.

Unable to roam freely, I became more friendly with my school mates, inviting the more interesting ones home to play with my Meccano miniature railway set. Quickly, the family objected to my choice of friends.

'Why must you bring these ill-mannered unkempt boys home?' I was admonished. 'Aren't there enough respectable acquaintances of ours – doctors, lawyers, businessmen – whose children you could play with?'

But I was unconcerned with suitability or influence. My idea of having a good time demanded only new ideas, alertness, mutual respect and freedom. Thus, playmates chosen for me from good families never became good friends. Their knowledge of 'the street' was poor, their temperament was affected by their parents' moods, and for every little thing they had to get permission from their maids.

---

* The Sturmabteilung, also known as the SA, were the Nazi Party's original paramilitary wing. The SA were also called the 'Brownshirts' because of the colour of their uniform shirts.

Each year the festival of 'Rejoicing with the Torah'* was celebrated at our synagogue. Accompanied on the organ, children (dressed in their best suits and waving colourful flags) slowly followed the scrolls as they were carried around the temple. We were rewarded with the traditional handing out of sweets and chocolates.

Afterwards, we compared our treasures. My pockets were full, but I could see the disappointed faces of the other children. I was upset, as we should have all been rewarded.

Later, I asked my father about this, and his hesitant reply brought an unpleasant insight into my young mind that spoiled my fun. While most people gave generously to all the children, some people would single you out to take home their 'visiting cards' if your family had influence or social standing. Sweets. It seemed that Father was quite aware of who was distributing the chocolate bars or lollipops. Therefore, if you came from a family of have-nots, even a synagogue ceremony could make you aware of the fact.

One morning, the street underneath my window was humming with the noise of breaking glass, urgent footsteps and excited voices. It woke me up. Aware that it was time to get dressed for school, I got up and tugged at the belt of the roller shutter curtain. But to my surprise, it was only dawn. I peered over towards the pavement opposite our house.

One of the black Daimler cars that boys were so fond of was parked in front of the shoe shop. Our street was littered with shiny, black, brown and white boots, sandals and high-heeled women's shoes and glass splinters. A team of uniformed Brownshirts were busy loading the car with all kinds of treasure. It was obviously a robbery.

Feeling rather like a successful detective, I ran to my parents' room to tell them of this news. Visibly less glad about my discovery, Father phoned the neighbours. There seemed to be general confusion, with only one thing being certain: there would be no school that day.

---

* Rejoicing with the Torah or Simchat Torah is a Jewish holiday that celebrates and marks the end of the annual cycle of public Torah readings and the beginning of a new cycle.

I looked at my wall calendar. It was 9 November 1938* – and the world as our community knew it was about to change dramatically.

More reports came in throughout the day. Beuthen's synagogue was burning. The town's fire brigades refused to help as they were 'busy guarding adjacent buildings'. Heaps of books were being thrown into bonfires on the streets. Jewish shops were being looted all over town. And hundreds of Beuthen's Jews were being arrested.

Dismay and anxiety filled our building. We all assembled into one room, fully dressed and ready for an emergency, dreading the knock on the front door. Finally, the knock came. We opened the door and were face to face with a Brownshirt. His face was harsh and his staring eyes were narrow, hard and cold. His finger glided ominously down a lengthy, typewritten Gestapo list. When his finger stopped, he snarled out the name of an elderly Jew, a former tenant who had since moved elsewhere. Luckily, the Brownshirt was not interested in taking any of us along as a replacement.

Later, we learned that the synagogue had burned down completely and our school was closed for good.

Parents who could afford to do so sent their children away to the countryside, a temporary safe haven. I was sent to a Jewish children's home at Obernick near Breslau, 220 kilometres north-west of Beuthen, for a month. Among its gardens and woods, we had the chance to explore nature. That was wonderful for me and it felt like paradise.

Most of the Jews in Beuthen who could emigrate did so.† My father, a veteran of the First World War and well-known Zionist, planned to get us to England. From there we could reach Palestine, the land of Israel. But progress was slow, despite our growing desperation. A decision was made for me to move to Berlin at the beginning of 1939 to stay with my grandparents.

---

* Now known as *Kristallnacht* or the Night of Broken Glass, 9 November 1938 saw the November Pogrom, carried out against Jews by SA paramilitary forces and civilians all across Nazi Germany.

† In the summer of 1938, at the Evian Conference, the world had condemned Nazi treatment of Jews, but had done nothing to make emigration easier. The Nazi regime interpreted this lack of action as tacit acceptance of their eugenic policies.

The world was not kind to refugees. People talked a lot about Birobizhan* as a potential sanctuary from the persecution for European Jews, but few ever took it seriously. Polish Jews in Germany were being deported by force back to Poland. The Poles were no more eager to have them than the Germans were. 'This can't happen to us' was the consensus among German Jews: 'We are Germans.'

Rumours, an inevitable consequence of censorship in a totalitarian regime, abounded and kept circulating like some biased, hidden newspaper. We knew an 'Aryan'† who was a member of the Nazi Labour army, O.T.‡ Unemployment had forced him to join this underpaid organisation to work on local road and canal construction projects.

Considering himself to be knowledgeable, he urged us to leave Germany as soon as possible. His predictions for the future – our future – seemed emphatically grim, possibly even uttered with a certain amount of malice.

The summer of 1939 saw my family leave Beuthen for good. Father left for England; Mother and I to my grandparents' apartment in Berlin. We were planning to join him soon after. I tried to imagine what our new life would be like once we were reunited with him in England. But history had her own plan and in September of that year the Second World War broke out and all borders were shut. Mother and I stayed in Berlin.

---

*Birobizhan was a Jewish autonomous region in the Soviet Union created in 1931 on the Soviet-Chinese border. As it was an inhospitable piece of land, and Jews living there were being still being persecuted in the Stalinist purges of the 1930s, it did not provide a feasible refuge to escape the Nazis.

† 'Aryan' was the Nazi's definition of pure Germanic stock.

‡ Organisation Todt (O.T.) – Fritz Todt was a prominent Nazi.

CHAPTER 2
BERLIN
1939–40

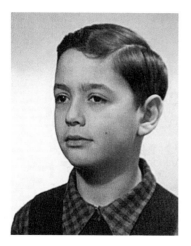

Moving to Berlin, 1939.

Mother had been busy making arrangements for settling in Berlin, so I was once more left in the care of her sister Ruth, an art and English teacher. Auntie Ruth had all the qualities of a true friend. She was fun, interesting and always teeming with new ideas and progressive thinking. Ruth was an idol to her pupils.

Auntie Ruth took me along to the Jewish school on Ryke Strasse in north Berlin, where she taught. My classmates there were real city children, conversant with the local slang, swank and swagger. At first, I was looked down upon as a country yokel, but soon they came to like my down-to-earth character, and eventually I became a fully-fledged Berliner. As I did so, my initial frightening impression of Berlin's city life gave way to an understanding of its make-up.

The city's routine began with the baker, the milkman and the newspaper boy doing their rounds. Later in the morning, the hawkers of brushes, shoe polish, flowers and the ragpicker would come. They all worked the streets of closely packed apartment buildings, which hugged each other for metropolitan warmth. Behind them, smaller buildings crowded around backyards. Their dirty brick walls reverberated with the sounds of city life: blaring radio sets, the beating of dusty carpets, crying children, squeaking staircases, twittering canaries and quarrelling couples.

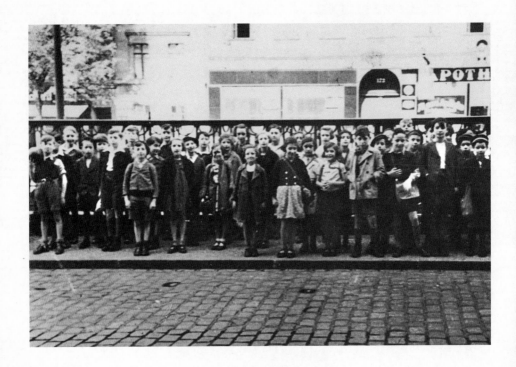

Children at the Ryke Strasse school in 1939, which I attended for a few
months only that same year.

For a while, the rise and reach of Hitler and National Socialism did not seem to matter; Berlin-life moved to its own rhythm and rules. One could not expect an occupant of a working-class tenement house to concern himself deeply with questions of race. He did not care whether the bugs invading his house in search of new feeding grounds had previously sucked Aryan blood or that of supposedly lesser human beings like Jews.

When war came in 1939, the changeover from peacetime seemed almost a technicality. Those who had made nationalism their business were overjoyed – Hitler and his henchmen had prepared Germany well.

Pro-war propaganda had not been defeated in 1918. On the contrary, the fact that peace had become possible had given it a new impetus. Rationing had begun in 1938, so now a few more items became scarce. Food, especially meat and vegetables, was harder to get. Mock air raids and trial blackouts made themselves such a nuisance that the real thing, expected to be less frequent, was greeted with some relief.

But Mother Krause, an archetypical Berlin housewife, was not so certain.

'It's an ill wind that blows no one any good,' she sighed. 'My old instinct tells me.'

The occasional howling of the air-raid siren brought her down to the damp, improvised cellar. There she shared the company of the seventy-odd neighbours who had their blankets, emergency rations, heavy suitcases, dogs and canaries.

Mother Krause had known my grandparents for many years, and she would not offend them. 'My old instinct,' she would mumble, 'does not like Jews, but these don't seem so bad.'

Our food became *ersatz* (substitute). Berlin's bigger department stores like KaDeWe, worried by a lack of provisions, were advised to attract custom with elaborate shows, exploiting all the spoils and ideas from a conquered Europe.

Large shop windows were filled with reconstructions of scenes from Nazi films, including '*Jud Süss*', a twisted, violently anti-Semitic story of a rich courtier; '*Ohm Krüger*', an anti-British account of the Boer War; and a biographical feature on 'Robert Koch' that glorified German medicine.

The experience was different for Jews. They were issued special ration cards with little Js scribbled all over them. These cards prevented us from buying vegetables, meat, milk, chocolate and any special holiday treats that might have previously been allowed. It also meant that we could not buy clothes. We were allowed to shop at 'approved shops' only during the prescribed 'non-Aryan shopping hour' between 4 and 5 p.m. Anti-Jewish laws kept on coming in every two weeks, including one that stipulated that Jews could not sit on trams. If one was rich, the food problem was eased by the black market. If one was both wealthy and Germanic, high-class restaurants could be counted upon to provide a fair diet. Being neither, we could only hope for some help from better-qualified friends.

I turned 11 in 1940 and the time came for me to enter senior school. We were now a poor family and unable to pay fees, so I had to rely on scholarships. A mixed school on Grosse Hamburger Strasse was chosen for me.

The school had troubles of its own. First it was transferred to Kaiser Strasse, and then later to Linden Strasse. The authorities could not care less about a Jew's place of learning, and still less about their feelings. Even the synagogue on Linden Strasse was now a grain store filled with hungry rats.

A classmate of mine, a half-Jew, had a sister at an Aryan school nearby. Some ridiculous court decision declared him a Jew but his sister a Christian. When they met in the street, they had to ignore each other in case someone saw them.

My friends and I amused ourselves with a number of hobbies.

We collected the figures sold to help finance the war. These included carved wooden dolls, and replicas of aeroplanes, guns and shells, which were sold and pinned on people's lapels. They made for quite attractive toys. Every other month there were new models to choose from. To get them, my friends and I followed the example set by the street children of north Berlin. Whoever still wore these adornments on his lapel after collection week was asked politely to surrender them to us. This sport became so popular that passers-by even thought themselves subject to a new kind of recycling scheme.

We also collected children's magazines. They were surprisingly free from the Nazi propaganda and given away at big confectionery stores. We got them by making a favourable impression on the salesgirl or, as a last resort, by buying a packet of pins.

My strangest delight, though, was compiling lists. Bombed-out buildings greatly fascinated me. All their intimate interiors could be seen, and each house had its own characteristic detail. My passion was to jot down in a book, the place, the date and the extent of the destruction.

When Mother found out about this, her stern rebuke made quite an impression on me. 'What if you were caught? How would you prove that you are not a spy for the Allies?'

With an exciting war on, school seemed dull and pointless. Accordingly, I took to exploring Berlin's streets. The school was an hour's journey away, so at home my absence could easily be blamed on heavy traffic, air raids or extra lessons. Plus, the family allowed me ample freedom, so few questions were ever asked. I was now a street boy and blacked-out Berlin became familiar to me.

Books, cinemas and shows were not supposed to be enjoyed by non-Aryans, so it was useless asking for pocket money to pay for them. Instead, I visited exhibitions of captured spoils of war – a must for technically minded youngsters like me. I studied aeroplanes, inspected pilots' seats and propellers, and ignored the notices warning non-Aryans to keep out.

Nor did I miss morale-boosting fairs during the summer of 1940, where Churchill's dummy head could be shot off, and clockwork puppets, dollies and soldier boys danced to the tune of 'Lily Marlene' or '*Wir fahren gegen Engelland*' ('We're going to take on England'). And I passed unnoticed along Friedrich Strasse, where the company of fleshy life-sized 'dolls', dressed in fur coats and the latest fashion from Paris, could be enjoyed for five marks.

My extensive explorations were made possible by the monthly subway tickets provided by the school, and a Hitler Youth uniform, without insignia, as a disguise. It was clearly dangerous for me as a Jew to wear this uniform, but I had little choice. Growing quickly out of my clothes and with no money to buy new ones, the only items of clothing I had were those given to me by a non-Jewish friend.

Once, I emerged from the subway station at Unter den Linden and was pushed straight into a huge parade. Had I backed out, it would have attracted attention, so I played along as an enthusiastic admirer. Peeping through the ranks of closely aligned guards, I had a good view.

Rolling slowly down the broad thoroughfare, accompanied by the noisy jubilation of the crowd, came open-topped black Daimlers. The leading car passed barely 10 yards ahead of me. Hundreds of hands shot up on cue to give the Nazi salute.

The adulation was for a dark-featured, rigid-looking man, with a strange moustache, who gazed ahead without emotion. This man was Adolf Hitler. Behind him followed the large form of Göring and other senior members from the German High Command, all of whom seemed equally unappreciative of the grand applause.

The traditional haunts of the German army and headquarters were in the area between Tiergarten, Potsdamer Platz and the Shell-Haus. I had the most unexpected access to this Nazi labyrinth thanks to a friend, whose mother was the mistress to a high-ranking officer. I was considered to be a well-bred and well-mannered companion, so he picked me out as the only classmate that could be honoured with an invitation to visit.

This was a dangerous world for me to walk into, but I was fascinated. There were field-grey cars lined up neatly between the numerous villas. Inside these buildings, teleprinters ticked relentlessly away, typewriters rattled and Prussians clicked their heels. Mobile radio stations hummed out words of war and there I was – a 'Jew boy' – walking freely and unimpeded.

Here I had my first proper glimpse of Hitler's army, and it was undeniably intimidating and impressive. Pairs of jackbooted military police, with Roman-style polished metal plates on their breasts, stamped through the street. They didn't bother with children like me. And neither did the colonel, who watched us playing chess in his garden.

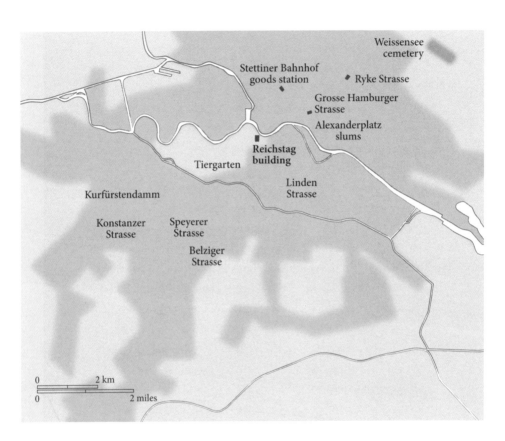

I lived in Berlin from 1939 until 1943.

CHAPTER 3
BERLIN
1941-42

Towards the end of 1941, the Nazi government put up a formidable show of force. That September, Jews had been ordered to wear the six-pointed yellow Star of David.

The stars had to be stitched over the left breast on every piece of clothing. They had to be freely visible whenever and wherever Jews might encounter a non-Jew. Well-bred ladies assured us over cups of *ersatz* coffee that 'Germany's honour will never allow such an outrage. We are a civilised nation and can't go back to the Middle Ages. People will protest in the street!' But sadly, that prophecy did not come true.

When the first Stars of David appeared, some ridiculed the notion, while others mocked the wearers. There followed a period of indifference that gave way to feelings of annoyance at being constantly reminded by the yellow rag of shame. We went without it whenever there was a likelihood of not being recognised by informers.* Under the light of the violet neon lamps that lit Berlin's streets, the yellow stars looked blue. Even better for hiding them were the blacked-out side streets, and, as a last resort, one could carry a newspaper or a satchel pressed underneath the left arm and over one's heart. An evening curfew for Jews was also sanctioned, but its enforcement seemed practically impossible. We generally ignored it despite the risks.

Soon, other labels joined the Star of David. There was P for Poles, and OST for Ukrainians. The decade-old signs forbidding entry to 'Jews' alone had to be taken down and revised. Corrected ones appeared. All public places, from a lone bench to spacious parks, from the telephone booth to the cinema, now displayed notices warning 'non-Aryans' to keep out. Some establishments striving to adhere

---

* The menace of informers in Berlin grew on a daily basis. The threat could come from anywhere: inquisitive neighbours, classmates, former friends, blackmailers, police and others.

strictly to Nazi law showcased signs that were more direct: 'Entrance to dogs, Poles, Russians and Jews strictly forbidden!'

In 1942, Jewish schools closed. Each day fewer students had been attending school anyway. They were not necessarily playing truant; they may have been arrested or gone into hiding. The decree to close the schools came as a bit of a relief for me. Now, there was no more fear of being beaten up on the way home for being a 'Jew boy'. Moreover, I did not believe in textbooks; I believed in technology and what I could see around me. I was able freely to explore Berlin and it opened my eyes and my mind to the wonders of technology and industrial invention.

There were four options open to us Jewish youngsters: nursing at the hospital, cooking in the soup kitchens, sorting files in the community's offices or gardening at the cemetery. I decided to devote a year to the upkeep of Jewish graves at Weissensee cemetery. There was no pay, just the privilege of holding a special travel permit and breathing in fresh air. The vast, walled city of the dead with its marbled mausoleums and crumbling tombstones was peaceful. Only the soothing noise of rustling trees interrupted what we considered to be our haven.

We were organised into working gangs. In spring and summer, we cleaned the weed-ridden footpaths, planted ivy and looked after the flowers. Come autumn, we swept the leaves. And in winter we would remove the snow. The cemetery was the ideal place for playing 'hide and seek' and 'cops and robbers'. Wolfgang[7] and Werner[8] were fellow diggers. The riotous moments of chasing each other over the vast expanses of the graveyard were among my happiest days.

Besides the gardening, that year I was also initiated into the various pleasures of driving a tractor, playing cards and teasing girls. I smoked my first cigarette, and for the first time, a girl, Eva-Ruth,[9] fell in love with me.

Mother had taken a course as a seamstress, and found a job mending army uniforms. On occasion, letters would be found sewn into the linings of blood-stained Wehrmacht-issued trousers.* Their messages, the unheeded warnings of Germany's sons, told of desperate conditions on the Eastern Front. They would say that Leningrad and Moscow were out of reach and only death awaited them in the unforgiving snow-covered Russian fields.

I moved out of my grandparents' apartment, and Mother and I went to Speyerer Strasse near Bayrischer Platz, a once-prominent Jewish quarter. It was a fashionable district, and the rent for one and a half rooms was so high that making ends meet was difficult. Our neighbours, fellow Jews, often invited me to see their valuable stamp collections and paintings – sometimes even for tea. None of them, however, showed an understanding of or cared about our financial troubles.

Around this time, the last letter we ever received from Father arrived from England via the Red Cross. He urged us to be brave. We really had to be.

Hitler's cruel laws penetrated everywhere, having only one aim: victory. Confiscation orders were extended to warm clothes, radio sets and pets of non-Aryans. Our aquarium and parakeets had already been abandoned, so Hitler's attention now turned to Grandfather's cherished crystal set.

Grandpa Julius had been blinded while serving as an officer in the Kaiser's army in the First World War. When in a jovial mood he would sing to me a sentimental song called '*Ich hatt'einen Kameraden*' ('I once had a comrade') about fallen comrades. I had once read him the newspapers, but now his only pleasure was listening through earphones to the 15-year-old cat whisker radio set.

We sent a letter to the War Veterans Federation begging their intervention to let Grandpa keep it. The reply was sympathetic but to no avail. Jews were not allowed to have a radio. There could be no

---

* The Wehrmacht was the armed forces of the Third Reich.

appeals against the orders of the new Reich.

Grandpa died on 19 March 1942, at the age of 71, unable to understand the new ways of his fatherland.

Real anti-Semites avoided all contact with Jews. Although they caused us much suffering, they personally remained unknown to us. However, it was the many helpful, courageous Germans that impressed me. Their sympathy for us did not come from any admiration for our Jewishness, but from adherence to a system of ideals and values that was now being ruthlessly outlawed.

Mother and I, unable to buy any influence, contacted everyone we knew who might be able to help us, but Nazi authorities would come down hard on anyone harbouring Jews. Any helper would be taking a potential risk not only to themselves but also to their own families.

Once, when hiding from yet another wave of arrests, we visited the home of a protestant clergyman from West Berlin's Apostel-Paulus-Kirche on Akazien Strasse. But we had overlooked the fact that his new son-in-law was a devout Nazi. The cleric's help dwindled to no more than keeping our plea for help a secret.

Desperate, we were finally given refuge by a widowed seamstress Clara Bernhard, a workmate of Mother's. Clara put us up on a field-bed in the narrow kitchen of her apartment on Belziger Strasse. Many years before, when Fate had taken her Jewish husband, she had no inkling that someday she would have to reaffirm her loyalty.

Left-wing friends from Auntie Ruth's student days – who had their own reasons to fear arrest – could be counted upon for radio evenings, and I, too, was sometimes taken along to learn of a world I had never seen.

These sessions were a special treat, for we were not allowed radios. To begin with, Radio London would talk of Allied actions and successful air raids. Then came the secret rite our left-wing friends had practised for nearly a decade: the crowding of ears to catch the muffled transmission, '*Hier spricht Moskau*' ('Moscow speaking'). With exhilaration written all over their faces, they listened to the long lists of recaptured Russian positions. Their radiant hope was contagious.

Another act of defiance came through the traditional Red Wedding district in north Berlin chalking its bombed-out buildings with anti-Nazi slogans. Much of the lettering had been done by disillusioned Hitler youths who saw no other way of expressing their grudges. Friends of mine from north Berlin had already contacted some of this new brand of rebel. Their slogans seemed universally appropriate: 'Down with the teachers – they teach ruin.'

Among the highlights of defiance was a bomb planted at a much-heralded anti-Soviet exhibition. Arrests following this incident were so widespread, however, that rumours suggested it was an inside job, like the 1933 Reichstag fire, which the Nazis used to justify their harsh crackdowns.

By the end of 1942, the deportation of Berlin's Jews was escalating on an intensified scale. The rumours at the time said it was mostly to Lublin in Poland. Friends and neighbours became fewer and fewer, with Mother and I in constant fear of the dreaded knock on the door.

Occasionally, I helped out at the bakery on Grenadier Strasse. So, every time it received instructions to provide loaves of bread in large quantities, we were alerted to the fact that another deportation was about to happen.

While working at the bakery I got to know the slums of Alexanderplatz. Gypsy and Jewish tenants seemed to live together in harmony, despite the drunken brawls that typified the district. They lived in abject poverty and overcrowding, but nevertheless the grown-up sons of the Gypsies were conscripted to the Wehrmacht to defend the fatherland.

We were now living alone in the Speyerer Strasse flat. The other tenants' rooms had been sealed up by the Gestapo. All of the valuable paintings and stamp collections that belonged to our neighbours had fallen into Nazi hands. An elderly couple from another floor tried to negotiate their overseas properties for an exemption to be deported. They failed.

Instructions were given to empty the apartments of food before they were sealed off. On one of the backyard staircases a huge chunk of black-market cheese had been abandoned. Its owner had clung to all that was his to the very last.

Mother had been drafted into a factory that assembled miniature coils for speedometers. Only night shifts were available, so I had to get used to spending the evenings alone in an empty flat. Heavy and almost daily air raids exacerbated the situation even further. But I had nowhere else to go. Jews were no longer allowed into bomb shelters. Even when an incendiary bomb whizzed down and smashed onto our backyard, I stayed where I was, trembling and terrified.

There were many less eventful moments, however, that characterised my confinement. Reading, preparing my frugal supper and cleaning up. Often, I toyed with the idea of breaking into the now-deserted neighbours' flats. A sale of a picture or a rug from a sealed-off apartment could have eased our financial problems considerably. It would have meant less overtime for Mother, a square meal and, perhaps, some kind of entertainment.

CHAPTER 4
LIQUIDATION
1943

The last dawn in February 1943 saw the beginning of the total liquidation of Berlin's remaining Jewish communities. As all the other urban and rural districts had already been concentrated in the capital or deported, this represented the end of German Jewry.

Every other Jew was already listed officially as having changed his or her place of residence to Lublin, Riga or Theresienstadt.

Now the final mop-up operation meant cordoning off the streets. Special SS reinforcements and lorries converged on Berlin for the final big round-up. Overseeing the planning and supervision were the infamous Austrian SS Command, whose officers had already rehearsed a similar action on Vienna's Jews.

We were ordered to stay in our apartments, while soldiers went door to door to tick off the last names written on the Gestapo lists. Only a skeleton staff was left for the Jewish hospital, the provisions centre and the cemetery in order to wind up all operations.

A sudden loud knock jerked us to attention. There was no doubting its ominous intentions. We waited for the knocking to stop, silently pleading that it would. But it went on and was now accompanied by nasty abuse. An escape by the back stairs would have been futile. While I noisily clanged the dustbin lids in order to lend support to our charade of having been down to empty the rubbish, Mother finally opened the door.

A man's fists came flying through the door and punched my jaw. The following minutes were agony. I could not see his face, but I could hear him grunting and snarling as he laid into me. For not obeying the order to close all the windows, I was beaten repeatedly by the SS officer. This was my first close encounter with the SS and I emerged with my ears and face boxed more thoroughly than I had ever experienced before.

With our keys handed over and the rooms sealed, Mother and I stumbled towards the waiting lorry, each of us carrying a single cumbersome suitcase.

'*Heraus, schnell, schnell!*' ('Out, quickly, quickly!') echoed fiercely behind us.

A long, stressful and tiring tour, in quest of new victims, awaited us. Elderly people hardly able to carry themselves, let alone their suitcases, were dragged along the pavement and pushed roughly into the truck. Children in the streets spat at them. Other spectators, silenced by a mixture of surprise, shame and malice, just stared at us.

Through a slit in the truck's tarpaulin, I peeped at our passing surroundings. There were reminders from the air raid the night before, with roadblocks isolating the destroyed Prager Platz. Demolished quarters were still smouldering. The bombing had finally reached a stage where it had to be taken seriously. Despite this, there were no delays in our arrests. The Fascist Beast was still strong and intact. Only its eastern fangs were bleeding.

Towards dusk, our lorry joined the others queuing up in front of an improvised detention camp.

Ours was one of six on Grosse Hamburger Strasse.* Ironically, I was being taken back to the site of my former school, which, together with a home for the elderly and the ancient cemetery, had been demolished to make way for our arrival. Once inside, we were now caged prisoners. We were processed according to numerous lists that we knew nothing about. All of us were being prepared for final transports to the East. There were perhaps five hundred to a thousand people in the camp, the last remnants of Berlin's Jewish community.

The guards were impervious Berlin policemen. There was nothing for us to do but spend the time wandering around the cemetery grounds racking our brains for ways of an escape. Climbing the wall seemed possible to me, but not for Mother. I could not imagine leaving her. And anyway, the repercussions for her, let alone for me if I were caught, would have been unthinkably severe. Plus, as a declared 'enemy of the state' and the 'worst kind of being', a Jew, how would I have made it on the outside?

---

* Grosse Hamburger Strasse in Berlin became an assembly point from which Jews were transported.

One remaining tomb in the cemetery, imprisoned by a little wire-cage of its own, attracted many a contemplating glance. It was the resting place of Moses Mendelssohn, the famous Jewish philosopher. Many drew inspiration from this reminder of past glory; perhaps the great man's teachings would prevail?

A committee within the camp had been set up to hear the pleas of family members trying to reunite with each other. Few reports ever went through to the commanding police officer, and of these most were rejected, but the imprisoned were aware that this was their last hope.

Half-Jews and nationals from neutral countries had the best chance of getting released. Any other attempt to cheat the sadistic talents of the police and Gestapo was pointless and dangerous. A crowded cellar prison provided the necessary intimidation.

Trying to fake evidence bore harsh punishments. I looked at my cards: I had no 'Aryan' blood in the family, no chance of a foreign government intervention and no money for bribes. I clutched desperately at one last trump card. I could bury the dead. First, I had to convince Mother. She agreed with me, so I approached the only Jew left on the Appeals Committee, Rabbi Martin Riesenburger, who had occasionally officiated at burials.

'Yes,' he exclaimed tiredly, 'I have seen your face before. You are one of those flower boys. Don't kid yourself that you are essential; you can't even dig a pit.'

Mustering all of my determination and courage, I promised to do whatever I would be called upon to do. I never knew what made him change his mind. Perhaps it was my healthy and tanned appearance – I was not like the Jewish boys immersed in books that the rabbi used to see on his daily trips to the synagogue. But the rabbi changed his tone.

'I'll check up on the number of cemetery workers still left. There may be a need for replacements. What about your family?'

'Only Mother,' I replied.

His searching glance fixed itself on me. His stare met my stare. They were long seconds. 'All right, if it's only two of you I'll try.'

The hours that followed were mental torture. Imagination's hopeful light struggled with the more obvious darkness of our common fate.

Despair was winning over hope. Finally, the commandant granted me a hearing.

I clicked my heels, trying to replicate the German military salute, and stood upright to suggest that I was older than my age. An adjutant recited my usefulness to the Third Reich, which was then vouched for by the pudgy, bespectacled rabbi.

'Cemetery worker essential for the upkeep of burials.'

'Yes, yes,' grinned one of the German officers present. 'This brat will have plenty of work.'

A casual motion of the commandant's hand was my sign to do a neat about-turn and march hurriedly away.

Mother and I seized our suitcases, grabbed the release papers and quickly made for the front gates before the Gestapo changed their minds. Before we could leave the camp, the police guard compared our faces to the photos on our identity cards. He remarked apologetically, 'Some slip; we didn't realise you were brother and sister.'

The grey street was tantalisingly close, freedom beckoned. We dared not delay. 'Never mind,' I replied, 'we'll manage without corrections.'

The steel gates swung open and we quickened our steps towards the next street corner. We had escaped certain deportation, so to be free again was an incredible feeling. However, it did not mean that we were safe, far from it. We had a form stating that we had been released, but this by itself did not protect us from being rearrested. My job was to seek real exemption papers.

Calling at the only remaining office for the Jewish community on Oranienburger Strasse, I pleaded for my rights. Initially, they would not certify my credentials as being an essential worker, as I was not on their list. After heated discussions with the staff, they finally agreed to register me as a common labourer employed at the Weissensee cemetery.

With this status came all the privileges originally intended for the informers who helped the Gestapo to make arrests. In return for a solemn promise to attend work regularly regardless of air raids or any private problems, I was handed a special badge together with numerous stamped and signed certificates. Alongside the yellow Star of David on my breast, I now donned a red armband lettered with *Ordner* (steward) and a number.

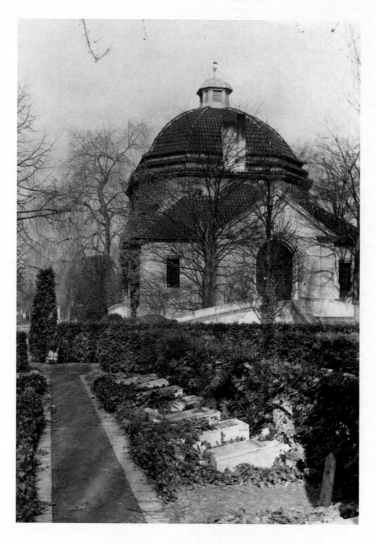

Weissensee cemetery.

All I cared about, however, was that I had outwitted the Gestapo.

Ignoring all the rules, we plodded through a blacked-out Berlin to our distant home back on Speyerer Strasse. We arrived in the early morning and woke the porter. His face was a picture of surprise and disappointment, having been certain of seeing the last of any Jews.

'What? You – free? And at this hour? Are they all coming back?'

After carefully checking our paperwork, he grudgingly handed back our keys. It was clear that he would have preferred rich, tip-giving Jews, and not destitute ones like Mother and me.

Tearing off the Gestapo seals from our door, we could finally lie down for a deeply deserved and peaceful sleep. Our new adage was to be totally inconspicuous.

Next morning, awakened by the five o'clock ring of the alarm clock, I discarded all my badges then boarded the tram to the far-off cemetery. When I first worked at the Weissensee cemetery there were 400 teenagers. Now, there were only six workers who had been spared deportation. My duty was to give all of my strength to the job.

Later, some half-Jews* joined us; among them a few other youngsters. Though by no means the smallest, I remained the youngest. The work was hard, but we could not let the others down by being absent.

Digging graves 6 feet deep became our daily routine, normally up to three a day. Occasionally, the steep piles of earth would collapse, half burying one of us. We would then extract the victim, completely covered in grimy black soil. It was the fun part of our day.

I had big wooden clogs, a pick and shovel, a fixed minimum output and a weekly pay packet. And more often than not, there was overtime for this kind of job.

Suicides came in at a rate of up to 10 bodies a day. We had to be thankful for the law that forbade people under the age of 21 to attend to the dead. This limited our sporadic help to hearse pushing and taking the place of the mourners. Almost all of the bereaved were now absent and

---

* Germans called them *Mischling* – a person who had both Aryan and Jewish ancestry.

had more than likely followed the path of their recently buried loved ones.

When time allowed, we helped bury the scrolls of the Torah as required by religious law. These scrolls were sent to the Weissensee cemetery by synagogues from all over Germany. No one was left to care for these richly ornamented scrolls, however sacred they may have been. Hundreds of them were carried to a mass grave to be given a suitably appropriate burial. It marked the end of an epoch.

Other unpleasant visitors to the cemetery came in the form of bombs dropped by night-time raiders, who had missed nearby Weissensee industrial targets, onto what seemed to us the most pointless target possible – the city of the dead.

A few girls, mostly half-Jews, returned to revive the cemetery's gardens and flowers. This, in turn, supplied the market for those who could afford the luxury of flowers and helped ease the financial burden on the cemetery's management. Working with them was a Polish prisoner-of-war who quickly became our friend. We taught him German and fed him with whatever little we could muster between us. He was a simple but sincere soul and returned our favours with daring accounts about his native land.

Away from the daily grind of cemetery work, keeping occupied during the evening hours while alone was quite a task. I might have been a child, but I knew how desperate our situation was. We had no idea of the whereabouts of relatives and friends. We feared the worst. I could not travel to see friends as they lived too far away and it was not safe to visit. Meanwhile, Mother was busy peddling our last linens for much-needed margarine.

My loneliness was partially offset by a self-assembled wireless set. Working without electricity, its parts – headphones, crystal, condenser and coils – had been acquired stealthily, bit by bit. A wire that I had stretched across the room acted as an aerial. I was so proud when I first heard the crackling noise of words coming through.

Lying in bed with earphones on, scanning the airwaves on my new wireless set, became my favourite pastime. One evening I was startled to hear an English-speaking station, but though I mustered my best school English, I soon felt disappointed, for it was only Nazi phrases that I could make out. It must have been Berlin.

Slowly I came to realise that Nazism was not just a German monopoly, as I had been led to believe, but an exportable ideal that had gathered pace. To my shock, I found out that the Nazis had many sympathisers in the very countries they were waging war with.

Just living on a daily basis became increasingly difficult. Our special ration cards needed renewing, a procedure most Jews avoided as it meant reminding the authorities of their presence.

Unable to exist on black-market food alone, we made the dreaded journey to the food office on Wartburg Platz. The Nazis were efficient, and every rubber-stamped swastika meant the law. Therefore, we had to take along an ample selection of documents for close analysis.

'We thought that there were no more Jews in the district and accordingly no cards were taken out for them,' squeaked the unfriendly voice of a minor female official.

However, after much begging, the management finally relented and telephoned the central head office to ask whether non-Aryans whose presence seemed to have the approval of the Third Reich should be issued new ration cards.

More calls followed to check the accuracy of our claim. It was early in the morning, with Nazi bureaucracy still yawning away yesterday's monotony. Not wanting to obstruct official orders, they handed over the precious booklets of coloured ration cards. It meant a few more months of vital supplies such as bread, flour, potatoes, jam, sugar and margarine.

We learned later that, soon after our departure, instructions came through to completely stop the issuing of Jewish ration cards and to arrest their applicants. Fate was shining down on us. Now Mother and I had valuable supplies and it bought us time.

Despite this reprieve, trouble was never far away from us. This time it was about our one and a half rooms in the apartment.

'Why,' said the landlord, 'I am not to blame for the Gestapo deporting all the other residents and sealing the doors. It's you two who live here now, so you have to pay the rent for the whole five-room flat.'

We could barely afford the rent anyway, so we had no choice but to

move out. Eva-Ruth, a fellow workmate, and her mother, Lotte,[10] offered
Mother and me a room at their home on Konstanzer Strasse. We took
along two suitcases each and moved in.

The new district, near the fashionable Kurfürstendamm, was full
of well-nourished, elegant snobs. It was the rendezvous of well-to-do
Germans and foreign fascists. Polished luxury cars shuttled in between
ice-cream parlours, exclusive restaurants, connoisseurs' tobacconists,
beauty salons and vendors of rare flowers. Berlin's West End, early on in
the summer of 1943, nearly made one forget that there was a war on.

One day at the cemetery, something moved from deep within a rubbish
heap. It seemed to be bigger than a dog. The girls from the cemetery's
flower shop begged us to investigate further.

Equipped with sticks, we advanced in a military-style formation
towards the tall brick wall, the spot where the kitchen refuse was
deposited. A ragged olive-green uniform bent itself up from the smelly,
rotting heap. It contained a human being. His unshaven head was covered
by a forage cap, his bare feet housed in wooden clogs. A mouldy turnip
was gripped tightly in his shaking hands.

In response to our barked commands, he hastily turned back to the
shelter of the refuse pile from where he had come. Suddenly one of our
group shouted, 'Look at his back; there's a big black SU printed on it.
What does that mean?'

'Yes, it means the Soviet Union,' we were told by a bright boy, known
for being able to distinguish between all the latest makes of cars and
aeroplanes. 'It's the place where the sub-humans come from.'

But Russia was an ally of the British against Hitler, so we decided to
call the rummager back for a more friendly interrogation.

With the aid of a hurriedly summoned work colleague who knew
some basic Polish we somewhat hesitatingly accepted this intruder's
explanation. He was a Russian soldier. In broken English, he explained as
much as he could.

'Soldier kaput – he work hard, eat little – he escapes – escaped Russians
shot – German bad – Jew friend – he not eaten in two days – he hungry.'

We could quite imagine this robust figure, his uniform shining in all of its old glory, marching on parade somewhere in far-off Russia and about to enter the battlefield against our common foe. The soldier deserved our sympathy. He ate raw turnips and we fetched him some more. We wished him good luck and then he scurried away.

Our desperate circumstances could not change the fact that I was a boy. And it was Eva-Ruth, the girl I worked and lived with, who first aroused my interest in sex.

A buxom, strawberry-blonde lass of 14, she took a liking to me. 'Don't come in now,' she would cry, 'I am only dressed in my kimono. There is only me and you in the flat, so don't be nasty.'

After a few minutes, she would continue flirting with me by announcing that she was only scantily clothed. I would naïvely continue to wait outside her room. Too young to understand her hints, my sole reward was her rebukes for my clumsiness. We teased each other and lay on the same sofa side by side, but could not make ourselves go any further.

The more I adored her body, the more I hated her mind. Her arrogance and prejudices were foul. Liking workmates of a non-German heritage was below her dignity. Occasionally, when I was the object of her heated quarrels, even I would be denounced as a 'dirty Eastern Jew'.

Her education, like that of many a German Jew, had been one of 'Deutschland über alles' ('Germany above all'). Conforming to the accepted social pattern was all that mattered to Eva-Ruth. An educated person's superior attitude may have suited more secure and comfortable surroundings, but now it was hopelessly out of place. The orderly German way of life was collapsing. There was no point in clinging to its memories.

One Sunday afternoon in June 1943, a guest arrived at Eva-Ruth's place for tea. He was a friendly character, smartly dressed, and he politely made himself at home.

This mysterious gentleman told us that he was a Jew who had been recruited by the Gestapo to seek out candidates for deportation. Strangely, he gave no reason why the Gestapo had persuaded him to do this traitorous task. He told Lotte that the few remaining Jews in Berlin had become more elusive and did not merit any large-scale action from the Gestapo. So a new scheme had been decided upon, 'arrests by persuasion', to be carried out by Jews like himself over a cup of tea.

Having come down with influenza, I had not been to the cemetery for a few days. I then heard through our seductive but treacherous visitor of a round-up that had been carried out there. Only a few workmates managed to escape via the cemetery's back gate.

Eva-Ruth and Lotte's arrest orders already lay on the table. My name was not on the visitor's pencil-marked list, but he assured us that it soon would be. A final rounding up of the few remaining Jews and half-Jews in Berlin, whether they were in hiding or not, had already been decided upon. 'To come voluntarily would be better than facing nerve-racking days, waiting for the inevitable knock on the door,' he said.

Not convinced, we decided to let events take their turn.

Lotte and her daughter, Eva-Ruth, were arrested soon after. Mother and I spent two more days in the deserted flat pondering our future.

We deliberated on our increasingly desperate situation. It seemed that the war would continue for many more years, and we could not find a reliable hiding place. Our resources and possessions could barely finance a month's illegal living. The terrifying realisation that our options were reduced to nothing meant that we had to make a decision. I reasoned that I was used to hard work and that the Eastern working camps that we had heard about might not be that bad. A good worker might even make a fair living. Finally, there was the insatiable hope that I might effect another release for me and Mother. We decided to hand ourselves in.

Once again, we set out across Berlin weighted with the inevitable four suitcases. Three months before on that street corner in north Berlin, we had taken off our yellow Stars of David. We now had to reattach them. Hungry, exhausted and scared, we re-entered the Grosse Hamburger Strasse detention centre.

This time around, there were different types of inmates packed into the transit camp – the last of its kind in Berlin. The motley but high-spirited prison crowd was made up of half-Jews, caught 'illegals', foreigners, community workers and the elderly. Jammed in though we were, a dozen to a room, with food and water mostly non-existent, somehow an atmosphere of defiant hope prevailed.

A group of young Zionists had arrived from a German farm that had been turned into a prison. Every evening they organised discussion groups, sang sentimental tunes and even danced the Horah.* Where their enthusiasm sprang from was beyond me; so was the technique of their happy dancing steps.

Eva-Ruth, too, had finally found her mate there. He was someone less naïve than me, and to the general disgust of the camp, she had gone to live in his cell. I was jealous and felt lost.

The few Polish Jews who escaped from the so-called 'concentration camps' attracted everyone's compassion. These Easterners told their stories with such repetitious fervour that only a few of us thought that they were exaggerating.

One man stood out from the crowd. A depressed, nervous and pitiful young man who claimed to have fled from a camp called 'Auschwitz'. This was one of the supposed Silesian working camps. His constant fidgeting and lack of self-control when talking made his accounts difficult to comprehend. From what little we could gather, they were also far-fetched. He deliriously shouted about the horrors of Western civilisation, offering no proof in the process. We had never heard of Auschwitz. Our shredded nerves about what lay ahead of us were already stretched far enough, which only added to our anger towards him.

Sorting out for the impending transports had started in earnest. Old people and owners of war medals would be sent to Theresienstadt, the rest to the East. Where? We did not know. Lectures on how to behave

---

* The Horah is a Jewish circle dance.

during the journey were followed by the distribution of identification numbers and basic rations. Next morning, we mounted the lorries that took us to Berlin's Stettiner Bahnhof goods station.

Mother and I, doing our best to keep together, were hustled into a wagon alongside twenty or so fellow passengers. Mother had told me to bring my winter coat as it would get cold in the East. We left Berlin in one of a dozen closed wagons waiting for departure.*

Laid out with straw, our wagon had four small barricaded ventilation slits, no windows and a solitary sanitation bucket that was to be shared by all of us on our journey to the East. We did our best to find some space in among each other and all the suitcases. My eager eyes had just about managed to catch sight of an inscription that was left over from our carriage's pre-war days in France. I asked one of my neighbours to translate the sign that was nailed to the inside of our wagon. It stated: '40 soldiers or 8 horses'.† At least we had a semblance of room in our wagon.

Then the train pulled out. As a defiant gesture towards their native Berlin, the worried souls in our carriage, which were all of us, summoned the energy to sing a final tune of farewell. Tall factory chimneys, signposts to the city's eastern suburbs, silhouetted against the falling dusk, receded along either side of the track as we made our last journey out of the city. There was an eerie silence as we pulled out, the blackout seemingly unable to sense her last few departing children. In that cramped, smelly carriage, who could say how many of us would ever see Berlin again? Perhaps now she was ashamed of herself and our plight?

As we rolled away from Germany, the regular rhythm of the wheels counting off rail by rail lulled us into uncomfortable thoughts. We were leaving a world that was lost for us – the very world that had lost itself.

---

* Research reveals that Thomas and his mother were sent on Transport 39, one of the last out of Berlin.

† Thomas and his mother were fortunate, so far as space was concerned. On their transport, around four hundred people shared the 12 wagons. At the height of transportation to the East, and in particular to Auschwitz-Birkenau, some of these 12-wagon trains packed up to 2,000 people.

PART 2

CHAPTER 5
AUSCHWITZ-BIRKENAU

The ventilation grille was our only source of fresh air, so we took it in turns to get our fill. When it was my turn, I pulled myself up to try and catch a glimpse of Beuthen, my hometown. I was unsuccessful.

The train passed familiar sights, like the coalmines of Upper Silesia. Often it stopped; much time was spent waiting to free up the railway tracks so that Germany's military reinforcements could continue their passage onwards to the Eastern Front. This mainly happened at night and quite upset any timetable we may have imagined. Even the talkative among our group ceased speculating where and when we would arrive. People became irritated and frustrated, perhaps scared of what unknown future lay ahead for all of us.

On rare occasions, we were allowed to empty the lavatory bucket and fetch much-needed water. Heated arguments would often break out as to who must clean what and who could use the precious pots. Common courtesy and sympathy were replaced by the desperate human instinct for survival. A mere two days' journey of fear, discomfort and the unknown had succeeded in breaking down barriers of human decency from the previously polite manners of Berlin city folk.

The only place where all of us were allowed to have a short stroll to stretch our aching legs was at a lonely countryside spot. The chance to take fresh air into our gasping lungs was welcome and finding a pit latrine a must. The Polish sign 'Ustempo' alerted us to the fact that we had left Germany behind and were now in Poland.

Our wagon train lurched eastwards. On this late summer's afternoon, the rural landscape gave way to scenes unlike anything I had ever seen before. There were wooden towers, 16 feet high with ladders attached to them. Were they aircraft spotters? But why so many? Then big wooden shed-like buildings appeared lined up in rows, with people in zebra-striped blue-and-white uniforms around them. Were they convicts? Apparently, the Polish supply of criminals was a record one. I had seen these people back at home in Berlin pushing refuse-carts, but here they worked in fenced-off storage depots.

The scale of where we had arrived was overwhelming. It was scarcely believable. I freed my arm to check my watch. Five minutes, seven minutes, ten minutes; still there was no end to the mesh of barbed wire. Craning my neck through the wagon's grille I searched for a prison building – without success.

Abruptly the train halted. We all tried to regain our balance, a natural human reaction. A jarring shunt and the train moved onto another track. We did our best not to knock each other over. A shrill whistle broke the deafening silence inside our carriage. The door was hauled open. And from every direction, harsh, guttural shouts of '*Raus! Raus!*' ('Out! Out!'). Facing us were armed field-grey-uniformed SS men.

It was the evening of 29 June 1943. The place was Brzezinka – Birkenau, near the town of Oświęcim.˙ Our familiar guards who had escorted us on our journey had been relieved long ago, for this was a secluded world not fit to be viewed by outsiders.

'Out, you bastards! *Raus, Raus!* Faster, *Schweinehunde!*' ('Run you sow hounds!'), yelled our new masters, the supermen of the super race. Shocked and trembling, we disembarked and were roughly arranged on a ramp beside our train.

A whole SS company was drawn up along the length of the platform. They were heavily armed and if this was meant to intimidate us, it worked. Continuous shouts exploded in our direction. Machine-guns were mounted at both ends of the ramp. Bloodhounds barked ferociously at us, their jaws foaming as they strained against their leashes. The dog handlers struggled to restrain them.

˙ Brezezinka and Oświęcim were named by the Germans as Birkenau and Auschwitz. Birkenau (a year later it became Auschwitz II) was the largest of the 40 or so camps and sub-camps that made up the Auschwitz concentration camp complex.

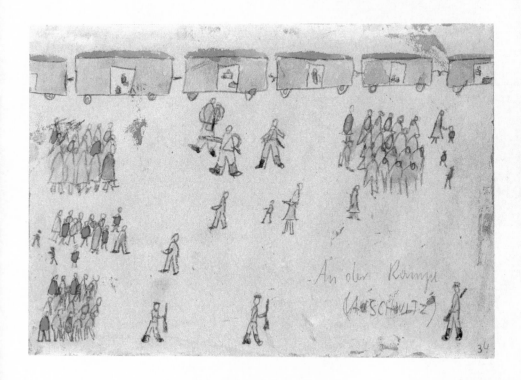

ON THE RAMP
The selection – able to work or not, we were
sentenced to life or death upon arrival.

I had a quick chance to look around. The immediate landscape offered
no kind of comfort or solace. For miles, I could see no trees, just empty
fields. A mist rose in the distance, doubtless hiding whatever was
lurking there and waiting for us. The SS soldiers harshly ordered us
to split into groups; some were pointing, some were pushing and some
were shouting.

'*Schnell, Schnell*' ('Quicker, Quicker!') 'Everything to be left behind!
Able-bodied men to the right, women that can work to the left, the rest
stay in the middle of the platform.'

The SS cracked whips down upon us to reinforce their orders as we
tried to comprehend what was happening.

I hurriedly hugged Mother goodbye and made for the right.

Standing up straight and doing my best to look impressive, I puffed
out my chest.

I passed the scrutiny of the supervising SS officer, then lost myself
among the crowd of men.

As dusk fell, more lorries arrived. I could see the elderly and frail
being loaded on board and driven away. The mothers and children
waited as we men, surrounded by SS guards, were arranged into ranks
of five and marched away.

After about half an hour, our column of 117* men, all of us still
bewildered by our arrival into Birkenau and the ominous reception
we had received, reached a guarded turnpike. Dirty puddles ringed
by muddy, barren soil suggested that nature took no interest in the
place. We were counted, recounted and then waved on through. We
continued marching.

Before long we were halted again. Beyond us stood a red-brick
building, similar to but much bigger than a typical farmhouse, but
directly in front of it were structures that were not seen on any farm.
Radiating from it were electrically charged barbed-wire fences,
8 foot high and paralleled with smaller ones. Regularly spaced black

---

*As recorded in the Danuta Czech files, the 39th transport from Berlin arrived on 29 June 1943 and included 346
Jews. 136 were killed on arrival and 210 were admitted to the camp, of which 117 were men and 93 were women.

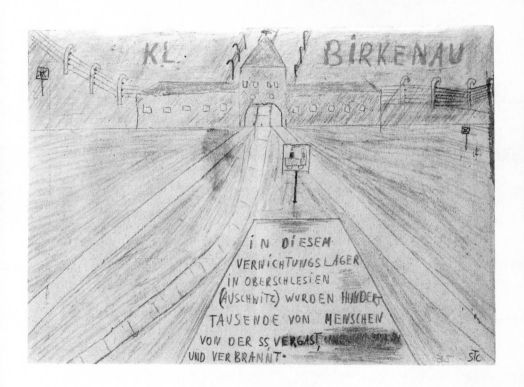

BIRKENAU CONCENTRATION CAMP
Auschwitz-Birkenau – a factory of death,
where over a million men, women and
children were massacred.

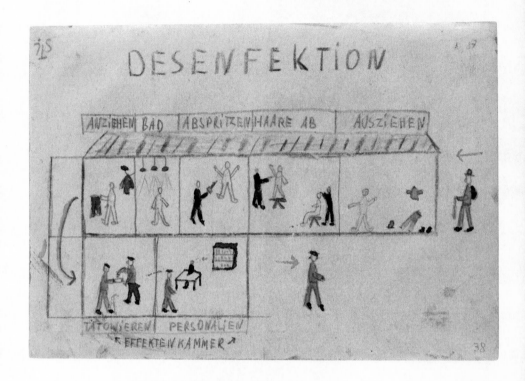

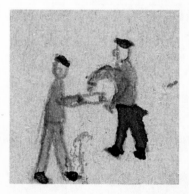

DISINFECTION
Within hours, free men and women became
prisoners, names became numbers.

signposts, showing a white skull and crossbones, read 'danger'.

The central feature was the tower, flanked on both sides by long and low wings, creating an archway over the rail track. On top of its pyramid-shaped roof was a mushroom-shaped siren, its piercing wail announcing our passage beneath.

Once we were through the arch, all I could see was an endless pattern of simply built wooden barracks, arranged in rows and illuminated by a sea of lights.

There was another headcount and we marched on, heading for this monstrous city of prisoners as all the while the dull hum of the electrified barbed wire filled our ears.

No trees, no shrubs, nothing green was to be seen. It was another world, unique in its depressing gloom. My eyes were continuously searching in an attempt to seek more knowledge of our whereabouts. We turned towards one of the many camps, a group of huts among hundreds. We stopped at a nondescript grey building from which a tall chimney rose. We waited, and then, finally, it was our turn to enter.

Inside, healthy-looking prisoners (although they looked like murderers and thieves to me) silently shepherded us in. They ignored being talked to and their only interactions were a gesture to move forward or a shake of the head. I entered a room that was filled with piles and piles of discarded clothing. Orders followed.

'Undress! Clothing to the right – underwear to the left – valuables and documents into the basket – shoes to be taken along; nothing else. All other items into the basket: money, photographs, rings and so on.'

I undressed quickly and my clothes were taken from me. Naked, I reluctantly surrendered my watch. Then my identity card was dropped onto a stack of others; another name had ceased to exist.

Then came the hair. Overworked barbers were trying to get through the new recruits as fast as their hands would allow them. Cutting was followed by shaving to ensure that no tuft or loose strand of hair was left on any part of our bodies.

I only had hair on my head, but that soon joined the mass of dark, blond and red hair that was fast piling up on the floor. A final check-up was made on me and revealed two cottage-cheese sandwiches, now shrivelled and stale, that I had saved all the way from Berlin. I had tried to hide them and carry them through together with my shoes. I had no appetite for them now, anyway.

More depressed than ever before, I entered the 'sauna' room. Inside were people who had been beside me on the platform just a few hours earlier. Row upon row, they all sat on batten-covered steps that rose towards the few ventilation openings in the room's ceiling. I found a place to sit. Crowded together as if in some weird enigmatic theatre, we were anticipating an unworldly performance. Nobody noticed me, and no one spoke. We had no idea what was about to happen. All we had for company was our own private worries and fears.

We waited and waited. Left to myself, appalling and scarcely believable thoughts started to grip me. I had heard rumours about the mass killing of Jews during our last days in Berlin. *What if these rumours were true? Didn't one of them mention gas?*

Refusing to let myself absorb such disturbing thoughts or resign myself to Fate, I scanned and I studied the sauna room we were in. The walls were solid, and the metal-lined door was secure, locked by heavy bolts. Only the high but small windows seemed penetrable, but escape was impossible.

Locked up with nowhere to go, we waited until eventually the big metal door swung open. A group of blue-and-white-uniformed wardens entered the room. They conversed among themselves in Polish, and then one of them stepped forward to address us.

'You are now concentration camp inmates. The easy life has finished. Old habits will have to be changed. If not, we will change them for you. Complete obedience to your prisoner superiors, and of course to the SS, is a must. Don't delude yourselves with ideas of ever getting out of here. Plenty of hard work will take the place of thought. This camp is called Birkenau and it demands the strictest discipline. You'll now be disinfected.'

We were chased through a pit full of detergent and then into a cold shower room. I tried to avoid it, but our new bosses were efficient in forcing us to obey. Their frenzied shouting of 'Quick! Hurry!' ensured that we followed their commands.

Underwear, jackets, trousers and caps were thrown at us. Quickly, I snatched the heavily patched-up prison clothing and put it onto my still wet skin. There was no time to consider who had previously worn this uniform and whether they were alive or dead.

Despite my untied shoelaces and the hopelessly large rags that engulfed me, we were already being driven out into the main sleeping camp. The shouts continued: 'Run! Run quicker, you lazy pigs!'

I ran. With every step, I fought the camp's mud that grabbed at my precious but unsecured shoes as the gooey sludge submerged my ankles. I gripped the waistband of my ludicrously large trousers that kept falling down towards the deep and cold puddles. Sweat now oozed from every part of my body.

Victorious but exhausted I arrived at the reception barrack in Birkenau. At the entrance, a figure in prison clothing emerged from the dark.

'Any valuables? Rings, gold?' he asked confidently. 'Don't hide them; the SS will get them. Better to leave them with me, in the trust of a fellow inmate.'

An uncomfortable pause followed.

'Now come on, don't hesitate! You must have something cherished that needs entrusting into friendly hands!'

Some of my new inmates responded to his coy and gentle persuasion. I only wondered whether he would have accepted the two dried-up cottage-cheese sandwiches left behind at the sauna.

We were now in the registration hall. Many tables were laden with card index boxes, with fellow prisoners and the SS seated behind each one of them. The soldiers instructed us to arrange ourselves alphabetically into rows of five. At first, this proved to be a complicated procedure for people totally unaccustomed to drilling and following commands. That soon changed when SS whips cracked, and the guards rained down blows upon us.

'Now, where are the fat Berlin merchants?' jeered one SS bully.

Two rather portly prisoners, who seemed to fit the description of rich traders, were ordered to run around the barracks.

'Are there rabbis here too?'

No one answered. Beards that might once have given them instantly away were now gone, the one ironic advantage from the earlier shearing we had gone through. Our silence did not go down well with the SS officer, who, feeling cheated, began his search for new victims.

'I hear there are bastards among you whose fathers raped Aryan girls. Let's see those blond ones with the crooked noses!'

There was silence again, as most of us had light hair, so that idea also had to be abandoned. Exasperated and likely embarrassed, he resorted to threats.

'This is your last chance to rid yourselves of hidden valuables. We will find them anyway. Drop them on the floor. If, after leaving this barrack, anything is found on you, you will be shot.'

Eventually, we were processed through to another roomful of desks. Here, a young Russian prisoner took hold of my left arm and started tattooing it with a double-pointed pen dipped in blue ink. He did the first three digits, being careful not to mix my blood with that of the blue ink. Then he did the last three digits.

The tattooist was as gentle as he could be, but it was agony. It felt like the continuous prick of a thousand pins. He looked me over and could clearly see that I was young. When he had finished, to my surprise, he muttered quietly, 'Good luck to you.'

I looked down at his work. The number 127003, neatly inscribed on my arm, was too big for my liking. I noticed that the digits added up to 13 – was it to be lucky?*

As meaningful as this number would become to me, in terms of the Reich's plan to eliminate our identity – an insignificant name had become an insignificant number.

Like the more than 100,000 other men before me, I had now become just another male '*Schutzhäftlingen*', a so-called 'protective custody prisoner'. Each of us was documented in duplicate, with one copy for the camp and one for the Gestapo.

---

* In Judaism, 13 is a significant number and also the age that marks the beginning of adulthood – Thomas's age upon arrival at the camp.

'You idiot, here you are no longer Israel!'* the prisoner clerk shouted at me as I was about to write the additional forename that, by a decree of 1938, was compulsory for all male Jews. I continued to fill in the form: '13 years – Beuthen – Berlin – Gardener's Apprentice – Emigrated – Deported – None – Measles, Scarlet Fever, Mumps – None – None – None.' The final part of the form was the signing of a statement, declaring myself to be stateless and property-less.

Finally, we had a sort of interval where a hot tea-like drink was poured into metal bowls and distributed among the prisoners. Again, there was shouting – there was always shouting. This time for doctors and other specialists. About a dozen inmates stepped forward.

My defiant mind re-awoke, eager to try yet another getaway from the Gestapo. If not now, then never. The plan was a desperate one, but its first stage seemed tangible. I headed for the SS officer, clicked my heels and tried to be as smart as my pitiful appearance would allow me to. 'I kindly beg you to consider my transfer. I am not 14 yet and feel out of place here.'

A mocking grin appeared from beneath his skull-and-crossbones-adorned peaked cap. He looked down at me. 'And where would you like to go?'

'To the children's camp,' I replied confidently, proud that my trick was working.

'We have no children's compounds,' he snapped, somewhat annoyed.

I persisted. 'At least have me placed with other youngsters, please.'

Obviously irritated, he seemed to admonish me: 'One day you'll be pleased I didn't send you. You are here now. That is that. Off you go!'

Finally, the registration process finished. Drained, we were led through the pitch-dark night into the sleeping barracks.

We were ushered into one of the innumerable huts on the camp's compound. The interior was sparse and bland. On either side of the hut, partitioned walls rationed the space into boxes. Each box was

---

* A law from 17 August 1938 meant that men who did not have a Hebrew name were forced to take the additional name *Israel*, and for women, *Sara*.

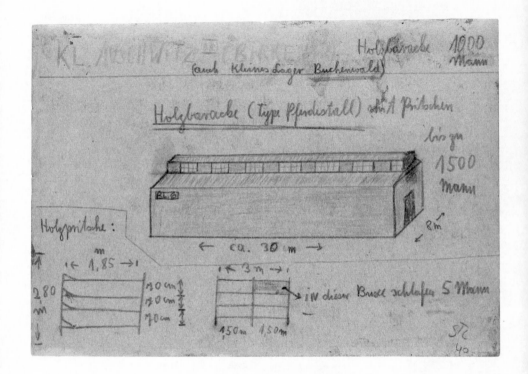

WOODEN BARRACKS
Crowded Birkenau barracks housed
up to 1,500 men each. Ten shared a
3-metre-wide bunk.

6 feet by 6 feet wide, 30 inches tall, and stacked three levels high. Each of the boxes was laid with straw-filled sacks. And each box was home to six prisoners, regardless of their size and height. In the centre of the barrack was a square, brick-built heating duct that had a stove at one end, and a chimney at the other.

We newcomers crowded in and were left in the charge of the 'Blokovi' (block-elder), a veteran prisoner who was entrusted with keeping the barrack's inmates under control. He and several of his room-elders busily went about getting us into our quarters. We had to learn the challenging art of lying on one's side like sardines, straight, with one's head enclosed between both neighbours' feet. A must for a bunk sleeper. A deafening whistle perforated the hut just as I was contemplating sleep. The Blokovi began a well-rehearsed speech in German.

'This is the men's camp in Birkenau – nobody is to leave the block. You may leave your bunks to relieve yourselves, but only one at a time. There is an improvised lavatory in the middle of the barrack. You must be absolutely quiet. Orders from block personnel are to be obeyed without question. We are your superiors and can order you to do whatever we like. Obedience must be complete. If you wake tomorrow morning to find your shoes missing, do not dare to complain. Woe to him who bothers me with complaints – he may never leave this block alive.

'When you see an SS man, stand to attention with your cap at the seam of your trousers. Should one enter a block or approach a group of prisoners, you must shout out, '*Achtung*' ('Attention'). If you hear that word, you jump to attention without hesitation. When he leaves, you call, '*Weitermachen*' ('Continue'). You will then get on with your work. If you choose not to greet an SS soldier or officer, you will feel the consequences. I have warned you. Lights out now, and quiet!'

This was my first night in captivity at Birkenau. I was dog-tired and yet I could not sleep. In their troubled slumber, people groaned, scratched themselves and fidgeted. The barrack ceiling was alive with mice. My mind replayed over and over again an extraordinary day. Eventually, the bowl of tea from earlier necessitated my need for a pee. I wriggled out of my crowded bunk, desperately trying not to wake anyone up. When I got to the lavatory, all the foul-smelling vats were full to the brim.

Barely two hours later, my first night in Birkenau ended with another deafening whistle. This would be our alarm clock. Sure enough, my Sunday-best shoes were nowhere to be seen. In their place were a black worker's boot that was too big for me and a tiny brown shoe fringed with leather ornaments that was too small for me. Mindful of the warning from the Blokovi just a few hours earlier, I hid my anger and swiftly got ready. A cry of 'thieves' added to the frantic atmosphere inside the hut. Muffled blows were heard soon after. I dared not look back.

Harsh orders were barked, and distant steps were heard from the still-dark camp outside. Once more we were lined up into ranks of five, more quickly this time than the evening before. Standing in the last rank of our hut, I fell asleep against a bunk post. A heavy cuff from the room-elder woke me.

'You're lucky I am no SS man.'

My exhaustion momentarily disappeared and I stood bolt upright and to attention.

As we continued to stand my eyes soon closed again, desperate for sleep. Suddenly, something else disturbed my dozing, but this time its origin was less pronounced. I shook myself awake and listened attentively. From somewhere, unexpected and grotesquely out of place given where we were: music. An orchestra was playing marching songs.

Some hours later, we were still standing in ranks waiting for an order. Finally, an SS delegation, including high-ranking officers, arrived. They inspected our group, pointing at stronger-looking individuals, who were then taken away. Later, we learned that they had been transferred to Monowitz, one of the sub-camps at Auschwitz III.

'Where is that half-Jew who was in the army?' called out one senior SS officer, who had neatly corded epaulettes on his shoulders. A young blond man stepped forward. I recognised him from the internment camp before we were transported. He was as German as a German could be. His many passionate appeals for release had been to no avail. 'You will remain in this camp,' he was told and 'be allocated easier work'.

When the officers left, the guards came in, bringing with them two bloodhounds. I was in one of the six remaining five-men rows of prisoners that were ordered to turn to the left and start marching.

As we crossed the camp, the early-morning mist disappeared, and Birkenau began to reveal its desolate self, full of foreboding. Even the worst pessimist could not have imagined conditions more shocking.

We saw a group of women, who were struggling to keep their footing through the boggy ground and constantly threatened by their yelling superiors.

They had to push big supply wagons, while behind them there followed bald, malnourished children, who would now and then lift their ragged garments to scratch themselves. It was a sorry sight. There was a squad of men, with black and red circles stitched into their clothing, and heads bent, feverishly breaking stones in order to pave a new road. They dared not look up for fear of a beating. Everywhere there were heavily armed SS guards brandishing whips and looking on, eager to mete out punishments for any possible transgression.

We trudged out of Birkenau and into an indifferent, deserted countryside, leaving behind a jungle of barbed wire and check-posts. The midday sun beat mercilessly down, meaning equal sweating for all. Led and leaders alike, we had to realise our insignificance against nature; we slowed down. Curiosity, too, knew no human-made distinctions. Now and then a guard would come closer to ask questions.

'Where are you from? Why are you here? Yes, now you are going to work! From now on you will realise what toil means; you'll be surprised. Don't ask questions, you will see for yourselves. How long do you think you will last here? You should have enquired about the place before coming. Why did you come? Now get a move on! Quicker first row!'

An hour later we passed through another large mass of barbed wire. Here, a loaded train had halted beside a road.

On either side of the wagons arose huge pyramids of brick, coal and timber. Everywhere hundreds of blue-and-white-clothed prisoners wrestled with boulders, tree trunks and coal, labouring in the oppressive heat like some cohort of Egyptian slaves. They were accompanied by the grim sound of screamed orders and curses from SS guards.

Our passing by attracted unwanted attention. Calls in different languages greeted us, although I only understood a few of the insults.

'See, here comes the *Vollgefressen* (fat-bellies); they want to push the wagons!'

'They won't stick it for long – the fat-bellies!'

After another 20 minutes, we reached the camp gates of Auschwitz.* The inscription on the front gate, in ornamental metalwork, read '*Arbeit Macht Frei*' ('Work sets you free').

We were checked in and then led to the disinfection barrack. There we were crowded into a steam-filled laundry hall. This was our first opportunity to talk freely with other inmates.

From them, barely 24 hours after our arrival, we started to learn the bitter truth. There was no children's camp, no camp for the elderly and no camp for the ill or weak. There was only the forest of death behind the Birkenau camp. Its depths were filled with gas and destruction.

When we heard this, I felt the ground beneath my feet begin to crumble away. My vague but desperate trust in civilisation lay shattered.

I did not think that any individual or even set of individuals could be responsible for the enormity of such a crime. Neither busy Hitler in far-off Berlin, nor the guard that had been sweating along the dusty road, seemed the right target for my wrath. A terrifying realisation overwhelmed me. The refined city manners, the studying of Greek and Roman achievements, the strivings of democracy, the neutral nations' eagerness to help the oppressed, the many impressive churches I had seen, the beauty of art and progress, the trust in my parents' judgement – it all seemed to have been a disgusting farce. I had no time to absorb these terrible thoughts or consider our fate. Veteran inmates were desperate for news from the outside world. They started throwing all manner of questions at us new arrivals. We swapped descriptions of the world events we knew about for valuable information about life in the camp.

---

* Auschwitz, the camp where Thomas was imprisoned, would become known as Auschwitz I, Birkenau as Auschwitz II and Monowitz with its subsidiaries as Auschwitz III.

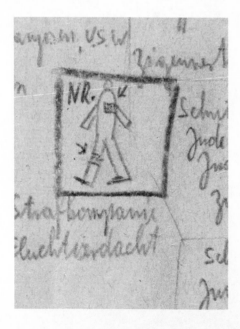

MARKINGS

For the supervisors, prisoner identification was a tattoo on their arm and a marking on their clothes.

Soon the jigsaw puzzle that had been troubling every prisoner was assembling itself in our minds. Bit by bit, we grasped the mechanism of a German concentration camp. We had to quickly pick up the rules for our identification process. Each prisoner was required to wear a coloured cloth triangle. This was followed by their number, which had to be stitched onto their clothing over the heart and the right upper leg. Each category of inmate had a discrete insignia. The elaborate card index system of the SS administration political department would list the official reason for the prisoner's arrest. That reason would then determine what cloth triangle the prisoner had to wear.

A green triangle with the apex pointing downwards meant that its wearer was a professional criminal. Apex up was a first-time offender. A black triangle signalled a 'work-shy' individual (Russians, Ukrainians and Gypsies typically wore these). A red triangle signified political opponents and was reserved for Germans, Poles, Czechs and the French. A pink triangle was required for convicted homosexuals. A violet triangle marked the members of pacifist religious sects such as the Jehovah's Witnesses.

Jews had to wear a red triangle or occasionally a green one, which was then superimposed onto a yellow triangle so as to form the Star of David. Triangles of non-Jews were imprinted with the initials of the wearer's nationality.

A young Polish-Belgian Jew, who had been attentively listening to our arrival story, seemed amused.

'So, he played that old shoe-swapping trick on you too, that old rascal.' He grinned. 'That damned Birkenau block-elder, a notorious Polish criminal, is a Jew like us. He deserves to be gored like a pig. One of these days we'll have to do away with him. You are lucky to have got out of that hell; you couldn't have stood it for long. Here conditions are more tolerable: we do our best to remove characters like him.'

Another listener emerged from between the boiling and steaming laundry kettles. On his smartly tailored outfit, we recognised the green triangle followed by a number in the thousands, meaning he was a veteran.

'So, these are the latest arrivals.' He studied us with old, blue and penetrating eyes. 'Germany, Germany,' he mumbled, 'it was my home too.' What he said next crushed us. 'We are all caught in the same spider's web now. Don't be misled by my green triangle; my sentence was served long ago. I am here for the same reason as you are: extermination! There is no escape from here. For 10 miles around us, the SS controls everything. You have seen only one camp so far, but there are seven more like it at Birkenau. Men, women, Jews, Gypsies and Germans, they are all kept separately. One of the compounds is for death candidates. Birkenau can hold only a hundred thousand prisoners; the rest are sent to the crematoria. I don't want to horrify you with further details.'

But he was in full flow now.

'Our camp, Auschwitz, is supposed to be the "model" camp. It is the showpiece for visiting Red Cross delegations, and you can be glad that you are among the eighteen thousand privileged. Monowitz, where some of your number were sent, is an exhausting treadmill. There, the eleven thousand prisoners work like slaves building a synthetic-rubber factory. Even with reasonable living conditions and food, the work wears you out in weeks.'

Our benefactor seemed to take pleasure in showing off his exact knowledge of the surrounding camps. He listed them with German precision.

'Birkenau, Auschwitz and Monowitz are the three main camps. Sprinkled all around them are subsidiaries whose role it is to suck the last drop of energy out of every prisoner, while he is alive. Like Janina, Jaworzno, Jawischowitz, Myslowitz, Sosnowitz, Schwientochlowitz, Fürstengrube, Guenter-Grube and Eintrachthütte – most of these places are mines.'

He continued. 'There are factories at Gleiwitz, Bobrek, Althammer and Blechhammer, quarries at Gollischau and Trzebinia, and agricultural establishments at Babitz, Budy, Harmense and Rajsko. Some have about two hundred prisoners each and are no more than cages. Others, with the same lack of facilities, house up to five thousand. The total number of slaves in this SS empire called Auschwitz may already be a hundred and fifty thousand, and it is

NAME	Männer Frauen	ARBEIT	Insassen 46
AUSCHWITZ	ML FL	Alles	48 000 ,1500
BIRKENAU	ML FL	Alles	
BUNA	ML	Bau	11 000
Babity	ML FL	Landwirtschaft	
Blechhammer	ML FL	Bau, Industrie	4500
Bobrek	ML FL	Industrie	215, 40
Budy	ML FL	Landwirtschaft	300, 600
Dubrow	X FL		
Fürstengrube	ML	Kohlengrube	2000
Gleiwitz I II III	ML	Industrie	1800
Golleschau	ML	Steinbruch	400
Harmense	ML FL	Landwirtschaft	
Janina	ML	Kohlengrube	600
Jaworzna	ML	"	400
Jawischowitz	ML	"	2500
Myslowitz	ML	"	
Mischfreilowitz	ML	"	
Porembka	ML FL	Landwirtschaft	25, 25
Raisko	X FL	Gärtnerei	200
Sosnowitz	ML	Kohlengrube	200
Schwientochlowitz	ML	"	200
Güntersgrube	ML	"	400
Eintrachtshütte	ML	"	500
Althammer	ML	Industrie	3000
Scherbina	ML	Schachtarbeit	200

THE SPIDER'S WEB

The Auschwitz complex – over 40 main and
sub-camps: slavery, starvation and death.

growing every day.'

As if this were not enough to take in, our well-wisher shook his head.

'No, there is no way out. Even if you escaped from the camp, could you get through the rings of check-posts that surround all of Eastern Upper Silesia? I, a cunning fox and privileged old-time prisoner, have had to abandon the idea of escape, even though my friendship with the SS officers makes it a possibility. You, the newest and lowest type of prisoner, should never dream of it. During the last two years, only four of the handful that escaped appear to have got away. Have no illusions about your future; the only hope is outside – Allied intervention. That, however, we have been waiting for since 1938.'

With this final distressing comment, he walked away.

I could not help but admire his elegant uniform. His trousers were neatly ironed, with each leg flapping over a fashionable pair of shiny leather shoes. Perhaps he could afford to be a pessimist. Still, squatting among the steaming laundry vats, we tried to get to know each other. Heavy-hearted, we talked about our past and our families. How we missed our families. How I missed Mother.

There were four youngsters among us who had not yet reached 18: Sally, Jonathan, Gert and myself. Sally Klapper[11] had been a Berlin acquaintance of mine, but I had not come across him much. He had emigrated from Poland with his mother. He was a little older than me, and I had always admired him for his choice of buxom girlfriends. Gert Beigel[12] and his elder brother were born in Berlin and, like myself, had at one time worked at the Weissensee cemetery. They had managed to go into hiding, but were betrayed and caught. In those dark moments of our new life as prisoners, we four youngsters came together. We made a solemn pact to share our sorrows and joys, our hunger and our food. A bond was created between us.

Those few moments in the laundry hall, talking and getting to know each other, came to an abrupt end. Our visitors dispersed or went back to their work duties.

Heading towards us was a gaunt-looking bespectacled inmate. He wore a green triangle on his breast and a yellow band around his left arm, which read *Lager Friseur* (Camp Hairdresser). He viewed the group we were part of in a condescending manner, and then turned to us youngsters and smiled.

'I am in charge of new arrivals here. Together with my seventeen assistants, called *Blockfriseure*, I am responsible for keeping the camp, and you, clean. Don't be misled by our armbands; cutting hair is not our business. There is enough of your sort to do the menial work. We are responsible for sanitary arrangements, disinfections and the working of the barrack that you are in now. Instead of being in command, we try to help you. If you children ever have trouble, do come and see me.

'Now you know-alls,' the hairdresser continued, his toothless mouth grinning, 'how are politics outside?'

Soon after, the doors opened and the rush to the shower room started. This time our reception was warmer, in all senses of the word, than that which we had experienced in Birkenau. Gladly, we shed our patched-up clothes. Even soap was issued, showing that kindness can work wonders. Next, warm sprays of water were turned on and momentarily we were free and careless like any other normal bather.

After our showers, we were again sprayed with the irritating disinfectant, and given fresh clothing and wooden clogs. My blue-and-white uniform was made of thin, cardboard-like material, but it was clean, and it was new. Not long afterwards, we clattered off to the building's upper storey, whose sign on the front stated 'Block 2a'.

Once inside, we had to skilfully sew on our new number badges. Then we were lined up with about a hundred Russian prisoners. Once again, a block-elder came to recount the rules to us. He spoke in his native Polish, which to his obvious annoyance fell on deaf ears, as we could not understand him. When he had finished, a volunteer inmate translated the instructions into Russian. There must have been someone present who could translate into German, but since this was the language of the SS, nobody wanted to speak it.

CHAPTER 6
QUARANTINE

We youngsters were to spend four weeks in quarantine to prevent a threat of spreading disease through the camp. We felt rather cut off, as prisoners from other blocks were not allowed to see us.

In our block, everything was said, ordered and announced in Polish, although Russian was also heard and spoken occasionally. In Germany, talking in public in a foreign tongue was a punishable offence. In Auschwitz, everyone who had a semblance of German was supposed to speak it. Yet, it was seldom heard. We had such difficulty in understanding our superiors that some of the die-hard Germans among us even voiced their intent to complain about it to the SS. They were overruled and we had to learn certain Slavic languages. Mainly it was Polish, the language of the country in which we found ourselves.

Our fellow block inmates were mostly Ukrainian and there was also a small number of Poles. They were a stubborn and dull bunch. The Ukrainians in particular were simple, strongly built country folk, and their hostility had to be avoided at all times. On the rare occasions we were given a second helping of soup at lunchtime, they would lay claim to it. We would not resist. Despite our subservient attitude, or possibly because of it, they considered us as two evils in one – we were German and Jewish.

The daily blessings of civilisation consisted of a quarter-loaf of black bread (350 grams) and 1 litre of foul-tasting soup that was brewed from weeds and thistles.

Forty grams of margarine, which Germany produced from coal tar residues, were issued on Wednesdays and Thursdays. Fifty grams on Saturdays.

On Monday, Tuesday and Thursday there would be 50 grams of sausage, and one spoonful of jam on Tuesday and Friday.

Sunday's 'treat' was 50 grams of cheese, half a litre of goulash soup and a handful of potatoes in their skins.

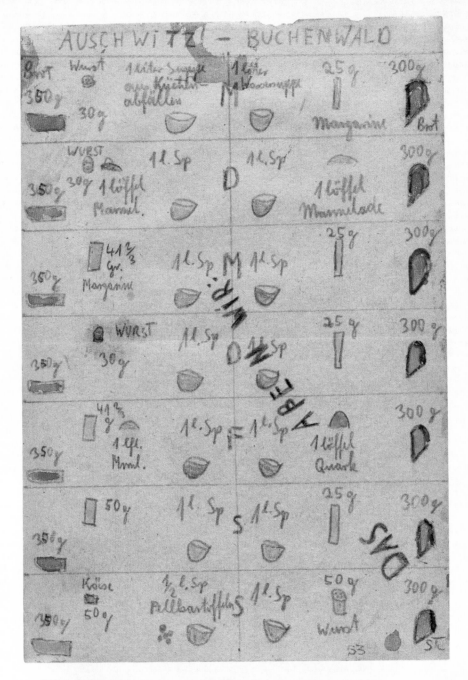

WHAT WE ATE

This paltry amount of food was ostensibly meant to keep a prisoner alive
for up to six months. Once he starved to death, he would be replaced by a
new arrival.

That, together with the morning and evening ladleful of acorn tea, was what the working slaves of the German empire lived on.

Few prisoners kept their food for later on. Rations were swallowed up as soon as they were given out. Given that the bread was issued in the evening, we went hungry until noon the following day. If, due to some mistake in distribution, there was any food left over, most of it would go to the block's personnel.

For the ordinary prisoners, their only priority was to worry about when to join the food queue, so as to achieve the right timing to hold out their enamelled metal bowl.

Individual ways of ladling out soup became a study for us. There were different soups and each one had their characteristics. Fat, for example, would swim to the top and potatoes would sink to the bottom. Skilful calculations and timing would mean we got thick, rich vegetable soup, with chunks of potatoes or meat, and sweet tea. Something to boast about! Something to dream about!

On days when a batch of prisoners left, thus making the block less crowded, we were allowed to spend some hours in the yard between Blocks 13 and 14. There we would sit in the sun, talking and making acquaintances.

The Poles were allowed to receive food parcels, which their eyes never strayed from – they were justifiably in constant fear of being robbed. Seeing these treasures being judiciously inspected by their owners and then devoured bit by bit, slice by slice, greatly annoyed us. We were famished.

Food also represented power, and the prisoners who cordoned off the yard were far from incorruptible. Water would be bartered off for chunks of Polish sausage, bread for bacon and tobacco for margarine. We envious starvelings turned away our sad eyes and concentrated on traditional prison pastimes.

We had been kept largely ignorant of the camp and the outside world. We felt rather forlorn, as prisoners from other blocks were not allowed to see us. The main events of the day were marking off the date with

our fingernails onto the wooden posts of our bunks, gobbling our meagre
rations and wishing for more. Accounts of tasty dishes ceased to make
us forget our hunger. Soon, we had heard enough about each other,
and intimate details of favourite girlfriends' female attractions became
annoying. Bored and impatient, we waited for what was to come.

Knife-making, though forbidden, was one way to pass the time. I
had found a few precious rusty nails and flattened them out between
two stones. They proved useful for spreading margarine, but never
succeeded in becoming saleable assets.

Another pastime involved the fleas, which were plentiful in
Auschwitz. They would emerge in the morning black and shiny from
our felt-lined clogs to start jumping across the dusty, stone-littered
yard. There we would wait, gaining our revenge by squeezing them
until they exploded between our fingernails.

What we could see of the camp seemed strange and incomprehensible.
To the right of our block, 60 yards away behind the fence, was the
crematorium. A small, unimportant branch of the crematoria at Birkenau,
it was said. To our left, the camp's band could be heard playing tuneful
marching numbers for the returning work groups. Outside the barbed
wire, SS personnel busily hurried from office to office.

We could not help but notice the thin grey smoke that arose from
the ominous chimney to our right. It would linger above us and we
knew what it was. A sinister 'guess what I see' game had developed
around it from our block. People with macabre minds would try to
analyse the cloud's shape and smell.

'Look there, doesn't it look like old Willie?'

'No, no, you ass, it's a virgin; can't you see the small breasts
sticking out?'

'Go away, that's his nose!'

I, however, kept my eyes to the ground, looking for more nails.

One day, a squat little Russian arrived at our corner of the room. His
shaven and round head accentuated the Mongolian features of his

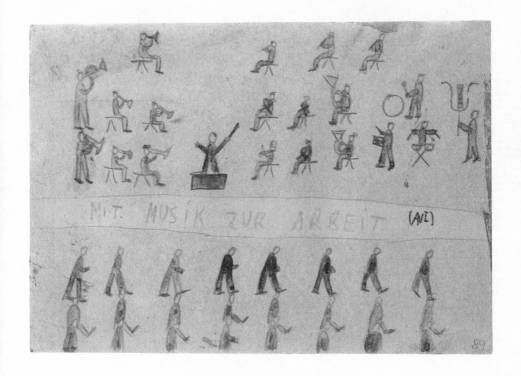

THE ORCHESTRA
The prisoners' orchestra were forced to play
marching songs to the prisoners marching off
to work – another irony of camp life.

pock-marked face. He had a square piece of cardboard under his arm and had come from the room opposite to ours. He was looking for chess players and he had found the right place. Quickly, the Russian became a regular visitor.

Slowly we gained his confidence and the little chess player became our friend. His smattering of German had been acquired at school and from his German grandfather. He had little in common with the Ukrainians around us.

The chess player had been a fighter, an ally, the way we had imagined them to be. As a 19-year-old pilot, he had flown one of the small Soviet planes that I had seen at the exhibitions back in Berlin. We were mesmerised as he excitedly explained the dogfight in which he had been shot down. Hands represented planes, deep gurgles imitated the engine's noises and the low headroom between the bunks was the open sky. No doubt that this little chap had fought valiantly before being captured.

'Don't think your roommates are representatives of the Red Army,' he whispered. 'With them, we would have lost the war long ago. Don't worry, the Soviet Union is a large country. Our lovely modern planes can easily handle the Luftwaffe. It is only a matter of time. I will come along every day now to tell you of the latest rumours, but don't ever talk about me to anyone. There are many informers about, especially among the Ukrainians, my own crowd. You may have heard what the Germans do to "communist" propagandists. I prefer to be just a chess player.'

Fenced in by two rows of electrified barbed wire, 3 metres high and shut off from the outside by a concrete wall, by now we had seen enough to understand what the basics of life were like in this new version of a prison.

It was only during the two daily rollcalls that we saw the SS men. Camp affairs were run by the prisoners themselves. Inside the fence, the hierarchy, wearing designated armbands, consisted of the camp-elder, the camp hairdresser, the camp interpreter, the camp secretary

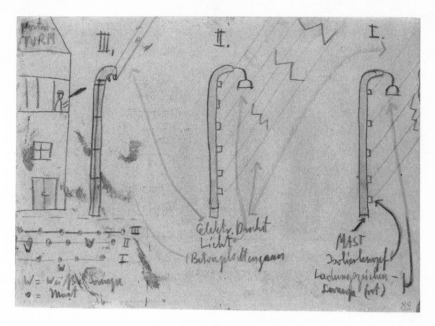

TOP: THE HIGH-VOLTAGE FENCE IN AUSCHWITZ I
Caged in, our world was surrounded by electrified fences, barbed wire and armed guards.

BOTTOM: ARMBANDS
Auschwitz's supervising prisoner hierarchy – as a German Jewish boy I was at the bottom of this pyramid of horror.

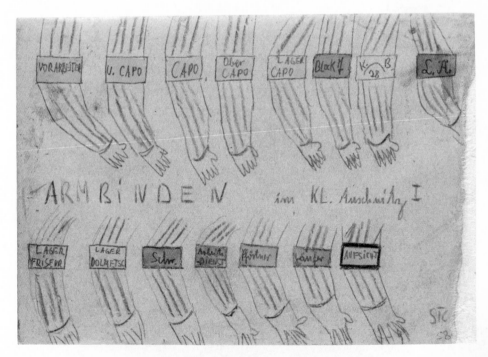

and the labour distributor. Overseers and block-elders made up the small fry. At the working squad, there were head capos, capos, sub-capos and foremen.

The camp-elder was an old-time criminal who the SS had picked out among the capos of one of the older concentration camps. His experienced superiors had found the right one to terrorise us. A favourite hobby of his was to get hold of some innocent, unaware bystander and beat him up savagely for no reason at all.

Most of the supervising posts at Auschwitz were filled by German criminals, who, like him, also had aggressive tendencies. Russians, Jews and Gypsies were not eligible for anything higher than a sub-capo.

Only at Birkenau, the hell on earth, no national distinctions were made, and their criminal specimens of any race would be allowed to show the weird cruelties they were capable of.

Then, one day in July, something unexpected happened. During the usual rollcall, I was told to step forward. My name, number and place of birth were checked, and, to the surprise of the whole room, I was led away.

Trembling with fear and uncertainty, I searched for reasons why, of all the many prisoners, it had to be me, the one who attempted, through every means possible, to remain inconspicuous, who'd been singled out. Had they found out about Father? Had anything happened to Mother? Did they think I was too young?

At the block office, I was spoken to by a cleanly dressed, rather short and stout prisoner who talked in fluent German. His hair, contrary to strict camp regulations, had been allowed to grow and sprouted like a hedgehog's prickles.

'I am one of the prisoners working at the SS registration office. In fact, I am in charge of it; a very responsible position,' he said self-confidently. 'Having seen your index card, I would like to know more about you. Tell me about your family. What happened to them after 1933?'

As I vaguely told him my family's story, he would interrupt

regularly, asking for further details. He wanted to know more about my father. I tried to be tight-lipped. 'Never mind,' he bellowed triumphantly, 'you need not tell me. I know he left you in the lurch! I have not forgotten you.' That took me by surprise. 'I knew you the day you were born,' he continued. 'I used to live opposite your house, near Stettin. Don't you remember Keding, the one who brought the groceries? That is me. They got me in here for alleged juggling of party funds, but now they regret it and are going to release me. While I am still here, I will do my best to help you, but I have to do it secretly. There are many friends of mine, old fellow prisoners who also need my assistance. They will be envious and may even spread evil rumours. So, don't tell anyone about me. You'll find out that keeping silent will be for your own good. Tomorrow, same time, be at the middle window, southern side. When you see me, open it but keep quiet. So long, and good luck. I have to return to work now.'

I kept my promise, and the next day I sneaked away to the appointed window. As he entered the yard below, I looked out. A little parcel was thrown my way. It contained bread and sausage. The food was divided among us four friends – the first materialisation of our mutual sharing agreement. Suddenly, after only three weeks in camp, and solely on account of my new acquaintance, we youngsters had become everyone's favourites. Even former intellectuals saw fit to degrade themselves by implying that we should help them too.

Towards the end of our time in quarantine, working groups were assembled and sent to other camps in the Auschwitz complex.

At Monowitz, the giant I.G. Farben plant (which produced Buna – a synthetic rubber) needed more workers to meet the increasing demand for tyres. It also constantly needed to replace those workers fed into Birkenau's hungry crematoria when they were no longer able to meet their output quota. This growing need was filled by fresh victims from quarantine. Even those considered too weak at the last selection were now sent to Monowitz's notorious sweatshop.

By now, only seven of our original transport remained in

Auschwitz. Among them Sally, Jonathan, Gert and me. Inexperienced as we were, we now had to make up our minds about the impressions we wanted to give to our superiors. We gathered to decide upon a common attitude. Sally and Jonathan wanted to apply to join the bricklaying school. This, they had heard, was a kind of asylum for the young, where you could spend a few weeks in safety, learning the trade. Gert and I, being familiar with gardening and imagining ourselves to be 'tough guys', thought of undertaking work straight away, hard as it might be.

Pondering long and hard, we decided that we could not desert each other. Keeping together, pooling our strengths and weaknesses, might give us a chance to survive. We would try to enter the bricklaying school, dangerous as it might be for us to seem not qualified to work yet.

We left quarantine and had our first look at the camp. Auschwitz's core comprised a few two-storied buildings of red brick, which had once been erected for the Polish army. Now there were three rows of them, 28 blocks, connected by asphalt paving. Cheerful flowers greeted us from weeded beds that bordered the streets and the joyfully painted boxes on the windowsills. A well-kept lawn separated the camp from the surrounding wire fencing. One could not help but be impressed by this model concentration camp – a showpiece for any delegation, German or neutral.

The blocks were filled with small wooden bunks, every prisoner being privileged to have one of his own together with a meagre sack of straw and three grey blankets. The bunks were arranged three tiers high. A block's capacity was 200 men in the basement, 400 on the four-roomed ground floor, 600 on the two-roomed first floor and 300 in the attic: 1,500 men in all. Seven blocks were reserved for the sick and three for administrative purposes. There were three storage barracks and a kitchen compound.

Fascinated by this first glimpse of the full camp, we marched on into the unknown. Only now, as we entered the main camp, would the complete picture of the prisoner's cruel lot, with all its suffering and brutality, begin fully to reveal itself.

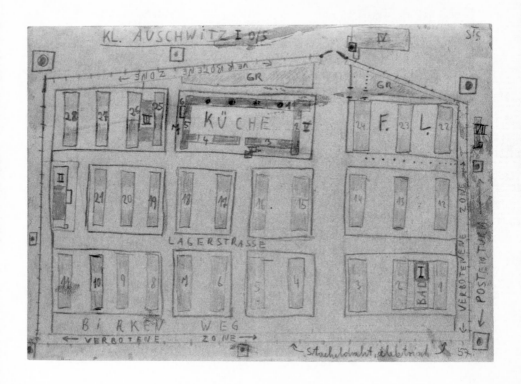

AUSCHWITZ CAMP I
Unwelcoming and dangerous – Auschwitz
Camp I was my home for 19 long months.

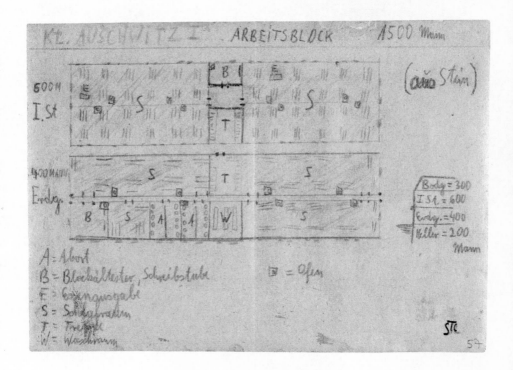

A WORK BLOCK

Block 7a – the bricklaying school was on the
top floor of Block 7.

CHAPTER 7
BRICKLAYING SCHOOL

At the beginning of August 1943, a dozen shy youngsters, flushed with expectation, climbed the stairs of Block 7. Heading our small group, taking two steps at a time, were Gert and I. We'd been chosen as the spokesmen as we were the ones who spoke fluent German and had decent enough city manners. After us came Sally and Jonathan. The nervous Poles and Russians followed slowly and at some distance behind us four.

We entered the attic, apprehensive and aware that making a good impression was our only positive weapon. Groups of young prisoners, some standing, others sitting, were circled around heaps of blunt-cornered, moist red bricks and vats of mortar. Some were laying out brick bonds, building walls and then taking them down again, after which they carefully scraped off the mortar and returned it to the vats. One instructor explained the secrets of arches, while another demonstrated the skills of plastering. This was the *Maurerschule* – Auschwitz's bricklaying school.

The block's personnel and teachers greeted us in a surprisingly kind manner and took down our details. Whatever their nationality, they, like ourselves, seemed eager to show off their best. The block-elder, who would decide our fate, was not in yet.

'It's all up to him,' we were advised, 'so you had better look neat and disciplined. He is very peculiar and full of whims. If he dislikes someone, he can be ghastly, and to those who offend him, he unleashes a fury of cruel brutality from which there is no escape. His cold determination is like a double-edged sword. It protects his flock of youngsters from the inquisitive snifflings of hostile SS guards with the same fearlessness that it mows down opponents. Be careful.'

When his arrival was announced, we quickly lined up in one row and stood to attention, our caps pressed to the seam of our trousers. Strolling in, like a sailor on leave, came a prisoner wearing a faded but well-pressed striped blue-white uniform, trouser legs widened at the

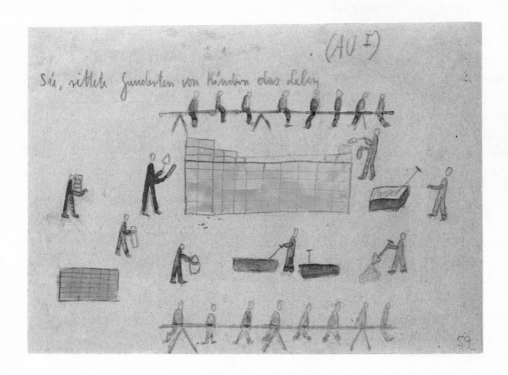

IT SAVED THE LIVES OF HUNDREDS OF CHILDREN
The bricklaying school was a haven for hundreds of 15- to 18-year-old
boys. I entered at 13.

bottom. His face, showing angular, severe features, might have been
that of a simple German worker. The triangle on his breast was red;
his personal number, in the thousands, next to it. It was obvious that
he was a political opponent who had spent many years in German
concentration camps before being sent to Auschwitz two winters ago.
Now he was in charge of this youth asylum, the bricklaying school.
Around forty years old, he was a father and dictator to 400 youngsters,
all of whom came from anywhere between Siberia and France.

He looked at us like a general inspecting his troops. He approached
a little Ukrainian, closely inspected his shaven head, scraped at it with
his fingernail and muttered, 'Dirty lout.'

His next target was me. I was standing at the head of the row, and
clearly my sticking-out ears were rather prominent. I had them pulled
and peered into. I was frightened at whatever he might find up there
that might annoy him. I was nevertheless flattered by the way he had to
crane his neck to look me in the eye. 'Next time I'm going to pick you
for growing carrots in,' he growled before moving on. We felt like the
lowest of the low.

He faced us with his legs apart and his arms at the waist. 'You
can stand at ease now, you maybugs,' he bawled finally. 'You are new
members of the bricklaying school.' Then, flapping the wide ends of
his trouser legs, he walked up and down the rows, fixing his glance
on each of us in turn. 'Don't think you can live here as you did in
Block 2A,' he warned, stopping in front of the Polish boys who had
food parcels under their arms. 'This is Block 7a, where I determine
the rules. Forget about the camp around you and stay in your rooms.
Even in Block 7, the ground floor is out of bounds to you. Don't ever
let me catch you lingering where you are not supposed to be! There
are not going to be any thefts or fights in my block. Woe on him who
dares to offer bribes. Block 7a means order, cleanliness, discipline and
comradeship. Those who don't adjust themselves may stay outside
with their grown-up friends and see how long they survive without
help. I will not take an interest in you when you come back, half-dead,
begging to be let in again.

'Anyone daring to disobey my orders or those of the block

personnel will be sent to me. I'll make him feel the consequences,' he continued, expanding his chest. 'If the offence is serious, I shall have as little mercy on him as he had concern for the rest of you. I don't want to have the school closed down because of the irresponsible few. There will be checks to see that you are washed, have made your beds properly and have no hidden food.' He continued, 'That your heads are clean, your hair properly cut and that you don't sleep with your socks on. If you cooperate, I'll do my best to organise food and to keep you alive. When you have learned something, you'll be sent to work as a group on your own, but still continue to belong to this block. I expect you to honour this because our common future depends on it. Remember,' he said, 'there are to be no national cliques or quarrels about your past. In my block, there have been none so far, and I want to hear no complaints about you.' With a final commanding look, he shouted, 'Room-elder, take charge of them!'

After the rollcall, we trod on the freshly cleaned, red concrete floor of our new home. The four of us were given bunks in the German part of the room, Little Berlin, as all the boys were Jews from Berlin.

Shortly, the block inmates returned from the building site. Most were exhausted from a back-breaking day's work, but on this rare occasion, questioning newcomers warranted giving up some hours of precious sleep. Crowding closely together, we were soon involved in lively conversation. Including we four, Little Berlin had nine members in all, including a 'Blond Gert', a 'Dark Gert', a 'Saucy Gert', a 'Little Kurt' and a 'Long Kurt'.

Other new arrivals joined Little Kiev, with its numerous Waskas and Wajnkas, or Little Warsaw with its Janneks and Taddeks. Looking on were boys from France, Belgium, Czechoslovakia and Austria. As a first sign of understanding, we would have to learn the names of all of them and pronounce them correctly. Later, we might even attempt to tackle each other's languages. Up until then, the odd names of the Gypsy boys seemed too short to be distinguished. The long elaborate ones of Little Salonika were too complicated to be remembered.

The main camp of Auschwitz had a comparatively large number of young prisoners. Out of every hundred inmates, about two were between the ages of 15 and 18. In 1943, most were either Russians, Poles, Gypsies from Czechoslovakia, Germany, Austria and Poland and Jews from Greece.

It was surprising how much we youngsters differed from our grown-up compatriots, as we had not yet absorbed all the national prejudices and illusions that hate thrives on. There was no particular way of life that we had become accustomed to, for throughout the years of our teens, there had been war. Instead, we faced our fate as one unit: 'youth'.

In our block, therefore, national differences never caused serious problems, as it was the differences that provided entertainment. Ukrainians were proud of their muscles so did acrobatics, inviting those who still had sufficient energy to challenge them. Wherever those skilful Eastern performers may have come from, they were just as capable of friendship as the boys I had grown up with.

The Gypsies were harder to understand, but once you had shown them respect as equals, they would even reveal the secrets of Romany to you, the language that kept them together. This was the greatest honour possible for an outsider, accorded only to the few true friends who succeeded in gaining their confidence. Other acquaintances of theirs were merely treated to sessions of clairvoyance.

Jews adapted well to the new surroundings, proving themselves to be workers equally as skilled as anyone. They were proud to show their knowledge, and quite a few of them were nicknamed 'Professor'.

We could not help but be impressed by this hopeful atmosphere that 'youth' had created for itself amid the holocaust of its elders. Perhaps the block-elder had been right to make those harsh threats against any who might disturb it.

Our instructors had been chosen for their knowledge of languages. All but one of them were Jews and had no previous knowledge of the building trade.

Among them was a Polish Jew from Belgium who, already
lecturing in Polish, Russian, Czech, Yiddish, German and French, was
now embarking on the study of Greek and Romany. Then there was
Mr Pollak, an elderly survivor from Slovakia, the school's one and only
natural bald head (an accomplishment he seemed immensely proud
of). It certainly served him well as a subject for amusing conversations
with outside visitors, who, as a kind of liaison officer, he was supposed
to entertain.

One of Mr Pollak's clients was a stout contractor, the civilian
responsible for our school, who had come all the way from Berlin.
Whenever this jolly-looking guest arrived for his monthly inspection
tour, he quickly walked past us and then shut himself in with Mr
Pollak. These sessions, lasting well over an hour, ended with the
civilian rushing off with as business-like an air as possible. Minutes
later, Pollak emerged, his straightened finger rubbing his stubby nose
and then adjusting his spectacles. Pacing as correctly as a schoolteacher
was supposed to, he tried hard to conceal his grin. Giving that up, he
sat down and lit a cigar, his cherished reward. 'Yes,' we would hear
him say to the other teachers, 'it looks bad for Germany, but not much
better for ourselves.'

Leopold Weil, 'Poldi', a Swiss Jew who had been arrested in France,
was our youngest instructor. His mother applied for his release and,
after much waiting, a date was fixed for his return to Switzerland. A
few days before this, however, he was put in solitary confinement. He
was accused of 'spying for a foreign power', which, had he been freed,
would have become true. They sent him to a punishment squad, never
to be heard of again.

Our room-elder, Sigi, was a frail little German Jew whose past
criminal offences had meant many years of concentration camps
behind him. In one of the camps before the war, he had lost an arm
and severely mutilated the other while working in a machinery shop.
Each morning, with the 5 a.m. shrill alarm hardly faded, he would
rush around the room shouting, 'Wakey, wakey!' Moving his stumpy
arm, he managed to pull away the blankets, and would sometimes pour
water onto our sleepy faces. As we admired his agility, we only had our

own laziness to blame for these early-morning showers. Eventually we even came to like his pranks. We, Sigi's compatriots, tried hard to get favours from him, but without success. He never budged from his stand of a fair share for all.

The youngest of our superiors was 'Ello', the deputy room-elder. A robust lad, he enjoyed treating us to episodes from his amorous exploits back home, rounding off each of his tales with, 'Oh, let me go, Ello, you are a pig', sung to his favourite tune, a Czech variant of 'Roll out the Barrel', called 'Rosamunde'.

At 19, Ello, a Slovak soldier, had been lined up at the railway station, ready to be transferred to the Eastern Front. Present, too, were Gestapo agents. They read out the names of the Jews, disarmed them and sent them straight to Auschwitz.

As the days passed, we became accustomed to the daily routine of the camp.

At 5 a.m. sharp, the camp bell rang, jerking us away from a warm, blissful forgetfulness. Thousands of bunk frames all over Auschwitz started shaking, littering the rooms with flakes of straw and driving off clouds of dust, as if these were so many futile dreams.

Thousands of inmates then headed for the crowded washrooms to empty their bowels and wet their skinny hands and shaven heads. Once back in their rooms, they brewed up whatever it is that acorns offer when boiled in water. It seemed good, even to the many who had not hidden a crumpled slice of yesterday afternoon's meagre bread ration.

Beds were then made, the sacks of straws carefully fondled to induce them to look full and straight, as befitting strict German culture.

By 6 a.m. the blocks were empty, their inmates now assembled into working groups called Commandos. Fifteen minutes later, these groups (that could number anything from 200 to 2,000 prisoners) marched out of camp, passing by the bandstand. The block personnel and the bricklaying school remained behind.

At noon, the bell rang again to announce lunch. Big heavy wooden vats filled with soup were carried out of the kitchens. The carefully

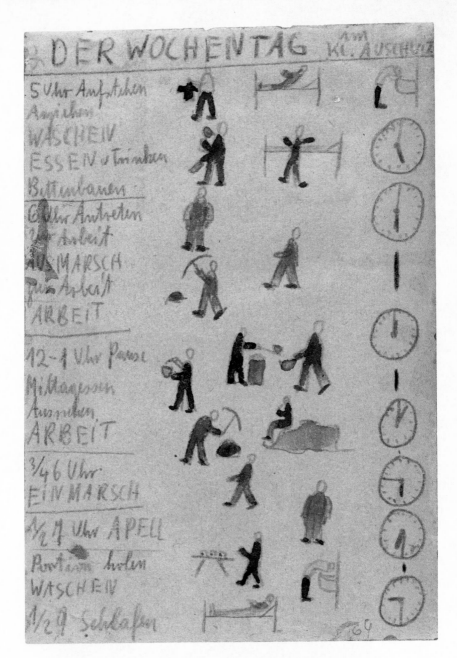

A WEEKDAY
A routine day of slavery – little food, little rest,
rollcalls and lots of hard work.

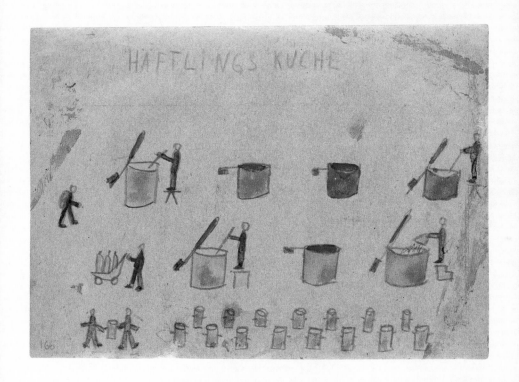

THE CAMP KITCHEN
Prisoners had to stand on stools to stir the vats
of soup, their own size.

ladled-out litre of soup was a mere pick-me-up, except for once or twice a week, when a second helping acted as a filler.

Our break for an hour at midday was spent walking around the camp in the hope of 'organising' more. To 'organise' meant to get something by any means – from begging to stealing. If you looked pitiful enough, a soft-hearted room-elder, who had received too big a vat and whose own protégées were out of camp, might treat you to a bowl of soup.

Everyone else, headed by the Ukrainian boys, invaded the stinking, rotting kitchen dump. When driven away, we returned to push long, pointed rods through the railings in order to poke at whatever treasures we may have been deprived of – mouldy bread, rotten cabbage and potato peelings. I often thought of that Russian prisoner-of-war back in easy-going Berlin. If you fished out something worthwhile, it meant being admired for your success and then begged to share it.

At 1 p.m. the bell rang again, and we resumed counting the bricks that we laid and the hours before the next meal.

At 5.45 p.m. the dirty and exhausted working columns started to return.

At 6.30 p.m. rollcall commenced. It typically lasted between 15 minutes and an hour.

After rollcall we streamed back to the block where rations were issued, and all prisoners then had two hours for 'personal business'.

Most youngsters spent this time in search of potential benefactors and adult friends who could organise extra food. A few took advantage of the vacant washrooms or mended their clothing. Others queued up outside the dispensary or lulled themselves into the land of fantasy by listening to orchestra rehearsals. Some looked to friends to get themselves educated on subjects ranging from 'organising' to politics. For others, the strenuous working day had dispelled all interest they may have had in the world they found themselves in; after gobbling their rations, they went straight to bed.

The members of Little Berlin, having few friends and still fewer compatriots, stayed in the block. Dark Gert and Jonathan, both silent

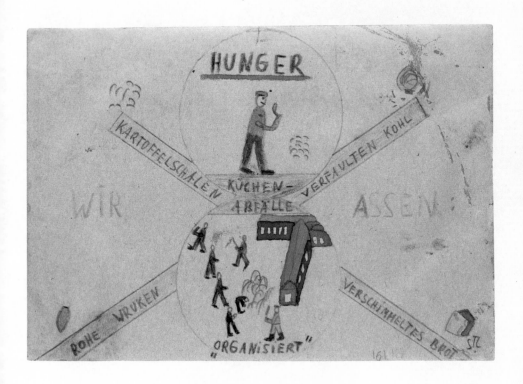

HUNGER

Our extreme hunger drove us to consider
unexpected things as 'food'.

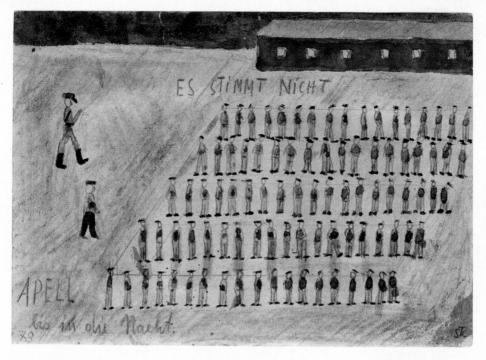

TOP: ES STIMMT NICHT (IT DOESN'T TALLY) When numbers didn't add up, the rollcall could last for many hours.
BOTTOM: ES STIMMT (IT TALLIES) When they did add up, the camp-elder forwarded his report to the SS Command.

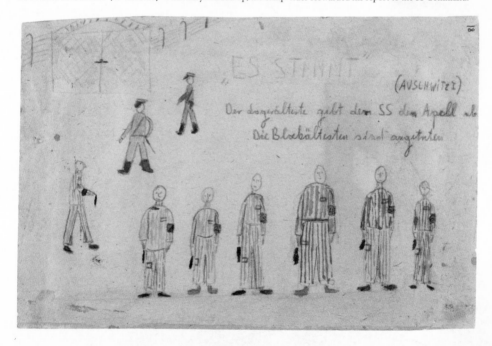

lads, just sat on their beds contemplating. Long Kurt, his big frame making him perhaps the hungriest of us all, set up a sock-mending business. As his cherished needle bobbed in and out of his clients' decaying socks, he kept up our spirits with tales from his native Königsberg. For those wanting to laugh, like little baby-faced Kurt, whose childish naïveté never left him, there was also Saucy Gert, who never tired of unravelling his stock of spicy jokes.

At 8.30 p.m. or sometimes 9.30 p.m., the curfew bell rang. A few minutes later, 'lights out' would be announced.

The Nazis painted some of the rooms with slogans. Blazoned upon the whitewashed half of the wall opposite the upper bunks of our room was the cruel but inevitable: 'There is only one road to freedom – its milestones are diligence, obedience . . .'

Das Tausend jaehrige Reich (the thousand-year empire), it seemed, had expectations even of us. Part of this discipline, apparently, was the 'bed-building' process. So important was it that the guards frequently had it supervised by the SS guards.

To eliminate the troubles that straw and dust created by falling each morning onto our freshly made lower bunks, we devised a bed-making schedule. The occupiers of the upper bunks (veteran prisoners and block personnel) would be the first to spread their blankets and within a certain time limit. Then came the middle and lower bunks, which we had.

The people in the middle bunks bore the brunt of the room inspections. Prominent inmates chose the upper beds because having more headroom meant that these could be walked over when escape required it. Floor-level occupants were out of sight, but they suffered most from carelessly stepping feet and spilt liquids – hot or cold.

During the daily rollcall we stood to attention 10 rows deep and were counted by the gloved finger of an arrogant SS corporal.

When the total number of prisoners present did not agree with the number recorded in the books (a near-weekly occurrence), this ordeal would drag on for hours. It was a constant reminder of our insignificance. A whole camp of tired sub-humans lined up was easy prey for any sadistic mastermind, and the Nazis quickly exploited it.

The block-leader* of 7a was keen on the 'flower box drill', and the school's doctor was a favourite candidate for it. He had to hold up the heavy green boxes that lined the windowsills and try to keep his balance while the SS corporal, his revolver drawn, built a pyramid of flowerpots on it.

Before long we developed a method of screening off potential victims with stronger, healthier-looking prisoners, who were less liable to be picked out and who made up the front, back and side rows. When the SS found this out, they gave up walking around and just entered our rows, kicking and beating us, regardless of our complexion, health or strength.

To look too much like a Russian or to have a Jewish nose meant being the continual scapegoat. But to give the impression of not being the caricature you were supposed to be was little better. 'How dare you lousy Gypsy brat be blond?' they would bark. 'Your mother must have been quite a whore!'

Sundays in Auschwitz were relatively quiet. The morning hours were occupied by numerous tasks for which there had been no time during an exhausting week.

Your one and only set of clothing always needed a brush-up. There were new numbers to be sewn on and thinning socks to be mended. Those who felt that a fortnightly change of underwear was not enough, washed their pants. We queued up for the barbers and cleaned the block. Then, at noon, we greased our rough leather boots – usually two odd ones – and went down for the obligatory rollcall.

Sunday rollcalls meant inspections, and one block would be picked out for being the dirtiest. We of the bricklaying school, in our precarious position, certainly could not afford to be conspicuous.

---

* A block-leader was an SS soldier whereas a block-elder was a prisoner.

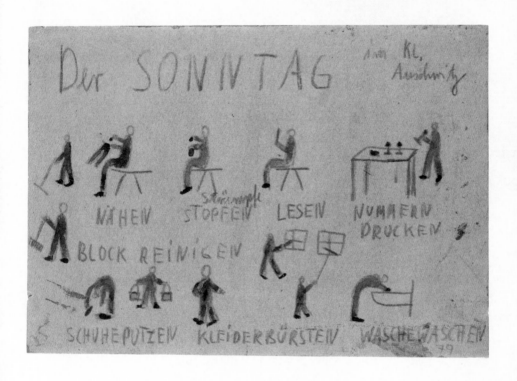

SUNDAYS
'Rest' day in Auschwitz meant no 'free' time –
we had many necessary activities to attend to.

The distribution of soup was followed by two hours' curfew during which the camp was supposed to take a midday nap. After that, with the exception of the few who slept through until the next morning, we woke up with empty stomachs urging us to spend the rest of the day 'organising'.

Our afternoons, therefore, meant roaming the camp in a vain and depressing search for friends and food. Our plight was further aggravated by the fact that, while misery and hunger tended to be invisible, wealth and having plenty had ways of showing themselves. We did not see the feelings of our fellow sufferers, only the food parcels of the few privileged ones. Also catching our eyes, as if mocking our helplessness, were the arrogant SS families beyond the fence taking their leisurely Sunday walk.

The only consolation that Sunday brought was a good, long sleep.

To lessen the rush on the hospital during the busy evening hours, when many of the ill had to be turned away, the authorities allowed our school to have a 'doctor' of its own. This we were grateful for, as visits to the camp dispensary meant risking one's life. Like others, we had heard rumours about SS doctors using youngsters as guinea pigs for their experiments. Of those who went, very few ever came back.

Our doctor, a Jewish Belgian male nurse, too soft-hearted to be strict, treated us as if we were his little children. He had a shop in a corner of the attic. From time to time, one by one, we sneaked away from the piles of moist bricks and queued up to see him. Most of us saw him every week, either because of real ailments or because we liked to hear him say, 'Oh, go away, you little scoundrel, there's nothing wrong with you, you'll still live to be a hundred.'

His equipment consisted of a tray bearing many-coloured ointments from which he would let you choose the one you liked best. 'Little Jendroe,' he would call good-humouredly to a Gypsy boy passing by, 'do tell our Janek, who is very, very ill, what colour you liked best for your skin disease.'

We kept him busy, because, hidden from the eyes of the SS, our various complaints remained a secret among ourselves. We felt at home with him and could confide in him.

When he had time to spare, he spent it trying to organise medicines. Sometimes a hospital friend of his would give him vitamin tablets; distributing them was one of our benefactor's happiest moments. 'Only for those who get no parcels from home,' he would announce, fully aware that, except for the five Poles, we received no mail at all.

With no means to fight my hunger, I decided to contact Mr Keding, the family friend whose sudden appearance at the quarantine block had caused such a stir.

Evening after evening, during private business time, I loitered in front of Block 3 hoping to catch a glimpse of him. Block 3 was divided into comfortable little rooms, and was home to prominent prisoners, capos and old-time criminals from Germany. No ordinary camp inmate – even if invited – would dare enter. Then, one day, Mr Keding appeared, and he told me his story.

'As you know, I was a shopkeeper, and you may wonder what brought me here. Well, it was a family affair. There was cash missing from my till and I suspected my wife. I told her of it and we quarrelled. She claimed that she had given the money to the Nazi Welfare Fund, but in my temper, it made no difference, and I must have cursed both her and the Fund too hard. Then my wife left me. She surely told people about the incident, because I was soon accused of "violently" attacking the institutions of the party. That's why I am here. Now,' he said, a note of regret in his voice, 'they are going to send me back again. My old party membership must have impressed them, especially now that things look grim for Germany.'

Mr Keding introduced me to an aggressive-looking German criminal who was a friend of his. 'My buddy here will stand by you when I have gone. Remember his name and his block. When you need advice, go and see him.'

Keding asked whether I liked sugar. I certainly did, and so we arranged to meet again the next day.

I could hardly wait to see him again. After the evening rollcall, I rushed off to Block 3. Mr Keding was there, waiting for me, with a bag of wet brown sugar.

'That's the only thing I can do for you,' he apologised, 'but it is quite a clever trick of mine. Once a week, as I come back from work, I am allowed to take in a big jug of coffee for the German inmates of Block 3. At the SS kitchen, they let me sweeten it myself. So, I fill the jug with sugar, then saturate it with coffee. At the block, I drain off the brew and there you are.'

Clutching the generous gift, I felt like a beggar receiving a gold coin, but I was uneasy about guarding such a treasure. 'Farewell then,' called my busy benefactor as he headed for his room. 'I am going home next week. Good luck, kid.'

Coming back to our block, I was at once surrounded by my roommates. Sugar was unheard of in a concentration camp. They all wanted to taste it. And I could not refuse them, as we were all beggars.

The rest of the bag was divided among we four members of the sharing pact. We gobbled up the sugar as fast as possible, but it nevertheless still lasted two days. Despite happier stomachs, and rare sweetness on our tongues, complaints swiftly followed.

'You made yourselves popular with the others at our cost,' said some accusingly. 'You had no right to be generous with our part of the bag.'

It was not long afterwards that someone told me another version of Keding's past. Before 1933 our friend's hobby seemed to have been scouting. As a leader, he used to accommodate a small group of boy scouts at his home. He ceased these activities on being brought to court and accused of having had homosexual relations with his protégées. Then Hitler came along, so Keding donned a brown SA uniform, and all was well again.

Why then, I asked myself, was he classified as a political prisoner? Faded as it was, maybe his triangle had not been red at all, but pink, pink being the colour of convicted homosexuals. This, too, may have explained his desire not to be seen in my company so soon before his release.

A stream of newly transported prisoners kept coming. And new arrivals meant that some of us would be sent to other camps to make room.

On this occasion, though, the destination was Birkenau with a 'supposed' job as bricklayers. But it was only a five-minute ride from there to the forest which hid the camouflaged gas chambers. We knew that only too well. So too did our block-elder, the one who would do the painful picking out.

We were lined up. There were a hundred too many of us. First, without even looking up, the block-elder called out the names of troublemakers. The Polish lad who did black-market business, the Gypsy boys with weak bladders, the children with contagious scalp diseases, the few extreme nationalists and those who slept with their socks on. Then he walked along our row. Having no alternative, he picked out those who he thought could take care of themselves without him.

That evening we stayed in our rooms. The full horror of what we had just been through stunned us into silence. Our morale was severely shaken. All that was left of Little Berlin was Blond Gert, Little and Long Kurt, my friend Saucy Gert and me. Sally and Jonathan, the original members of our gang, had gone. We were not even certain that we had been lucky. Only eight months ago, when all the surviving youngsters had been concentrated at the bricklaying school, the whole block, teachers and all, had been transferred to Birkenau, never to be heard of again. Innocent boys and men, all with their own identities, had disappeared.

CHAPTER 8
SURVIVING

Little Kurt was our problem child. Coming from a reputable family of Berlin intellectuals, he had been spoiled at home and was ignorant of the world around him. Now he made such a nuisance of himself that we started to doubt his sanity. We did our best to try and earnestly father him.

One of his crazes was to bother us boys, teachers and room-elders with a newly learned song about girls, which we had actually taught him. In one of the neighbouring blocks, we heard him singing out of tune, but he was rewarded with enthusiastic applause by his listeners. It must have worked for him, as he was charitably rewarded with a bowl of soup.

Another, less easily remedied whim of Little Kurt's was to spit at anyone who was teasing him. Comic a character as he was, it was only natural for us to poke fun at him. He himself admitted that he looked like an 'arse with ears'. But when it came to picking out his opponents, from whom he depended on us to rescue him, he unfortunately decided to choose big, muscular Ukrainians.

The majority of the SS men who guarded us originated from fascist countries like Poland and Slovakia. Although they were recruited as representatives of 'Germanic glory', they were as ignorant of the German language as the prisoners who were taken from these very countries. Maybe, like them, they had come to hate the language of their masters.

There were many ironies to concentration camp life. One of them was the story of our block-mate, a Slovakian Gypsy boy. He was imprisoned, whereas his father was wearing the uniform of the SS, having enlisted before Hitler's decision to exterminate the Gypsies. With the silvery skull-and-crossbones emblem of the SS pinned to his forage cap, he drove the same trucks that had taken his family to the gas chambers. Sometimes he passed our camp, but his son dared not talk to him. Fearing denunciation, they would just wave at each other.

It was a strange world we were living in, but I could not figure out who was causing it to be so. I picked on the obedient tools of the SS empire, but the image of the Gypsy boy's father, governed by orders and fears, driving in his lone cabin, made me change my mind. Then who was to blame for our plight? Was it Hitler? Was it the warmongers? Was it the captains of industry? And what about God?

The youngest of the camp inmates was a 12-year-old baby-faced, Slavic-looking Polish Jew. Together with his four cousins, a little older than himself but just as small in appearance, he had come to Auschwitz in May 1943.

At the station, their newly arrived transport faced the fatal selection. These five boys had been picked out by the SS to serve as camp messengers. Three of them were allocated to our camp and lived on Block 16.

Known as 'runners' they spent their busy day rushing around to maintain communications between the capos and the SS. We tried to be on good terms with these smartly dressed, midget-sized children, for, besides knowing all the latest camp news, they were close to many influential camp bigwigs.

However, some people suspected that the 'runners' held their envied and privileged positions by playing the young 'girlfriends' to the camp's senior personnel. Accusations were often thrown at these boys and rumours even had it that their underpants were laced and pink.

'Well,' Blond Gert lectured me, 'why shouldn't they? Back in Monowitz camp, I too had homosexual relations with my capo. It gave satisfaction to both of us and there is no point in refusing it. What else could have saved me from the hard work, hunger and illness? Look at Little Kurt, childish and naïve as he is,' Gert went on to tell me, 'even he has been had. You just ask him and see how much he giggles about it, silly ass.'

Youngsters who, through lack of self-control, had surrendered themselves to the desires of their sex-starved acquaintances were looked upon with contempt and had to keep quiet about their experiences. Kurt, however, could not be blamed for his actions, for he was too innocent to understand. His helpless self, pulling grimaces and reciting nursery rhymes, could only evoke pity.

One day, a tall, friendly Pole[13] came to see me, the first visitor I had had since quarantine.

'I know that your block-elder doesn't like strangers here, but I had to see you personally,' he said in broken German.

His self-confidence impressed me even before I knew the reason for his visit. We went to a quiet corner and there he produced a carefully folded little slip of paper.

'This is for you. Give me an answer by tomorrow, when I will be back at the same time. I have to get out of here. So goodbye, good luck!'

Unwrapped fold by fold, the smudgy sheet revealed a pencil-written message. I looked at the words that stood for the signature. There was no mistake about it; they said, 'Your Mother'.

I was flushed with excitement. I had never given up the belief that Mother was close by. She was alive! News of my luck spread quickly and soon I was surrounded by dozens of roommates who, claiming to be my best friends, wanted to hear details. Above all, to see the word 'Mother'.

It was as close as I had come to experiencing a miracle in this hell-hole. There was a double reason for rejoicing. Someone had found my mother – a mother is surely the dearest human to every one of us – and some noble stranger had risked his life to smuggle in a message from the women's camp at Birkenau. We knew that Birkenau was a camp of mass murder. The very mention of it sent shivers down one's spine, and if you were caught with any kind of message, you would be killed.

The note said that next week a group of women, which would include my mother, was to pass through our camp. Nearly all the roommates who did not go out to work were eager to come along with me to welcome her. More than the sight of my mother, it was the idea of seeing 'women' that attracted them. However, they were to be desperately disappointed, as the block-elder, fearing trouble from the SS guards, decided that only the room-elder and I were to see her.

It was a week of almost unbearable waiting and so many questions. I wondered what Mother would look like. Would I recognise her? Would she recognise me? Would this dream really come true and would we really meet? A thought slipped into my mind that maybe looking out for Mother's tattooed camp number, 47542, would be a good idea.

The room-elder and I, carrying baskets under our arms for the supposed purpose of fetching the rations, walked down the main street. The place was deserted, as it was during the morning hours. We saw a column of women in striped dresses, with bleak kerchiefs on their heads, being led along by armed grey-uniformed SS women.

We had expected to see glamorous females, but they turned out to be miserable prisoners like ourselves. Exhausted veterans rather than women. Their suffering was written all over them. I was shocked at what I saw, and hardly recognised my mother.

Still in her late 30s, Mother looked as haggard as her companions. Without either of us slowing our stride, we touched hands. I managed to sneak a kiss. To hold her hand again was an unimaginable, miraculous moment. I would never forget that. Mother managed to express her hope that my work was not too hard. She rummaged beneath the rags that clothed her to pull out some bread that she had saved. But as I refused it, the guard stepped in to chase me away. Our encounter had lasted barely 15 seconds.

To have seen and spoken with my mother and just to be in physical contact with her had an enormously powerful effect on me. My determination to survive, no matter the constant dangers, was now encouraged by three factors. At the neighbouring camp, there was Mother, waiting for letters that would quieten her fears. Over the ocean, Father was fighting with the Allies, to help us. Out in the world, there was the future, beckoning us boys to become men.

I found out that the women's situation was no easy one. Factory and store-yard workers, labourers, farmhands and seamstresses, their working day was 11 hours long. Only the young and attractive among them were eligible for office jobs.

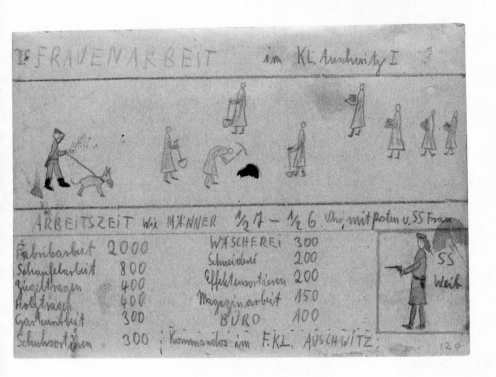

WOMEN'S WORK

The work for women was just as hard as for men and SS women guards were as sadistic as the SS men.

Following the brief encounter with my mother, I decided to see the camp hairdresser on Block 1 and tell him about it. Maybe the vague promise of help that he had given me on our arrival would materialise.

'How nice of you to have come,' he greeted me. 'But before we talk, do have something to eat; that is what most people come to see me for.'

As I looked down from the little window that opened onto the shower room, a trio of Gypsies with a guitar entertained a group of camp VIPs by singing sentimental Romany melodies. Meanwhile, the hairdresser laid out food the likes of which was scarce even in the capital of wealth, Berlin.

When I had polished the plate clean, I told him the news about my mother. He was quite unimpressed by it, explaining that he could not show goodwill to me or the other youngsters, except between the four walls that hid him from his rivals. Consoling me, he said, 'But I always have some titbits left for you youngsters. Come along in the evenings; you might even be good company. You know,' he continued, 'I am an old jailbird and have some experience of "organising". This has been my life for over ten years now. Hitler or no Hitler, I don't get out of here – but you who could get out won't survive. Do you think that the fences, gas chambers and crematoria at Birkenau have been built so that we may survive them? They mean destruction. This is the world that wants to show us criminals and you youngsters how to be civilised!'

My newly found benefactor was far from being a beacon of hope, but as he was hospitable and one of the most influential camp inmates, I decided to cultivate his friendship. As a rule, I went to see him twice a week. My companion was bald, wore dentures and his blue eyes peered through a cherished pair of glasses. Something, however, reminded me of his past. On his chest and arms was a fading set of blue tattoos with hearts, daggers and initials.

He told me stories of his exploits as a safe-cracker, the days of glorious independence, of his family that had long since forgotten him and of the hardships at the moorland concentration camps on the Ems.* As a veteran expert on prison life, he asked me, 'You know why

---

* The German districts of Emsland and Beutheim had a series of concentration camps from 1933 to 1945. The

I take such an interest in the naked arrivals just before they take their showers? It is my job to interview the new prisoners. If they talk to me, I quickly pass them on to another group. It is those who keep silent and are hiding something that interest me. My task, then, is to find out what. Usually, it is valuables, which I am supposed to hand over to the SS. But . . .' – he pulled open a drawer to reveal glittering jewels and golden coins – 'I am no such fool as to let them have all of it. Trusted friends of mine exchange these treasures for whatever I am in need of, and I can tell you that even SS officers are not indifferent to them.'

Then, one day, he startled me. 'The time has come when I can no longer afford to help you without asking for something in return. You know that not only do we miss our women, but we can't remember their pleasures.'

He locked the door and then started to unbutton his trousers. I was in shock. My only way out seemed to be to hit him hard enough that I would be able to escape. I did not dare, for he was a man of influence among inmates. I just stood there motionless, not wanting to give the slightest sign of cooperation. Again, he beckoned me, moaning that he was getting cold. He gave up. 'I am sick of you standing there as if someone wanted to kill you. You are no good to me and I am wasting my time.'

He unlocked the door but stopped me as I was about to rush out. 'Never mind, I will find plenty of others. Still, I won't abandon you altogether. Go to Block 1a now and then and take my bowl of soup that they reserve for me.'

Saucy Gert and Long Kurt just laughed at me when I told them of my ordeal. 'Yes, that damned old wretch is famous for his passions,' they grinned, 'and if someone tries to denounce him, the old schemer sends him off to Birkenau. You can count yourself lucky that he didn't use threats. It's not a bad idea pretending to be naïve and innocent. After fooling the old fox for all these weeks, however, you should be quite an expert now.'

Nearly all us boys had been propositioned, despite the efforts to

---

camps were largely punitive – starting with homosexuals and Jehovah's Witnesses. From 1942 onwards, over 50 per cent of inmates were German military personnel who had deserted.

stamp it out. Homosexuality was an open secret.

A few months later we learned that the camp hairdresser had been sent away to an Auschwitz subsidiary camp. Our block-elder's remarks about 'adult friends' seemed to be justified. 'To fool around with people in the limelight becomes a dangerous sport. When they go under, they drag down their associates.'

Block 7a, despite its strict and sometimes merciless rule, kept on being a refuge from the daily dangers and intrigues that haunted Auschwitz. It was a haven where the ups and downs of prison life faded against the brightness of a free, honest exchange of views, friendship and the overwhelming radiance of youthful hope.

Before long we experienced another of the dreaded selections. The picking out of prisoners who, no longer profitable to their SS masters, would be sent to the mills of death at Birkenau.

After the evening rollcall, the whole camp was marched onto the roadway that led to the 'Birkenweg', the 'Bathhouse'. With electrified wires on one side and armed SS guards on the other, there was no escape.

With our spirits at breaking point, we waited for hours while the huge queue crawled forward to enter the inspection rooms. The deafening silence was broken only by a lone clatter echoing from the main street – the rapid running steps of the lucky few who had passed their ordeal of life or death.

Trained on us from the watchtowers above were four machine-guns, lest any of us were contemplating an escape attempt. Some of us prayed. A few thought of home. Others, having given up hope for survival, seemed indifferent to their fate. Even the veteran German prisoners, previously confident of their privileged status, were afraid. Whatever our respective thoughts were, we kept silent.

It was now our turn. We entered the moist, cold bathroom and undressed. Then, taking our bundle of clothes, we ran past the SS doctors as quickly as our legs could carry us.

Fate was undoubtedly shining on me and the other boys that night. Why? Because the block-elder used all of his influence to save us. He

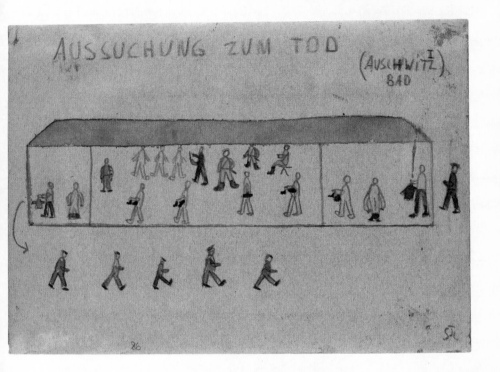

SELECTION FOR DEATH
At the selection, any sign of weakness, or even a bruise, limp or rash, would mean a death sentence.

whispered into the ears of the SS officer: 'The children really worked a lot today; let them run through quickly so that they can go to bed.'

This time the gamble largely paid off and only a handful of us were picked out. Those who passed the selection ran back to the safety of the block, hardly bothering to dress again. It was a simple procedure for such an inhumane and brutal process.

Sleep came hard that night. We who had been given another month's life expectancy turned our thoughts to those who were being driven away by the lorries and would soon experience the terror of Birkenau's overworked gas chambers.

The world had forgotten them and there was nothing we could do about it.

The constant fear and our common hardships made us draw together still closer. Acquaintances became companions and companions became comrades.

Among my friends was Mendel Tabacznik, a bright Jewish boy from Bialystok in Poland. Not much older than I, he had been in the camp since the winter of 1942, quite an achievement for a boy. An idealist, who remembered the past and thought towards the future, his moral conduct was admirable. He never talked about problems associated with camp life and was not interested in organising to survive. His sustenance seemed to be his dreams and recollections.

One of the most impressive moments of his life had been in Moscow in 1940, where he had participated in a mass display of gymnastics. 'Imagine yourself being on top of a human pyramid, with a vast crowd looking on, in the most famous square of the most talked-about capital city in the world,' he would say, his eyes glistening with enthusiasm. I was very fond of him.

Then there was 'Little Berger', an amusing young Gypsy boy from Austria. A bright lad equipped with intelligence and wit, he had used his time in camp to learn the art of writing.

Little Berger was an open-hearted friend as long as talk revolved around camp affairs, but when one mentioned the outside world, he would retract into his protective shell. He certainly had an inferiority complex. 'You needn't think that because I am only a Gypsy' was a standard phrase of his. Maybe he was right when he said: 'The Jews outside are all big shots, just as eager to hurt the Gypsies as anyone else is.' Should he ever have a chance, he will make an eager, promising student,' said our instructors. 'But until then, our world will have to do a lot of changing.'

Jendroe, 13 years old and a Czech Gypsy, was the smallest, and as a result, the most flamboyant and pompous among us. Backed by his several brothers, Jendroe knew how to exploit the sympathy we all gave him. Clustering around him were other Czech Gypsies, members of the same clan, who were anxious to guard their mysticism from the prying eyes of forward-thinking rivals, like Little Berger.

Then there were the boys who found themselves alone, without friends because they saw themselves as better than or separate from the rest of us.

One such inmate was a noisy Odessa boy who proclaimed himself to be a 'Jew-hater'. His father had been a participant in the pogroms and had always urged him to be anti-Semitic. Now that the Jewish bosses had abandoned him to the Germans while they themselves retreated to Moscow, his prophecy seemed to have come true. 'Even here in the camp,' he howled, his frail, blond forehead beaded with sweat, 'it's the Jews who are going to kill me.' His fears were not unfounded – we did beat him up occasionally.

Another such inmate was a lone German, an ignorant country lad wearing a red triangle. How he'd managed to become a political opponent of the regime remained a secret. Even he, himself, did not remember it. His slow mind was now troubled still further by the fact that we all avoided him as much as possible. Like Little Kurt, he was a candidate for madness, a common affliction given the conditions we lived in.

At the women's camp in Birkenau lived the only Jewish child. A boy of four, he was very popular with guards and prisoners alike.

Once, he came to our camp to see his mother, who at the time was in Block 10 – the experimental hospital for women. Since I had arrived with the same transport, and I knew him from the internment camp, I tried to see him. 'What do you want?' the blond Berliner hissed at me, contemptuously waving his little tattooed arm the way they had taught him. 'Get away with you, *Scheiss in Wind*!' ('Shit in the Wind').

A prisoner's best friends were melodies. One of the few ways we could lift our spirits was with music and songs.

On Sunday mornings, when the camp's band gave auditions at the SS compound beyond the fence, many of us would crowd into the roadway between Blocks 1 and 12 to catch a glimpse.

The band, dressed in zebra-striped suits and equipped with highly polished brass instruments, would sit on a lawn surrounded by a neatly cut hedge. Walking around the garden were the guests of honour – the officers and their girls, the wives and their babies. Behind the high-voltage wires, the other audience would stand, shifting from one tired leg to the other, neither invited nor worth acknowledging. The songs made us forget our plight, and while our ears absorbed their magic, those on both sides of the fence were equally drawn to the music.

In summer, when every other Sunday afternoon meant a concert, the members of the band sat on a wooden platform near the camp's kitchen and formed a real orchestra. Their conductor was a Pole, formerly a well-known member of Radio Warsaw. It seemed as though the melodies had been picked to inspire us. And we felt, in this hell-hole, that there was no other place where they meant so much. When the evening clouds floated westwards as if in a hurry to leave us, they took with them the scraps of music and our thoughts. The clouds were free. Music was ageless. Thoughts were limitless. But we and millions like us were held by chains, chains we did not see and could not break, chains we had not known of, chains forged by a dying civilisation to shackle its youth.

On one dismal morning in Auschwitz, the foggy dew from the Sola river lingered over the camp and the first sun rays penetrated the darkness. The camp bell rang and the daily fight to get up and away from heavenly sleep and into our world's reality started. I rubbed my eyes and realised where I was. Then I remembered that it was my fourteenth birthday. I had a single letter reminding me of it, from Mother. It was carefully tucked away in my shirt pocket, telling me to be brave.

A child's birthday is usually a big affair, but as he becomes older, he receives fewer presents. That day I had none at all. I seemed to have become a man.

In the evening, I went to see the courier who had brought the birthday letter, the same irreplaceable Polish well-wisher who had delivered the first message. When I arrived at his block, fittingly numbered 14, he was expecting me. Waiting was a bowl of soup and some bread – this was a real birthday treat. To cheer me up, he told me more about Mother: she worked as a mechanic at the 'Union' metalwork factory and lived in Block 2 of Birkenau's women's camp. I learned from him that Mother had an important role helping others by being a German translator. Then my new friend, who was tall and, in his 30s, took me for a walk.

'Now that I know you better and that you are older by a whole year, it is only right that you should learn more about myself and the ideas I hold,' he said in a low voice, looking behind him to see that no one was following us. Slowly but clearly, he unravelled the story of his life, a struggle for his beliefs, which seemed more vital than ever now.

'The old Poland was no pleasant place for Jews to live in,' he confided in me. 'I have no particular liking for their kind, but as a socialist, there can be no such distinctions between human beings. Especially as it is a common desire now that unites us. We do not suffer in silence, as you youngsters have to. We keep up connections with our friends outside, among them the prisoners at our camps. All I can promise you is to keep on letting you know about your mother; that, you can depend on.

'Helping you with food,' my friend continued, 'would not be fair to

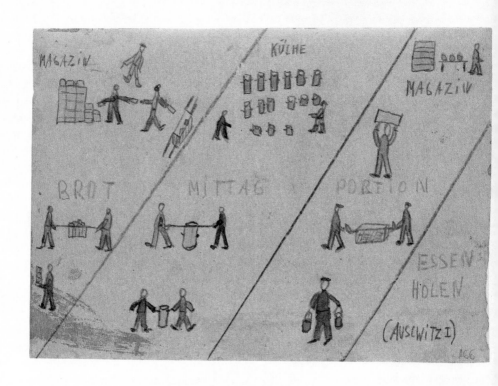

FETCHING FOOD
Once a day our poor but precious food was
carried by prisoners from the kitchen.

my fellow Poles, who I cannot let down.' I admired his frankness.

The Poles I knew were country boys and uneducated, rather unpleasant characters. Now I realised that not all of them were as aggressive as they seemed to be. Like my new Polish friend, they were capable of helping the worst kind of foreigners to them: Jews.

Poland's neighbours, the Ukrainians, were slave labourers in Germany prior to being imprisoned. This may have explained why these rough people – who would do anything for extra gain – were notorious as the camp's hooligans.

Friendly neither with the Russians nor the Poles, they embarked on a ruthless fight for survival, a drive that made them capable of attacking fellow prisoners for the sake of a slice of bread. A Ukrainian's loot was usually shared among friends and always gobbled up at once.

Every prisoner was a potential thief, but every Ukrainian a potential robber. Open attacks on weak-looking inmates grew to such an extent that we formed defensive squads. Their typical bait was the haggard and frightened prisoner. One of those they called *Muselmann*. This was a German slang term for someone who was hovering between life and death – such individuals would peddle their bread rations for tobacco. The victim would then be beaten up by one of the gangs, who in turn would be attacked by another gang. All for a piece of bread or an ounce of tobacco.

Thieves were harder to detect. At night, unseen, these daredevils would wiggle their skilful hands deep into your straw sack in search of any precious stowed slices of bread. In the more affluent blocks, the incentives for pickpockets were so great that their activities had to be guarded against by voluntary night watchers. Our sleep was frequently interrupted by the lights being turned on to reveal the elusive offenders scurrying back to their bunks. Punishments could be lethal. They would be pounced upon with a ruthlessness that only a concentration camp could teach. A thief, once caught, would be lucky to get up again after his punishment had been meted out.

A few daring youngsters practised 'soup-raiding'. This activity was regarded more as sport than outright theft. Certain agile lads would wait until a couple of prisoners passed by – bent double as they carried a vat of steaming soup back to their block. The lads would then swoop in and dip their bowls. It usually ended up with the raiders carefully balancing their watery quarry while being chased around the camp. If successful, they would find safety in some secluded lavatory where they could wolf down their prize.

Whenever the troubles – exacerbated by orders from above or caused by the prisoners themselves – threatened to boil over, we had a block curfew. That meant an early bedtime and a grim lecture from our block-elder. As usual, he warned that only rigid self-control could save us.

'And to those who believe in spiritual happiness,' he sneered, his voice booming in the direction of Little Warsaw, Little Salonika, the Catholic and Jewish corners of the room, 'if you imagine my advice to be trash, and repeated merely to hear myself talk, I can only say that I do not begrudge you your haven. If that is what you are after, you won't have to go far to look for it. The "ascension squad" assembles every fortnight. I only hope that by the time you rise up the chimneys of Birkenau, you will still be clean enough for your angels to receive you.

'The rest of you,' he roared, pacing up and down the gangway, 'had better do as you're told. If I catch you maybugs sleepwalking again tonight, you'll have nothing to laugh about. Once I beat you, I'll thrash you hard. I repeat that no one is to hang about the washrooms after bedtime. Understand! No one!'

Then it was lights out. We knew these were not empty threats, but as energetic as the block-elder was, he still needed his sleep. So, 30 minutes after the light in his room had been switched off, and he was asleep, it was time to enjoy our traditional nightlife. Heedless of warnings, there would always be some dozen absentees at a time. We ran down the cold stairs, rushed to the urinal and then refilled ourselves with the only thing that was not scarce in Auschwitz: water.

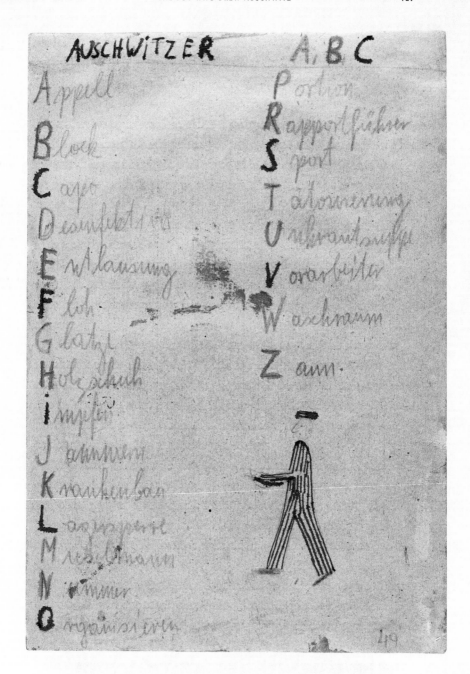

THE ABC OF AN AUSCHWITZER
These words were part of my reality for the 22
months of my life in concentration camps.

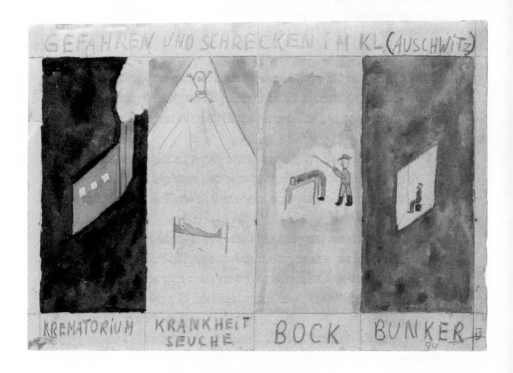

**CONCENTRATION CAMP DANGERS
AND HORRORS**
Crematoria, illness, punishments and
detention cells – the danger of death was
everywhere at all times.

CHAPTER 9
EXHAUSTION

Bleak weather heralded the coming of winter 1943. Much of our strength had been sapped away, and nothing had changed to our advantage. The prophets had been wrong. Germany's army was still powerful. The Nazis looked as triumphant as ever. And all we could do was suffer. In the fight for survival, the odds were heavily against us. The SS held four trump cards, real threats that we lived in constant fear of: the whip, the torture cell, disease and the gas chamber.

Each day candidates for punishment were led off to the kitchen square shortly before the end of the rollcall. There, one at a time, they were strapped to a scaffold and whipped. Minor offenders got 25 lashes, others 50, 75 or even 100. Some never returned.

Other suspects, whose cross-examination revealed insufficient information, were sent to the punishment cellar at Block 11. There, the implements of torture included dark and moist single cells, designed to fit around an inmate's standing body so as to prevent him from moving even an inch.

It would have been folly to expect the harsh camp regime to show leniency towards the younger generation. Boys caught having a nap at the worksites were given 25 strokes. Those on jobs outside the camp accused of dealing with civilians tasted the cells.

A strong body, encouraged by a determined mind, could outlive torture. However, all one could count upon to ward off malaria, typhus and the gas chambers was Fate.

One of the favourite correction methods was having us do 'sport': an ordeal imposed on us for 'not having worked hard enough'. First up were the capos, dozens of them being led through the camp streets exercising to the guards' commands.

'Lie down!' 'Get up!' 'Bend your knees, stretch out your arm!' 'Jump!' 'March!' 'Turn around!' 'Roll on the ground!'

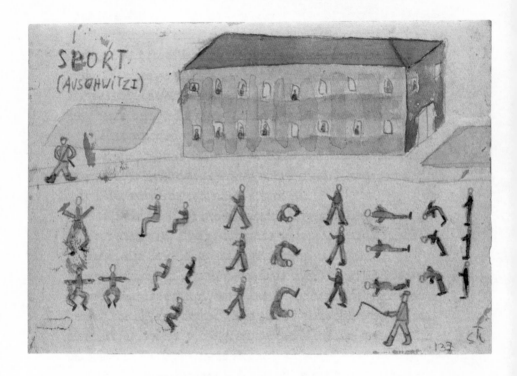

SPORT
Even 'sport' was used cynically to punish
prisoners at all levels.

'And now, you bastards,' they would be barked at, 'to teach you to extract more work from the skunks you are responsible for, we'll do it all over again but quicker.'

The following day, with the output still not increasing, there would be 'sport' with the foremen, the lower-ranking supervisors. If that still failed to bring results, we would all have to roll in the dirt – accompanied by the grotesque yelling of ridiculous camp songs.

Afterwards, we were warned that we had to be clean and shiny for the rollcall. Therefore, the rest of the evening was spent laundering our clothes desperately trying to dry them in readiness for the coming workday – only six hours ahead of us.

A new enemy had now made its entry: the Polish winter, cold and indifferent. 'Last year', said veteran inmates, 'it was hard; only a few of the Westerners not seasoned to it survived.'

This year our chances seemed better. There were striped prison coats, shawls and gloves to help us. To the shielded youngsters at the bricklaying school, the frost even brought entertainment. Skating fans, old and new, had slippery streets to glide along. Tougher lads re-enacted their childhood with snowball fights.

It became a common sight to see someone vigorously stamping their feet or wildly flapping their arms – a self-styled heat-generating ploy.

Waving limbs to fight off the cold was not much use to us. We just had no time for it. By day we worked. Then later, during rollcalls – when the cold would mercilessly gnaw at us – we had to stand to attention, helpless and motionless. Afterwards, we rushed back to our blocks, where winter evenings were generally spent in our rooms, waiting patiently near the lone iron stove for a vacant spot to toast a slice of bread, or skilfully trying to smoke a cigar made from the straw from our bunks, splinters from the wooden scaffolding we worked on and paper torn from bags of cement. Meanwhile, in the deserted wintry yard, our dark footprints – still lined up in rows of 10 from the rollcall – would slowly be covered with fresh white snowflakes.

Now and then our fortnightly bath was coupled with disinfection, in a vain attempt to banish the tenacious fleas. It meant emerging stark naked from the hot showers and running through a minus 20-degree, ice-covered camp all the way back to the block. Having performed this feat a few times without coming to any apparent harm, I became strangely aware that we and the fleas had become tougher together.

My time at the bricklaying school was up in the winter of 1943 and I joined a working squad some four hundred men strong. With our capo, an experienced bricklayer, at the head, we assembled in the yard long before dawn, then marched out past the bandstand. Penetrating the dark were the vigorous strains of 'Colonel Bogey' and 'The Stars and Stripes', the tunes of our Allies. *Either the Nazis had declared Sousa, the band's favourite composer, to be German or they were being fooled.*

After an hour we reached the snow-covered worksite. Our job was the construction of a women's camp – 20 blocks, identical to the ones we lived in. Most of the foremen were civilians, Poles, Czechs and Germans. Already housed in an abutting camp, they ignored us as much possible out of fear of the commonplace punishment of being sent to the main camp and becoming prisoners themselves.

There were no guards except those surrounding the 3-mile outer camp zone where we worked. This area was ringed by watchtowers 200 yards apart. Once the prisoners returning from the outer camp had been accounted for during the rollcall, the chain of guards withdrew for the night. If someone escaped, the wailing of the siren would tell the guards to stay on. With reinforcements arriving for the additional dugouts, the ring would then be strengthened until there was a gun every 70 yards.

The work, mainly concreting, bricklaying and plastering, demanded the fulfilment of a daily quota, and keeping a lookout for the supervisor. Cement bags were unloaded running at the double, and concrete was shovelled with a speed governed only by the mixing machine. Accidents were so frequent that they ceased to distract us.

Under the ever-watchful eye of the commanding SS officers, we developed a habit of being in constant motion. Working or not, we always looked busy.

A favourite trick of ours when, on rare occasions, we finished our quota ahead of schedule, was to sneak away to rooms on the upper floors to relax. There had to be at least four of us for this to happen. One was posted to watch the staircase, while two others – their hands clutching a hammerlike object – imitated working noises.

To acquaint oneself with our workmates – their quirks, strengths and weaknesses – took time. My own initiation came through some boyish plotting. Together with some muscular Russians, I was vigorously pushing a lorry full of sand. Going uphill, the load seemed to get heavier and heavier. We slowed down. 'Push, kid,' they shouted at me. 'Do you want the lorry to roll back again? If it does, it will only be because of you, lazy bungler. Want to exploit us, you son of a bitch?'

I was really frightened and pushed with all my might, feet apart and wedged to the ground, shoulder pressed against the cold steel of the lorry. My efforts seemed useless. The wheels stopped, then started to roll backwards. Someone quickly put a log under them. The broad Slavic faces of my workmates were grinning. 'You – big pusher! You willing to help. You push all alone, you brave! We – you – comrades,' they said in their broken German. They patted my shoulders; the new member of the team had passed the test.

During winter, the work was back-breaking and done in freezing temperatures.

Except for the short midday break when the soup arrived, sitting was a pleasure reserved for visitors to the onsite lavatory. The hut covering the stinking pit, forever threatening to overflow, was the only place to get some warmth and privacy. Never lacking busy admirers, it was rivalled in popularity only by the warmth of a treble-blanketed camp bunk.

The block-lavatories were equally popular. Returning from work, tired and frost-bitten, we made straight for their warmth. They had two rows of basins like seats at a bar. As we squatted on them, with trouser belts slung over our necks, appreciating the flushing water, we made acquaintances and exchanged news. Now and then we were joined by smokers, who, having found a bit of scarce paper, rolled it around wood shavings to make a cigarette.

Ten minutes later, the bell would ring for the rollcall, and we would be standing outside again.

Counting usually finished at about seven. When the daily arrivals and departures had been so numerous as to necessitate calling out names, it took longer. When someone was missing, the process of finding out the details would drag on till well after midnight, with our exhausted bodies having been up for 20 hours before that.

All we could do was to shift from leg to leg and hope that next time there would be more sympathy.

The experienced camp veterans had been right in their grim prophecies that we 'newcomers' would not stand it for long. The pitiful rations, although enough to prevent dying from starvation, could not be counted upon to sustain an ill-clad, emaciated body against the piercing cold of a Polish winter.

One evening after work the inevitable came. I dragged myself to the hospital compound, my head pounding with fever. Waiting in front of Block 28 were throngs of ailing prisoners, grouped according to nationality.

I joined the queue that would be the last to be admitted, the one for the Gypsies, Russians and Jews. If there was still time left to consider our group, we would get the worst treatment of all. Aware that I was about to surrender myself to the mercy of people to whom life and death meant nothing, I tried to work out an alternative. But there was none.

After hours of standing, we were let in. We undressed, and again grouped ourselves according to nationality, then paraded before the SS doctor. His job was to jot down either 'admitted'; 'back to camp'; or 'to Birkenau'. Apparently, there was still room at the hospital that day, for I was transferred to Block 19.

When I fell asleep, I remembered only three things: there were bedsheets, I was supposed to have influenza and the thermometer read 104° Fahrenheit, 40° Celsius. When I recovered my senses a few days later, it was the beginning of a new year, 1944.

With my fever improving I was released from hospital. On my way out, I happened to glance into the surgical department. I had never imagined that it was 'so easy' to treat boils and abscesses – the camp diseases. The infected limb was strapped to a railing, usually without anaesthetic, and the centre of the inflammation was cut. The operation, and the shrill yells of the patients, vied with each other for barbarity.

On my return to camp, I went back to the bricklaying school.[*] I discovered that it had changed considerably. Most of my companions and friends had gone, making room for new faces. Once more, I felt like a newcomer, the type of prisoner that others did not have to show sympathy for because they simply did not know whether I was worth it.

A few of the teachers said I looked very pale and advised me to seek out grown-up friends who could help my recovery and prevent me from becoming a *Muselmann*: one of those whose bodies could no longer support their spirits. Some extra food was now essential if I was to recover, so, accompanied by my friend Saucy Gert, I set out to find it. Evening after evening we toured the camp in search of help, but like disappointed beggars we quickly learned that only vague advice is given away for free.

Saucy Gert knew a fellow Berliner, a Jewish mechanic, whose job meant doing business with civilians. As we considered him to be rich, we tried to befriend him. Often, we would wait for hours at his Block, 22a. Occasionally he would show his appreciation by bestowing upon us the most he was willing to deprive himself of – a bowl of soup, half a litre each.

---

* Thomas, like most of the boys from the bricklaying school, continued living in Block 7a, even after they had finished their practical bricklayers' training and become workers. Living there saved Thomas's life and those of many other boys.

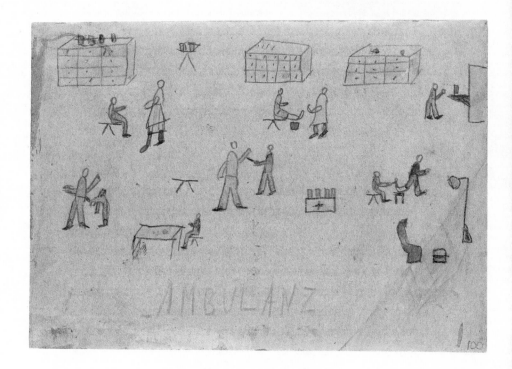

AMBULANZ (OUTPATIENT CLINIC)
The first aid given by nurse prisoners
sometimes helped us avoid dangerous
hospitalisation and saved the lives of many.

Our eager counsellors at the bricklaying school had said, 'Go to your fellow countrymen, the German Jews.' We had approached the two dozen-odd of them, but the only one who could have helped us proved a failure.

Lacking a better patron, I looked for the German criminal, the prison veteran to whom Mr Keding had once introduced me. When I finally found him, he was glad that I had come.

'To go around begging is foolish,' he lectured me. 'You just have to use your elbows and be aggressive. The cleverer your opponent, the harder they deserve to be kicked.'

Excusing himself for not being a businessman and living only on rations and occasional parcels from home, he said he could not help me. However, he was surprised at my inadequate clothing.

'You'll never be a tough guy with rags like those over your bones. They make you look like a *Muselmann*. Here, take these,' he continued, handing me two warm shirts that were gifts from his family; 'you'll be more respectable in them.'

I thanked him, but did not forget to ask what to do at the next inspection, when they would be confiscated. 'Just tell the block-elder who they are from,' he replied. 'He should know who I am.'

A few weeks later, when what I had feared was now about to happen, I decided to say goodbye to my shirts rather than attract the block-elder's attention. I reasoned that being familiar with criminals, whom none of the political prisoners liked, was too much of a risk.

Again, I showed my allegiance to those who warned against being conspicuous. I never had the courage to return to my friend, who had been generous both in providing clothing and in his advice to be aggressive to stay alive in camp.

Still in search of food, I often lingered around Block 1a, trying to get the portion of soup that the camp hairdresser had once promised me. This brought me into contact with a Belgian Jew, a frail tailor of about

30. 'Come along to our bunks,' he said, 'and let's hear a bit more about you.'

I followed him gladly, especially when I saw that he and his friend, also a fellow Belgian, occupied upper beds, a sign that they were 'rich'. Nor did their cupboard, a rare privilege, escape my notice.

'The camp hairdresser is not a good influence on youngsters like you,' they said – as if I did not already know this. 'It's good you don't go there any more. You can come to us; we have good connections with civilians, and access to clothes – excellent for bartering. We don't mind sharing our luck. We like you and want to be friends of yours.'

After that warm welcome I was almost a daily guest of theirs, often being invited to share their evening meal, a luxury that only a few prisoners knew of. They taught me French and many a sentimental song about the Foreign Legion. Sung with fervent enthusiasm, the catchy tunes of the desert soldiers far away from their loves never failed to captivate me.

My contribution to our entertaining gatherings were schoolboy anecdotes, jokes and the latest exploits of our block-elder – the 'sleepwalking maybug' as we had nicknamed him. We became good friends and I felt as though I had found a second home.

Then, one evening, a visitor came, a friend of theirs whose lack of humour put me on my guard: a Jewish capo from Birkenau. The newcomer, about to be transferred back, had a proposition to make. If I was willing to become his 'girlfriend', he would take me along as his confidant. To my friends that seemed to be a wonderful deal.

'You are lucky that he takes an interest in you; he is rich and important. To be his protégé will keep you immune from camp dangers. Once you are in a position of prominence, helping your mother will be easy.'

Rather impressed by all these promises, I had a talk with the visitor. He took me to one of the dark, floor-level bunks. There, instead of answering my questions, he started to fiddle about with my trousers. Quickly, I jumped up before he could go any further and ran out of the block.

'You're telling me,' was Saucy Gert's comment on my latest adventure. 'You are not the only one who finds out that those "friends" are all the same once you get to know them. There is no one you can trust – except yourself.'

After that, I never returned to my friends. If we met on the street, we looked away from each other, one ashamed of abusing children, the other of having been about to fall for it.

Later, I heard that my unsuccessful admirer returned to Birkenau but had escaped. I wished him luck!

Looking for work, I was allocated to the building materials yard, the largest and most monotonous working squad of all. A thousand strong, it was made up largely of newcomers, unskilled labourers who were the least valuable kind of slaves.

The work was hard. Railway wagons, loaded with bricks, cement and aggregates, had to be emptied according to a schedule, a feat that could only be achieved by speed and overtime. When there was nothing to unload, we were kept busy building the materials at the yard into pyramids, or even more exasperating, just transferring them from one stack to another. We spent our days carrying block after block, plank after plank, depressed by the realisation that we had ended up as human wheelbarrows. Modern galley slaves.

During my first days at the yard, when my face was still new to the foremen, I occasionally managed to sneak away. With boyish curiosity, I scouted around the district, the industrial area of Auschwitz concentration camp. It was a real city. There was workshop after workshop, a busy bakery, the big DAW joinery works,* and the Union ammunitions plant. Working day and night, the sweatshops never failed to reach their quotas.

With eight-hour regularity, their products rolled away over the single track leading to the railway station, and from there to feed Germany's war machine. From the same station, over the same track, other goods appeared also to be sorted, classified and stacked by silent slaves. These were belongings of people packed into new transports and being herded off to Birkenau.

---

* The *Deutsche Ausrüstungswerke* was a Nazi German defence contractor who exploited the huge slave labour available in the concentration camps.

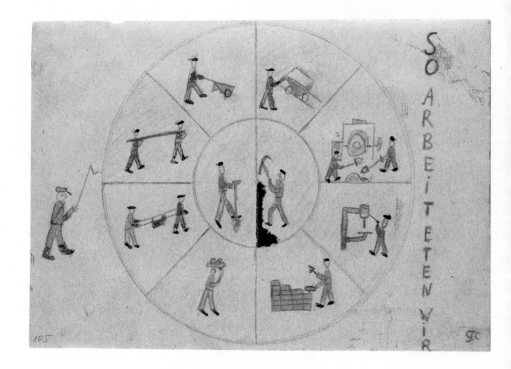

THE WAY WE WORKED
Under the guard's eye and whip, we modern-day
slaves would work non-stop.

After a few weeks of seemingly senseless work, dominated by constant shouts of 'keep moving', I was exhausted. I felt I could not go on any more. My heart was willing but my body was breaking down. I had blistered hands, raw feet and was drained of the last drops of energy.

Making my way to the camp's labour exchange, I waited to be assigned there to one of the sixty-odd working squads by the prisoner responsible for this. Aware that the good jobs were only obtained through bribes, I nevertheless hoped to be transferred to a place of work less difficult than my current post.

'There are many like you who want easier work,' the prisoner replied to my pleas; 'it's not my fault that you are young. Once, I could have sent you to the bricklaying school, but now, since you are a prisoner of eight months, it's too late. There is nothing I can do for you.'

The cold disregard of my request, which could have been so easily granted, flattened me. In my despair, I sought the advice of the Block 7a elder. 'It is unfair', I argued, 'to treat a youngster, just out of the hospital, with the same harsh consideration as a newcomer.'

The father of Block 7a had no say in work arrangements, but he had an unconquerable sense of justice. My trust in him, despite him being the arch-enemy of favouritism, was well placed. Somehow, he pulled the necessary strings, and before long I was transferred to a squad of building labourers.

Arrangements at Block 7a were much the same as they had been when I had last attended the practical bricklayers' training. The same type of lads speeding up and down the stairs to the leaking taps in the washroom. The same familiar inspections to see if ears and feet were clean. They still cheated the room-elder by washing only the foot that he expected them to show him. But the faces of the occupants had changed again.

There had been selection after selection. My old friends were gone – sent away, never to be seen again. The dark moments after curfew, when we had to watch the lorries take our friends and relatives away to Birkenau, were now part of our existence.

Little Kurt had been sent away. Blond Gert was in the hospital. Saucy Gert, still my best friend and eager to be helpful, had been transferred to the farm labourers' block. I was the block's only remaining German Jew, the last of Little Berlin.

Having no one to share my worries and sorrows with, I felt lonely. I missed my fellow comrades and our youthful escapades. Above all, I missed my friends from Little Berlin and our unique bond.

When despair was at its greatest, I looked at Mother's letters, notes of hope. Though few in number and sparse in words – 'Keep well, stay safe . . .' – they kept me going. Spring was around the corner, but for the first time in my life, it failed to bring joy.

When in a low mood, I found relaxation in philosophising and trying to analyse our predicament. My never-failing partner in this was Schorsch. A year older than me, with a good education, he was the only friend who could appreciate my striving for knowledge and understanding.

Blue-eyed, with a fish-like expression around his mouth and nose, Schorsch was an intellectual in the making. Adopted by an Austrian family, he was preparing for an engineering career. Then, with the return of Hitler, it was discovered that Schorsch's parents had been Gypsies.

'We Gypsies', reasoned my friend, 'might be closer to being Aryan than those crossbred specimens who call themselves "Supermen". Perhaps that is why they want to kill us off. No one can deny that the Jews are foreigners. But in our case, there was no reason for the Nazis to turn against us. Our plight was as unexpected as could be.

'We don't all walk about in rags. Gypsies have become professors, doctors and world-famous musicians. Nor are we cowards. Once away from that caravan mentality, we give up fear and superstition.

'So, you see,' Schorsch went on, 'we are just people. And just like you Jews, there are good ones and bad ones. Though we have no Bible, our history may be even older than yours, but you have always been luckier. You always had Palestine. Had we Gypsies, like you, been told what was in store for us, we still wouldn't have had anywhere to go.'

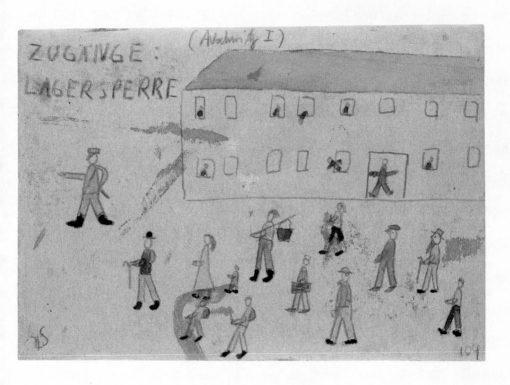

NEWCOMERS
Gypsy families arriving at Auschwitz Camp I.

Schorsch, along with the other Gypsies, still in their civilian clothing, first lived at a special camp in Birkenau. The inmates, encouraged by a fair diet, no work and agreeable living conditions, were hopeful. 'As soon as the Wehrmacht clears the area of partisans,' they were told, 'you will be resettled in Ukraine.'

Then, one day, the order had come through to liquidate them – men, women and children. Helplessly trudging to the gas chambers, they encountered an officer looking for bricklaying school candidates. Schorsch was saved.

It was from Schorsch that I heard the first eye-witness account of Birkenau's forest of death. Realising our common suffering, from that moment on I took a close interest in my Gypsy companions.

Some Gypsy families were temporarily billeted at Block 8. A mixture of attractive girls in national costume, women in rags and booted men in traditional farmers' dress. A motley crew but one not easily forgotten. We could tell where they came from by their clothes. From their shabbiness, we could guess how long they had been in camp. Only their thoughts remained a mystery. But the bulk of the camp's Gypsies lived at Block 7a – ours.

Attempts at understanding each other, however, brought little success, for the Romanies sought salvation in keeping to themselves. The most secluded were the clans that had come from the mountains of Czechoslovakia and Poland. They were a primitive, superstitious people whose ignorance kept them in a constant state of fear. Using sign language and their Romany dialect, they even puzzled their fellow kinfolk who had become modern.

When the block was overcrowded, we slept two to a bed. For a few nights, I had a Gypsy for a mate, a shy and cowardly fellow. The only thing he was persistent about was his determination to sell me a pair of scissors. A rare treasure. I wondered how he got them. I told him that I did not have any use for them, but he kept on trying to convince me that they were an excellent tool for slicing bread.

'I never barter away my rations and certainly not for fancy gadgets,' I said.

'I know I have got a big stomach,' he replied in his last sales effort, 'but can you buy it, just for friendship's sake?'

I didn't. But when we huddled together under our common blankets, heads at opposite ends, we seemed to have become friends all the same.

Next morning when I woke up, the bunk was wet. Wet with the repulsive smell of someone's urine. Flinging heated accusations at each other, we soon attracted the attention of our roommates, lads who had become convinced that evil must be punished. It was determined that the culprit could only have been the Gypsy boy, the newcomer, 'offspring of dirty, ill-mannered thieves'.

The next day, I discovered the real bed-wetter. It was the Pole from the bunk above us, also a newcomer. I also realised that, unwittingly, I had this once given in to the same prejudices that I myself was trying to condemn.

CHAPTER 10
DESPERATION

It was already summer 1944. We were engaged in enlarging the Union arms plant by another 12 factory halls. The first stage of this back-breaking work was to level the ground, dig foundations and cart away the earth.

History books portray slaves as big, muscular men whose bare chests were drenched in sweat, but we never enjoyed such 'privileges'. Toiling in the midday sun, malnourished and weakened, we had to remain in our prison jackets. To take them off and be bare-chested would have been the equivalent of planning an escape and would be punished accordingly.

Bringing in materials from all over the camp's working area, we made frequent detours that allowed us to satisfy our desire to learn more of it. Once, while dismantling some disused huts near the railway line, we saw trainloads of new arrivals. Jews from Hungary, Holland, Belgium and France. All came in with the same hopes and fears that we had had. We saw them crowding around the ventilation gaps of their closed cattle wagons. They waved at us. It was sickening. There was nothing we could say or do for them.

Most of the time, the whole transport would go straight to its death, like cattle to the slaughter. We would see them come in. Then their journey's end would announce itself with a dark, creeping smoke, slowly rising above the western horizon from the crematoria of Birkenau.

Birkenau's crematoria worked continuously. Saucy Gert worked the night shift, doing repair work at the bakery. On the face of it, this was a good job, because it offered opportunities to get bread and throw it over the bakery fence to a waiting accomplice, who would smuggle it into the camp. But Gert complained constantly of being tired and nervous.

'The conditions are good,' he confided in me, 'but I can't stand it much longer. Night after night, standing on our bricklayers' scaffolding and facing Birkenau, we see the fires. It is a sight I can't get out of my head: the flaming horizon clashing with the night sky,' he went on. 'But you, you are asleep in your warm beds when all this happens. All you see are the loaves of bread. Believe me, there is no compensation for what we have to endure.'

The SS guard at the civilian workers' disinfection barracks, the compound that was adjoined to our worksite, was in the habit of picking out youngsters to do odd jobs for him. Once, he called me out to clean his sentry hut. While I bent down to sweep the floor, he offered me a sandwich. 'Here, take this,' he said hastily, 'but don't go near the window.'

Surprised to hear a 'thank you' in fluent German, he instructed me to carry on sweeping until I was told to stop. As I swept, he talked.

'Yes, I am an SS soldier, but I am a human being all the same. Now and then we beat you up – that is part of the job. But don't think what's happening over there', he went on, pointing westwards, 'is any of our fault. We look on with the same anguish and helplessness as you do. Officially, of course, we are told nothing, but who can ignore what is happening at Birkenau? Knowing much better what goes on than you prisoners, many of us here go mad. When we joined up, we didn't know what we were in for. Now it's too late. There is no way out for us.'

It felt like he wanted me to feel sorry for him. I just swept the floor, silent and unmoved by his apparent helplessness. Then he ordered me out, shouting loudly as he was expected to do.

We often thought about our own helplessness. We were capable of killing a guard, but that would have brought severe reprisals. We could overpower the camp garrison by an organised revolt, but that would leave us helplessly exposed to onrushing reinforcements. If the local SS troops themselves mutinied, the Nazis would then send in army tanks.

Although we outnumbered our SS guards many hundreds to one, we had heard about the fight at the Warsaw Ghetto,* where conditions for revolt were far more favourable than ours. Therefore, it was natural that we became pessimists; even I became depressed.

The camp's lone symbol of defiance was Jakob Kozelczuk, known as Bunker-Jakob. He was a burly Jewish boxer, born in Poland, who had toured the world winning fame as a pugilist and trainer. We liked him mainly because of his enormous body, and the respect that the SS accorded to it. They kept him locked up and only allowed him to fetch supplies. His daily trip from Block 11 to the kitchen was watched over by a couple of armed guards. But now his job was anything but glorious. He was forced to become capo in Block 11, to play the role of whipping prisoners and leading inmates to the wall of death. On occasions, Jakob was called upon to whip us. Some expected him to refuse but other youngsters who had come to know both him and the punishment cells said he was gentle, kind and did his best to help. Anyhow, they would prefer to be lashed by a fellow prisoner, even one the size of Jakob, rather than by the SS.

Another type of inmate whose skills were turned against us were the surgeons who performed castrations. Working at Birkenau, the hell that befitted them, we knew them by their victims, fellow Jews, who were block-mates of ours. Seeing these once proud boys come back deprived of their masculinity was just another horrible day in camp.

When summing up friends and foes, the enemy in our midst never escaped our attention. Aware that some capos and block-elders contributed more to our plight than the guards, we strove to avenge ourselves. Helped by senior camp inmates who were loyal to us, we harassed them until they were removed. At our camp, we achieved it by blackmail,† but in other camps, they resorted to murder.

---

* The Warsaw Ghetto uprising started on 19 April 1943 and was one of the major acts of armed, organised resistance by the Jews against the Nazis. Despite the heroism and initial success, the uprising was ultimately brutally crushed after a month, and the ghetto was completely burned down and liquidated.
† Prisoners would denounce them to the SS for stealing or drinking alcohol.

Transports of prisoners were being sent to the Eastern Front, to dig trenches. Others, mainly women and Poles, were issued with clogs, fresh blue-white prison clothing, and dispatched to factories in Germany. Mother's letters had stopped. She, too, was supposed to have been sent on such transport.

New arrivals and transports kept on coming into Auschwitz. Birkenau was crowded, and room had to be made for all of them. Once again there were the dreaded selections. At our block's evening rollcall, the number of Jews had been whittled down to 15.

Blond Gert died of pneumonia. Saucy Gert, who had found a way of entering the hospital block to pay his last respects, asked if I wanted to come along.

I was used to seeing death. There had been my dear grandfather, pale and worn with age. All the family had come to mourn at his bedside. Then I had worked at the cemetery. Later, there had been bodies lifelessly clutching the electrified camp fence. This time, however, it was different. Gert should not have died. He was young and innocent. He had been healthy and full of life. More than that, he had been our comrade, a fellow fighter for survival, hoping for a better future.

No! I could not bear to see his youthful blond face – his pudgy nose, his thick lips, the straw-coloured freckles – lying dead and helpless on a nondescript camp bunk. *No! I would refuse to recognise Death's victory!*

I told Saucy Gert I would not go. He replied that as long as someone went to the hospital, it did not really matter if it was only him or both of us.

With Blond Gert, soon to be forgotten, I felt how close we were to the youth of Germany, the sons of our enemy, some of whom were also dying a death against their will. Years ago, Blond Gert had shared school benches with them as their teachers had extolled the glories of the past, toeing the line peddled by their superiors. Now these schoolboys were paying the price. Blond Gert entered a concentration camp. His classmates invaded Europe. And Fate had reunited them all in death. One, now naked, whose striped prison garb had already been given to another, would be put on a pyre in a forest-hidden crematorium in Birkenau. The others, in field-grey military uniform and long deprived of their boots, would rot on the wastelands of Russia.

I was devastated by the loss of Blond Gert. His death made me revise my attitude. From now on, I would not just stubbornly face camp life and hope for change, but would act to bring it about.

How much longer could I keep fighting the odds? My survival seemed in doubt now. Our never-ending daily hardships had taken their toll, and I was emaciated and weak. Liberation seemed a far-off dream, something that only the fittest could hope to see.

In my desperation, I started to take a keen interest in the accomplishments of the daring few who had escaped Auschwitz. To be prepared for any eventuality I improved my Polish and memorised my surroundings.

The most spectacular of escapes from Auschwitz had been one that centred upon my former place of work, the blocks under construction for the new women's camp.

A campmate who had hoarded gold and other valuables, stolen either from Nazi loot or straight from the new arrivals, decided to make the most of it. Instead of spending it on food, he waited until he had enough to buy the assistance of a civilian, a fellow worker of ours. One day, he took the SS supervisor's motorcycle and made for one of the partially completed buildings. There, in the sloping cavity beneath the staircase, he had walled himself in, helped by his courageous civilian, a bricklayer.

For five days, the area was combed by guards and bloodhounds, but the fugitive had both time and ample cover on his side. His hide-out was equipped with provisions and a ventilation hole. He stayed on for a week. Finally, when he thought it was safe to escape, he smashed through the brick wall, mounted the motorcycle and raced into the dark night towards freedom.

After that incident, all civilians working with us were carefully screened. Some of them were imprisoned, others sentenced to death. Thereafter, most other escapes failed and served only as an opportunity for our oppressors to showcase their efficiency and dominance over us.

Fugitives, once caught, were brought back to the camp. Some were even captured within yards of the Allied front lines. Barely alive, they were brought back and displayed on a dais facing the returning work columns. There they were forced to hold up posters that said, 'Hurrah, we are back again! We did not succeed in spite of clever plotting! No one gets away from this camp.' Afterwards, they were led off to the kitchen square, where they were hanged. Their stiff bodies dangled from the gallows until the following evening.

Despite the obvious dangers of getting caught, I decided that if a chance came to escape, I would take it. To lessen the danger of being found out, my getaway plan would have to be devised single-handedly; no one to help me or share the secret. My achievement would be impressive; I would be the youngest prisoner ever to escape from a concentration camp. If unsuccessful, I would, at least, have shown myself to be brave.

The daily outgoing goods train attracted my attention. The wagons were pushed along by toiling prisoners, lined up in front of a checkpoint and left waiting for the engine. The wagons were loaded with boxes or scrap metal, and some remained open. Once I was outside the camp's territory, the sanctuary beneath the tarpaulin covers would make a good hiding place. My best scenario was a distant destination, because that would carry me into the vastness of Europe. But if not, I would have to try my luck in Upper Silesia, plodding towards Beuthen, my former hometown.

The potential problem of acquiring civilian clothes did not bother me. I was already wearing a shirt without prison markings. I would dispose of my jacket, cut off the trouser legs, and, as a temporary measure, blot out the white zebra-stripes with mud. Driving myself on like some haunted animal, I would be a dual personality, a harmless youngster and a reckless fugitive who knew the consequence of capture.

For days I studied the habits of the guard in charge of the

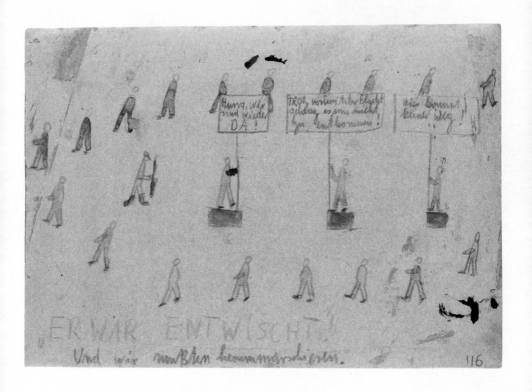

ESCAPE AND CAPTURE
Most brave escape attempts were unsuccessful.
Those caught were humiliated and hanged.

wagons. With a Germanic sense of duty, he arrived exactly five minutes before the train's time of departure. He would look over the wagon roofs and examine the undercarriages. Occasionally, he lifted up a corner of tarpaulin, but he never bothered to untie them. Then he went to the sentry hut – the same one that I had once dusted in exchange for a sandwich and a lecture on the helplessness of the guards from a colleague of his. When he heard the whistle of the engine, which was hardly ever on time, he would re-emerge, throw another quick glance at the wagons and signal for the Polish driver to pull out.

It apparently never occurred to him that in between the two check-ups someone might have sneaked in. He knew that we prisoners worked elsewhere and had no excuse to be lingering around the shunting rails, certainly not when they were guarded. This then, was my chance.

Unseen, I strode along the row of wagons. It would be now or never. The destination tablet read, 'Berlin'. The flapping canvas of one wagon begged me to get in.

Then, one by one, the wagons rolled away. They moved on beyond the chain of guards, but I did not budge from my hiding spot. I stayed behind.

I realised in those last moments of opportunity that it was not only a matter of courage but also a question of conscience. There would have been reprisals. If Mother was still alive, they would find her. My plan was an utter failure.

That evening, my youthful dreams crumbled and I marched back into camp as one of the many who had given up hope. For the first time, the familiar strains of 'Colonel Bogey' that greeted the returning working columns failed to inspire me. They rang out like laughter, mocking my helplessness.

'Work sets you free!' said the wrought-iron inscription looking down contemptuously from over Auschwitz's main gate.

That hated slogan was worse than merely ridiculous. The sordid irony was revealed in the rhyme the cynics had made about it, the bitter message we so desperately tried to forget: *Arbeit macht frei, durch Krematorium nummer drei!* ('Work sets you free, through crematorium number three!')

Yet there was a tiny part of me that could not believe that life could end if one so desperately wanted it to go on.

PART 3

CHAPTER 11
KINDNESS AMONG CHAOS

I had pains in my neck and suspected them to stem from my tonsils. After work, I went to see the school's doctor.

'Little bricklayer, you have nothing; it's only a little swelling. Just as you said, your tonsils,' he assured me in his cheerful way of imitating childish chatter. 'I'll put some of the black paste on it. You know, the kind that's full of sugar, fat and vitamins. It will soon be okay.'

For the next few weeks I walked about with a precious collar bandage, but the fabulous ointment failed to work wonders. The paste nourished my ailment, instead of healing it. My neck continued to swell.

'My dear son,' said the dispenser of hope and ointments when I could no longer move my head, 'don't be afraid, but you must go to the hospital. Go at once, go now – the boil has to be lanced.'

This time he was serious. These putrid swellings brought on by malnutrition grew grotesquely large and quickly multiplied. Widespread as boils were among us, this was my first, and a dangerous one. Of all the places that this annoying specimen could have chosen, it was on my neck, a body part I was least eager to say goodbye to.

The next morning, I was strapped onto the operating table, my face covered with a towel. Inhaling the alcohol, drop by drop, I counted aloud as instructed. I still realised that I was in a concentration camp and that, in my condition, a knife could put an end to me. I only hoped that my imminent silence would be a temporary one.

When I awoke, they said that my boil, now cut open, was one of the biggest they had ever seen. I dragged myself to the lavatory and vomited.

I was handed over to the room-elder of my sick block, a male nurse who impressed me with his gentleness.

His room, part of Block 28a, had 10 three-tier camp bunks that differed from other blocks only by their bedsheets. The inmates, mostly old and toothless Poles chosen for their need for care rather than because of any specific illness, suffered from anything between appendicitis and insanity. I admired the room-elder's quiet, self-confident way of handling them.

A German communist, himself no stranger to concentration camps, he was not just a nurse but also someone to whom helping the sick had become a way of life.* Unlike other camp inmates, he seemed to take satisfaction in his job, and devoted himself to it.

Whenever there was spare food, he would share it out equally. Often, he would divide his own share among the youngest of us. However, my attempts to make him a friend of mine failed. 'Please', he excused himself, 'don't talk with me for too long. The others may think that I favour you. Sick people are easily irritated, and we must prevent them becoming jealous.'

All that the dreary sick-room atmosphere seemed good for was sleeping, groaning and dying. Surgery visits added some variety to my secluded existence. Strings of cotton wool were inserted into my wound as if stuffing a goose. This procedure was irritating and painful but it broke the monotony.

Now that the wound had begun to heal, I was transferred to hospital Block 21a. The two hundred or so convalescing inmates there were short-tempered and quarrelsome. As soon as they felt well enough, they started fighting. Soon the block personnel whittled down the numbers, and they exploited our frailty without exception. Our food amounted to less than even the usual sparse camp ration.

Aggravating the general anarchy was the room doctor, a German Jew, who was overworked, ruthless and horrible. When he thought it necessary, he beat us, usually picking on those who did not understand German. He called them, 'dirty peasants'. I was also treated harshly. On one of my visits to him, he tore off the scab from my wound with such force that it reopened again. Then he barked, 'Out, I can't waste my time on you. Next one, quick!'

---

* In 2005, Thomas's family found out that while Thomas was in hospital having his boil removed, someone had changed his Jewish family name on the list to 'Colditz', a Polish name. This probably saved his life.

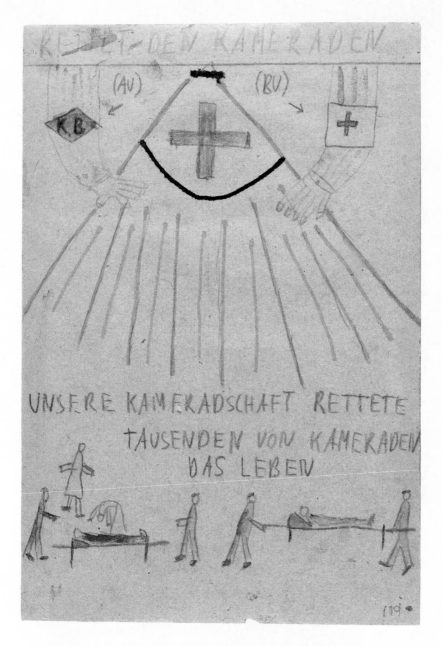

SAVE THE COMRADES
The comradeship showed by the hospital team
comrades saved the lives of thousands.

I was appalled to find out that most of our superiors who made our hospital room hell rather than help us were newcomers. These prisoners who were now imposing their will on us had never seen the harsh realities of camp life, the common hardship that makes veterans respect each other. I tried to contact the German criminal, my former protector who had once tried to help me. I was told, 'He has left the camp.'

At last, after constant begging, I was released. On my way out I looked down upon the enclosure opposite our room window, the space between the mystery Blocks 10 and 11. These were the blocks that many entered but few left. Their secrets – the cold-blooded executions, agonising tortures and cruel experiments – were hidden behind blocked-up windows.

Soon after my return to Block 7a, I went to visit the school doctor. He wanted to know how I had fared at the hospital.

I told him all the many details that he was keen to know. Then he made a confession. He had realised from the start the severity of my swelling, but had kept it a secret. To shorten my potentially dangerous stay in hospital and not have to wait for the operation, he had dressed the boil with ointments, making it ripe for cutting. I thanked him, but he was too busy to look up. With motherly care, he was removing the scurf from the infected scalp of a little Gypsy.

During my stay in the hospital, I had missed a lot of news. Now I learned that although conditions were no better, the inmates had become hopeful.

Hitler's war, it seemed, was nearing its end, and even Germans were turning against him. For the first time, the Nazis were filling the punishment cells with their own people. Groups of a dozen or so hostages freshly arrived from Germany became a daily spectacle, as they were led to Block 11, apparently unaware of their fate. Men, women and children, SS men and high-ranking officers with their insignias torn off – all entered, never to return.

At the same time and along the same streets, German camp inmates were singing, marching and drilling in preparation for being 'volunteered' into the Wehrmacht. The German army was in dire need of cannon fodder and decided to establish a brigade of ex-prisoners. These future soldiers were anxious to enlist so that they might have the chance to desert and escape to the Allies.

Our block-elder, too, had been pressed into the volunteers.˙ It affected him badly. He took to drinking, wandering about the camp drunk, and avoiding his former friends. Later, we learned that he had committed suicide. Our once stern and strict father, the caring dictator of Block 7a, had killed himself.

Our new block-elder, a Pole, was glum and miserable. He had little in common with his illustrious predecessor. We called him 'Fishhead', for he resembled one both in appearance and speech.

Although just as strict, and just as quick to impose a block curfew as punishment for untidiness, he was more of a schoolteacher than a guardian. His sole concern was to run the block. What we did in our spare time and the means by which we thought to survive did not interest him. If, when in trouble, we asked for his help, he would shrug his shoulders, smile and excuse himself for being 'only the block-elder of 7a and not the Lord of the Universe'.

The influence he wielded among the camp hierarchy was insignificant. His German was bad and his voice was not persuasive enough. Even we did not value him. To his dismay, we avoided him less out of fear and more out of a desire to ignore him.

The first months after arrival, a prisoner spent his spare time brooding about the future. Then, when he had acquainted himself with all the daunting details of camp life, the future no longer a priority, he would just try to stay alive. Having gone through many trials and hardships, he would strive to forget. This was now my strategy.

---

* He was transferred to Block 8, the block opposite Block 7a that had become a military training base.

One of the best ways to dream ourselves away was to sing. We sang when boxed up in our block, we sang during the many curfews, we sang while having our weekly shower or we sang out of loneliness. Our songs were many and varied. Gypsy melodies, love ditties, folk songs from all over Europe and partisan marches. Those who picked themselves a favourite would hum it as kind of a signature tune, something they would be known by.

My own choice was a sentimental French song called 'Chante, Chante Marie' in which a young man reveals to his mother why he had joined the Foreign Legion. 'Neither because I am a murderer,' sings the soldier, 'nor because I am a robber. No, it is for the love of a girl.' Every time I hummed this, my own private melody, I was overcome with the feeling of being alive despite everything. After a whole year in a concentration camp, I had remained my own self. Even though I could not see my face, for mirrors were denied to us, I could still hear my tune. It proved my existence.

Often during the evening, we sat on our bunks, listening to the Russian lads singing. Their catchy songs were so full of defiance and confidence that we could not help joining in. It did not matter whether we came from France, Belgium, the Netherlands, Germany, Austria, Italy, Czechoslovakia, Poland, Hungary, Greece or Russia, the stirring rhythms gripped us alike. The rousing tunes that had inspired the revolutionaries of 20 years earlier had lost none of their meaning. Their message of uniting in order to fight the common enemy was not only appropriate but had now become vitally important.

Among our favourites were 'If Tomorrow Brings War', 'From Border to Border' and 'Steppe Cavalry'. Listening to them awakened many feelings of longing and nostalgia. Somewhere in the partisan-held forests of Europe, we imagined that other youngsters would also be humming these melodies. Their fight was ours, and ours was theirs. All we could do for the common cause was sing.

Then there were the traditional concentration camp songs. Most of them were little more than German marching songs to which the prisoners had given a new, inoffensive text. Notable for its particular lack of taste was one about Auschwitz. It was based on a favourite

DIE MOORSOLDATEN*

Wohin auch das Auge blicket.
Moor und Heide nur ringsum.
Vogelsang uns nicht erquicket.
Eichen stehen kahl und krumm.

Wir sind die Moorsoldaten
und ziehen mit dem Spaten ins Moor.
Wir sind die Moorsoldaten
und ziehen mit dem Spaten ins Moor.

Auf und nieder geh´n die Posten,
keiner, keiner kann hindurch.
Flucht wird nur das Leben kosten,
vierfach ist umzäunt die Burg.

Wir sind die Moorsoldaten
und ziehen mit dem Spaten ins Moor.
Wir sind die Moorsoldaten
und ziehen mit dem Spaten ins Moor.

Doch für uns gibt es kein Klagen,
ewig kann nicht Winter sein,
einmal werden froh wir sagen:
Heimat du bist wieder mein.

Dann zieh´n die Moorsoldaten
nicht mehr mit dem Spaten ins Moor.
Dann zieh´n die Moorsoldaten
nicht mehr mit dem Spaten ins Moor

THE PEAT BOG SOLDIERS

Far and wide as the eye can wander,
Heath and bog are everywhere.
Not a bird sings out to cheer us.
Oaks are standing gaunt and bare.

We are the peat bog soldiers,
Marching with our spades to the moor.
We are the peat bog soldiers,
Marching with our spades to the moor.

Up and down the guards are marching,
No one, no one can get through.
Flight would mean a sure death facing,
Guns and barbed wire block our view.

We are the peat bog soldiers,
Marching with our spades to the moor.
We are the peat bog soldiers,
Marching with our spades to the moor.

But for us there is no complaining,
Winter will in time be past.
One day we shall rise rejoicing.
Homeland, dear, you're mine at last.

No more the peat bog soldiers
Will march with our spades to the moor.
No more the peat bog soldiers
Will march with our spades to the moor.

---

* The song originally had five verses. Here are the three best known and the chorus.

tune from our guards, bluntly declaring that 'We'll stay in Auschwitz no matter if it snows or red roses bloom'. Composed only because the authorities were keen on having a camp song, the original words were so repulsive to us that we only sang them when forced to.

Handed down to us by veteran prisoners were songs about life at the moorland camps near Papenburg – now a decade old. One song, with both music and words composed by inmates, was successful. Since it was first heard in 1934, at the Börgermoor concentration camp, it had become a kind of political prisoners' anthem everywhere. Its rhythm, though confident, makes it clear that the struggle would be long and slow. 'Far and wide as the eye can wander, heath and bog are everywhere.' 'But', it promises to those who sing all the verses, 'winter will in time be past.'

Ten years earlier, this emotional tune had been hummed by lone forgotten German anti-fascists at hidden moorland camps on the Ems. Now, 400 youthful voices, gathered from all over Europe, lent it new vigour. The prisoners' hymn, floating out from our block to penetrate the dark night, had become a challenge.

We knew that millions of our comrades in the other camps were singing along with us. One day we would be united. Then our songs would be heard stronger than ever before. The tunes of old would not be forgotten. Inspired by them, we would one day seek out the remnants of our oppressors and their supporters and bring them to justice.

Ogling women prisoners, wherever they could be seen, became a hobby of mine. I wanted to find out what made them attractive.

Whenever a group approached from the distance, the youngsters in our working party would determine to meet it. We would make excuses for leaving work, the most plausible of which was a trip to the three-celled lavatory, a privilege granted once a day. Having a keen eye and strong bowels, I was a strong contestant. Sometimes the foreman was first to spy females, but we did not fear the competition. 'Three youngsters who haven't already visited the privy may do so now!' the kindly soul used to shout on these occasions. To those heeding the hint, it was then merely a matter of agility.

Since we worked near to the roadway, we would often try to glimpse new arrivals to camp. On one occasion, we watched a long column of women prisoners coming from Birkenau for their monthly disinfection and shower bath. We shouted at them – from a distance that dissuaded their guards from pursuing us – asking their nationality.

'Anyone from Miskolc?' the women called out to us.

'Anyone from Miskolc?' our voices echoed in the empty shells of factory halls under construction. Answering the plea came the running footsteps of Hungarian workmates, folks to whom that town had once meant peace, home and family life. Carefully dodging the guards, the accompanying SS women and the bloodhounds, they sneaked onto the road to search for acquaintances, while we others looked on.

As the women trudged past, they hardly bothered to lift up their heads in greeting. Dressed in rags, their hair shorn and faces worn with worry and despair, they still had sufficient energy to shuffle along the dusty roadway. I reflected that weeks ago, these same women might have strolled along the streets of Budapest clad in elegant clothes, attracting the glance of many admirers. Now they were reduced to the lowest type of prisoner – helpless newcomers.

Trying to cheer them up, we bared our shaven heads, waved our blue-white caps and forced a smile. But later, our workmates told us that the women had asked about 'the children's camps'. These women had been separated into a special compound for Hungarian Jews right inside the horrors of Birkenau. The scheming camp authorities had kept them ignorant of it, while continuing to talk to them about 'resettlement'. Many of these women, it seemed, preferred to believe this deception over the bitter reality – a nightmare they hoped never to be confronted with.

Enthusiasm for greeting the womenfolk was common to all working groups. So before long, any prisoners lurking alongside the road would cease to be lone bystanders. And as their numbers grew, their presence became obvious. One day, our little game came to an abrupt end when the SS swooped down on us. The chase was led by one of the SS women guards. Spindly-legged and ugly, she nevertheless imagined that it was her who was being stared at. Her enraged shouts had all the other guards running after us.

Pursued around our worksite – the new halls for the Union factory – we desperately looked for a hiding place. Finally, I spotted a heap of empty boxes. One of the containers, still endowed with a lid, beckoned me to get in, so I did. After an anxious few minutes, the shouting faded away. I extracted myself, careful not to make a noise, unexpectedly discovering that the boxes around me were also inhabited. Once the other fugitives emerged, we had a brief conference before sneaking away, one by one, back to work.

Those unlucky few who were caught by their pursuers had their buttocks thrashed with 25 lashes. Thereafter, going near the road when women were on it became an offence. But craving the unattainable did not deter our efforts to see the women.

Instead, back in the camp, we gathered around the steam-filled laundry barrack in a desperate attempt to see into the women's showers. Clambering onto each other, we scaled the walls to reach a solitary, high-up window that offered a hazy, distant view of naked bodies. Soon, however, even this precarious pleasure was denied to us – the bathers ceased to come.

Then, one day, dismantling some disused barracks between the railway track and the road to Birkenau, we got caught by heavy rain. It meant stopping work, so we hoped this gesture from heaven would be lengthy. Five of us sought shelter in an abandoned stable where we relaxed by listening to the friendly drops tinkling like a melody on the corrugated metal roofing. Suddenly, we were interrupted by two newcomers, who started shaking off the rain from their soaked prison clothing. We realised that they were girls – curvaceous country lasses.

Stunned by suddenly finding the object of my youthful imagination right next to me, I just stared at their femininity. My other companions had long ago learned their lessons about the facts of life and started talking with the visitors – one a Polish girl, the other a Russian. Their guard, it seemed, perhaps afraid of being overpowered, was sheltering in a nearby sentry hut. Two pairs hustled off into a straw-filled corner of the barrack.

As we others watched out for intruders, we could not help but be envious.

When returning from work, we would often pass the camp's new extension, a site I had once worked on. Now it was surrounded by high barbed-wire fences and occupied by an advance contingent of women prisoners who had come to install the furniture. Seventy triple bunks, a table, a cupboard and two benches to a room.

As the few dozen inmates had been picked for their reliability, they were temporarily guarded by a single sentry stationed at the gate, an arrangement we exploited to the full. On passing by the fence, we and the girls would throw flowers over it to each other. These withered but heartfelt gifts were picked during our midday break, in the precious few minutes that remained after gobbling up our soup. We cheered each other by shouting greetings and waving our caps, while the girls waved their kerchiefs.

I asked them whether they knew any German Jewish girls in Birkenau?

'Yes, there are one or two of them,' cried someone.

Shouting, with hands pressed funnel-like to my mouth, I enquired if they knew any women from the transport I had come on.

'No, never heard of these numbers,' came the reply.

I was not upset. I continued to cheer, hailing people with whom I had no connection and who once would have meant little to me. Now, though, we were not applauding individuals but saluting youth that would never be conquered.

There were women prisoners at the Union factory, working day and night shifts, but no strangers were allowed. Although the workers were sworn to secrecy, we knew the factory produced shells by the punched-out scrap metal we found in the open wagons returning to Germany's steel mills. By measuring the diameter, we could even guess what guns they were used for.

Occasionally we saw women recuperating from illness who were employed in a group that came to forage for weeds. Their job was to scan the countryside for a variety of wild herbs that could be used

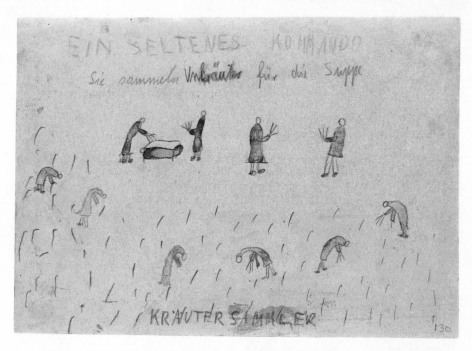

TOP: A RARE WORKING SQUAD
Women prisoners still managed to acknowledge us while plucking weeds for the soup.

BOTTOM: BLOCK 24A
Despite terrible abuse, these special women managed to show compassion and generosity to us youngsters.

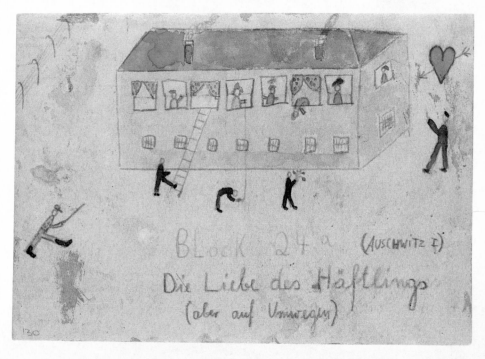

to make medicines, or thistles that could be made into a soup for prisoners. Under guard, they dared not talk to us, but they would still smile when stooping their skeletal frames to pick at a thorny weed. There were other types of women prisoner in our camp. There was a brothel on the upper floor of Block 24, above the camp orchestra's room. These women were from all over Europe, most of them having already practised the oldest profession before being imprisoned.

German prisoners were entitled to visit the two dozen women every fortnight. Prisoners, except Russians, Gypsies and Jews, received metal entrance discs once every few months. Prominent camp personnel had their favourites, women they were fond of. In return for gifts hauled up by bits of string through an unobserved back window, the girls would let them stay more than the prescribed 15 minutes.

It was a strange irony that a prostitute, once arrested for her profession, was now required to work by the very authority that had imprisoned her. They catered for both prisoners and guards alike, so they were rarely allowed to leave their quarters. During the few moments they were able to show themselves at a window, we never failed to watch them.

Often, they would scan the yard below for prisoners who looked young or very frail. Calling for them to stand beneath their window, they dropped them a ration of bread. It was their motherly way of helping despite the hardship we all endured. We could not help but respect them.

Opposite our worksite, the new stables was now a rest house for SS officers, a *Fuehrerheim*. As in all SS living quarters, household work was taken care of by a religious sect called *Bibelforscher*.* Women prisoners would call us in to help with heavy supplies such as sacks, boxes and barrels. Hoping to snatch morsels of food, we were so eager to be useful that, upon seeing the weekly provisions cart draw up at the German officers' mansions, we would sneak up and try to attract the women's attention by animatedly pointing at ourselves.

---

* Investigators of the Bible, also known as 'Jehovah's Witnesses', were tagged with a purple triangle.

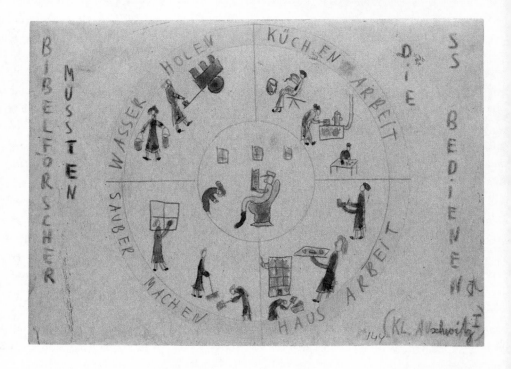

THE INVESTIGATORS OF THE BIBLE
Their women served as houseworkers for the
SS families.

Once, it was my turn to be lucky. Precariously balancing a case of wine bottles on my young shoulders, I passed the sentry's entrance, climbed down the dark stairwell and entered the supply vault. Lowering my load and raising my eyes, I was confronted with a sight I had thought only existed in fairy-tales.

Stacked along the wall lay endless rows of Europe's finest bottles of wine. Hanging from a rack were plucked geese, hares, sausages and fragrant, juicy, mouth-watering hams. An elderly housekeeper, with a bundle of keys tied to her blue-white prison frock, pushed a piece of cooked chicken into my pocket, then bade me return to work. On my way back I glanced at the rooms upstairs. They were luxuriously furnished as befitting kings.

Yes, the 'Masters' of the 'Master Race', their greed satisfied, had reason to relax in their armchairs.

The Investigators of the Bible sect were imprisoned for their stubborn pacificism and only the women had survived. Mostly Germans or Poles, their avowed honesty was cleverly exploited by the Nazis. They now served the SS as cooks and housekeepers.

Apparently incapable of hurting even their worst enemies, these Bible Women were entrusted with positions of such responsibility that the restrictions imposed upon them were merely symbolic. Slaves rather than prisoners, they were attached to the SS living quarters beyond the guard-surrounded camp compound, housed there, and so were free to move about the district whenever their work required it. Seeing a prison-garbed woman queue up at the village shop was just another odd spectacle that the surrounding population had become used to. The prisoner would neither engage in conversation nor try to escape, for she kept her pledge with religious fervour.

We fellow prisoners respected the devotees of the Bible primarily because they helped us. They deserved more because their attitude towards life showed courage. To them, God was far from being the heavenly judge who demands holy wars and forgives sinners.

My most loyal friend, Saucy Gert, now worked at a large farm near Raisko (Rajsko in Polish). It meant getting up before 5 a.m. and marching a couple of hours. He would toil in the fields and then, exhausted and blistered, trudge back, often reaching the camp only after the evening rollcall.

However, working among luscious tomatoes and spicy onions was profitable. Every Sunday, a lone horse-drawn cart conspicuously heaped with flowers drew up in front of Block 5.* Hidden beneath the potted green plants and colourful bunches were sacks of vegetables, the weekly total of whatever the farming squad had been able to 'organise'.

This clever trick often made the farmworkers' room resemble a greengrocer's shop, its inmates bartering away their cherished capfuls of vegetables for even more precious bread. Nobody ever found out because the guards who specialised in detecting smuggling had Sundays off.

When I visited him, Saucy Gert would always have something saved up for me: a couple of tomatoes to be gobbled up as a treat. Sometimes a pungent piece of garlic that could be rubbed onto many dry crusts of bread, or even an onion that would bring variety to a week of camp food.

There was nothing I could offer in return, and as our sharing agreement within Little Berlin had long been abandoned, I felt rather uneasy about accepting his kind gifts. Generous Gert badly needed his hard-earned weekly 2 pounds of vegetables to try and help his family. Gert's father had been contacted at Birkenau and his brother at Monowitz.

'When one doesn't hear of the family,' he used to say, 'one fears the worst or hopes for a miracle. Then, when from some camp there is news of them being alive, one feels lucky. But very soon, as their miserable lot becomes worse, one regrets ever hearing about it, for what once had been feared will then be known for certain.'

---

* The authorities did this with the aim of *beautifying* the model camp.

CHAPTER 12
A VETERAN NOW

The camp was transforming. The Nazis were preparing to transport millions more slaves from the many inferior races of Europe. Auschwitz was to extend and expand.

Vast new projects were planned. A foreman of ours even peeped at the blueprints. They projected a living camp of double its present size, a trebling of factory buildings and a new network of roads and railway tracks for the working area. It meant that the whole district flanked by the Vistula and Sola rivers would become one giant concentration camp. A monster to those in it, a mere name in triplicate to others.

The first step was to introduce a new system of administration. Our camp, the smallest but best-kept showpiece for external delegations, was now named Auschwitz I. The camps at Birkenau became Auschwitz II. And Monowitz, with its subsidiaries, Auschwitz III.

New constructions mushroomed all over the camp's territory. The demand for skilled building labour became so great that even the thousand former inmates of the bricklaying school could not meet it.

I was assigned to a working site called the New Stables. There, we struggled in the scorching sun, not helped by being forced to wear our jackets. Watching us as we dug foundations and moved the earth, an SS guard sat lazily beneath a tree. Sometimes, probably after an evening of entertainment, the normally aggressive guard would fall asleep. This would be a signal for the more daring among us to wriggle through the fence into a nearby garden. Anything in there attractive to birds, bees and worms, also interested us. Berries, flowers and radishes – rare and indispensable trophies.

The garden was like the other Polish property within the camp's district, which had been taken over by an SS officer's family. Our small-scale looting expeditions without being found out not only supplemented our rations, they also spread discontent. The Nazi boss, on returning to his villa and seeing disorder among the flowerbeds, would blame his own children.

These moments, however, were interludes. There was little else to break the monotony of work. Exhausting ourselves by continuously digging, while sweating and aching all over, we prisoners only had the occasional and pitiful camp mark* to look forward to. Most of us, like myself, would not even be favoured with this paltry reward. This was the maximum value put on our labour as 20th-century slaves.

When someone received a mark, he (along with the privileged German prisoners who had accounts from home) would spend the evening queuing up outside the canteen. There, you could acquire mustard, writing paper, toilet paper, cigarette paper and tobacco (made from wood), if they were not already sold out.

Large transports of Hungarian Jews arrived at Birkenau every day and every night. Many of their occupants were transferred to our camp, and overcrowding forced us to share bunks.

The newcomers stood out from other inmates for being Magyars (Hungarians). Living under oppression seemed new to them. Their language was totally different from ours or any of those we knew. Trying to make ourselves understood, we spent many hours striving to acquaint them with the elements of camp life, but we doubted whether they would ever master the art of being an underdog.

Since my arrival, over a year ago now, the number of prisoners that had passed through Auschwitz had doubled. There were now five separate series of numbers: E for Educational, G for Ordinary, Z for Gypsy and A and B for the Jewish mass transports arriving since 1944. E prisoners, mostly Germans, lived at a special camp at Birkenau and would be released after they had served their term. All the others with numbers tattooed on their left forearm were in for life.

---

* A 'camp' mark was paper money that was just used within concentration camps such as Auschwitz, as opposed to a Reichsmark, which was the actual German currency at the time.

Jews arriving from the 'rich' countries, like Hungary and Italy, where they had been subjected to clever and calculated propaganda about being resettled in the 'East', brought along with them most of their belongings and many provisions, often wagonloads full.

With the owners disposed of, attention was turned to their property. Suitcases, clothes, bedding, bicycles, sewing machines, sacks of provisions, bundles of correspondence, photographs, rings, diamonds and hidden dollar bills, all went to the sorting barracks to be classified and given the respect their owners were not thought worthy of.

When the plunder had been graded, and any name tabs or sewn-in notes removed, it was stacked onto railway wagons to be sent to Germany. 'From Auschwitz concentration camp to Breslau', read the destination tablets fixed to every wagon.

'Can it be', we asked ourselves, 'that people at the other end, soon to enjoy the loot, are ignorant of how it was come by?'

Many of the provisions that the new arrivals had been ordered to carry were stale, rotten or suspected of being poisonous. These were not sent to Germany, but rather they went to the camp's kitchen. Where, like everything else taken from the mass transports, the foreign macaroni, flour, bread and dried fruit were called *Kanada*, possibly because to Europeans that country represented richness and abundance.

Kanada soup, then, brought welcome variety to our diets. It was a bread soup that, depending on its ingredients – chunks of fruit, cake, sandwiches, newspapers and often leather and nails – would either be sweet or bitter.

Similarly, the rich property brought by the transportees created new opportunities for those prisoners who worked as a *Kanada Kommando*.

As they sorted the loot, they would 'organise' some of it. Arriving for work at the *Kanada* warehouses in cheaply acquired camp-boots and leaving in a pair of quality leather shoes was common. As was

wrapping bedsheets around their waists, pushing golden watches up
their rectums, hiding jewels in their nostrils and lining their caps with
foreign banknotes.

These prisoners soon became financiers that lesser camp traders
had to treat with respect. In camp, such goods were passed onto
other operatives, who received a commission. They in turn would
barter them to civilian workmates in exchange for alcohol, butter and
cigarettes.

Three cigarettes, Europe's black-market money, bought a day's
bread ration – 350 grams. Butter was reserved for buying the
cooperation of capos, foremen and block-elders, while brandy, in
great demand but hard to smuggle, was used to bribe wealthier camp
personnel and SS guards.

Returning from work, we went through a daily procedure in which
1 person in 50 was meticulously inspected, and the rest threateningly
looked over for suspicious bulges. Anyone caught was brutally beaten
and then made to stand for the rest of the evening in the 6-foot gap
between the wire fences that hummed with lethal charges of electricity.

The bricklaying school and I had moved to Block 13a. Its apprentices,
all new now, were mainly Jewish lads from Hungary – youngsters
from 14 to 16. Like naïve little Kurt, who had long since vanished,
they too clung to their pleasant childhood and took little note of the
cruelty around them. Watching them, unperturbed and balanced, was
a pleasure; something to cheer us up.

A few, having had a Zionist education, entertained us with tunes
about pioneers in Palestine, who were bravely fighting for a Jewish
homeland. Sentimental melodies recalled an ideal that old-time
prisoners had long forgotten. 'Sleep quiet, Valley of Jezreel" sang the
clear youthful voices, helplessly muffled by a roomful of dusty, straw-
filled camp bunks. 'Sleep quiet, wonderful valley, we are your guard . . .'

Another little group that never tired of being cheerful, mainly

---

* 'The Song of the Valley' was written in 1934 and gave Thomas and his companions strength and confidence, as
its original meaning was about guarding this *special* valley and the *promised* land of Israel.

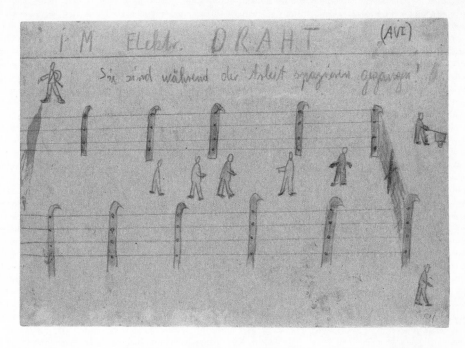

TOP: IN BETWEEN THE ELECTRIFIED WIRES Putting standing prisoners in confined spaces for hours with lethal electrified fences around them was another cruel punishment. **BOTTOM: WE ARE INSPECTED** A thorough check, if it revealed any goods, meant more than just bad luck. It could cost prisoners their own lives.

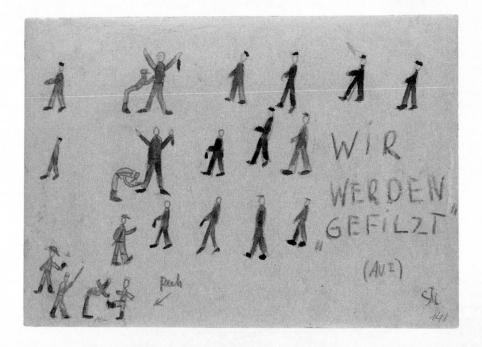

because it earned them an occasional extra bowl of soup, was made up of a few Gypsy lads. Rhythm-conscious Romanies who spent their evening at the *Birkenweg*, the camp-promenade facing the treble row of barbed-wire fencing, danced and sang to remind us of days gone by. I now had time to listen. For having given up vainly begging for food, I no longer just limited my attention to inmates who could provide favours. I now wanted to meet them all, to watch their various habits and try to understand them.

Under the showers, we would look at the scars littered all over our loose skin. Scars left over from boils, abscesses, skin diseases and sometimes even lashings. Each type had its own characteristic place, shape, size and colour. We all had them.

In the winter of 1943, the crop of assorted abscesses, caused by the curse of malnutrition, had been worse. That epidemic had invaded the whole of our bodies. Now they thrived principally on our legs. But when we poked fingers into our calves, a hollow mark was left behind, meaning that we also had dropsy.* We had become living sponges.

'Those damned swellings come from drinking too much putrid tap water,' said the veterans. 'If you lads don't sleep with your legs up, it'll spread to your hearts. Stop drinking or you'll blow up like a balloon!'

There was nothing funny about this. Except for air, water was the only free sustenance we received and enjoyed without it being whittled down to starvation rations. Deprived of the washroom tap, we would wither like shrivelling flowers.

Bathroom nudity also revealed the red, raw bodies of the newcomers. Still unaccustomed to the persistent fleas of a concentration camp, they scratched themselves until they bled. Several of them had already become infected by scabies. Once afflicted by these minute parasites, prisoners, constantly sweating from back-breaking work, could do next to nothing to save themselves.

---

* Dropsy, now known as oedema, is swelling caused by fluid retention, typically on the legs, ankles and feet.

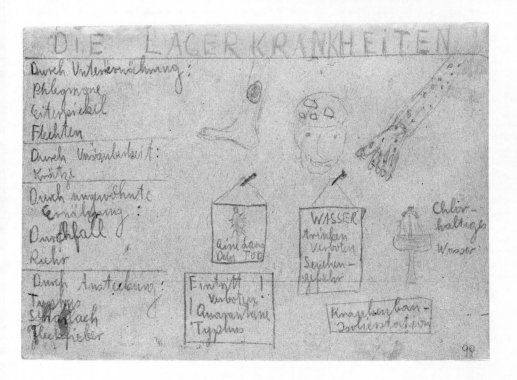

ILLNESSES IN CAMP
The many hardships prisoners went through:
infections, diseases and fevers.

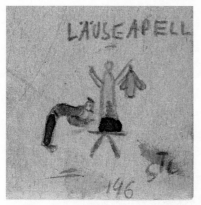

VERMIN
Most unwelcome prisoner companions: vermin in the camp.

Typhoid, spotted and scarlet fevers continued to take their toll with frightening regularity, not to be outdone by the no less deadly diarrhoea and dysentery.

'It's the dirty food,' argued the sufferers.

'It's our weak constitution,' said the others.

Placards hanging over the bathroom taps warned: 'Don't drink! Danger of epidemics!'

Elsewhere, on the bathroom walls, enamelled notices shrieked '*Eine Laus dein Tod!*' ('a louse – your death'), and showed a large portrait of the beastly sucker. For the first time we now had lice. Every Sunday, after rollcall, we queued up for a vermin inspection, carefully cleaning out the seams of our clothing beforehand, in case we were accused of spreading disease.

One of these parasite hunts proved to be another step forward for my growing reputation. Shirt in hand, trousers down, I approached one of the inspectors, a fellow prisoner who, armed with a magnifying glass, should have searched my body for lice, head lice and crabs. But, grinning with amusement, he lifted his lens to look closely into my eyes instead.

'Oh, so it's you, old fathead! Still alive and kicking, eh?' exclaimed a Slovak-accented voice. It was Ello, the chirpy lad who had once been the deputy room-elder at Block 7a.

'Next time,' he whispered, 'save yourself the bother; I'll cross you off the list without seeing you, like the block personnel. Old hands such as you can be trusted to crack the lice by themselves.'

Going back to receive my desperately needed daily soup, I glanced once again at the lads still lining up for the inspection. One after the other, I looked at their bare forearms that displayed their camp numbers. They were all higher than mine, most of them newer by over a year.

Now, only a handful of block inmates exceeded me in seniority. I had become an 'old hand'.

More than a 100,000 prisoners had arrived after me. Now, having been in Auschwitz for over a year, I was a veteran. Someone familiar, through experience, with all the annual events of Auschwitz life.

Many of the prominent camp personnel already knew me by sight, and I was now someone they sympathised with. The youngster that every inmate had once been keen on bullying had become an old-timer who was respected for having survived so long.

Even the authorities made a concession to my seniority by including me in a list of inmates allowed to write home. Staring at the postcard I had been given, I contemplated how best to choose a few words and to whom I could address them. I wrote about being well, 'hoping that you will send a kind reply' (this meant a food parcel) and sent the message to an elderly German lady who had been our neighbour. But the few lines I put my hope in were never answered. I guessed that letters were torn up and never left our camp.

On another occasion, the Nazi administration decided to hold cinema shows, with tickets being given to just Germans and Poles. Before each performance, crowds of other inmates, Russians, Jews and Gypsies, blocked the entrance hoping for a chance to sneak in. One evening, a German imprisoned for being a criminal, who probably knew me, pressed a ticket in my hand.

'Go in kid', he whispered, 'and enjoy yourself.'

Despite my embarrassed red face, I entered the cinema, an empty room in Block 2a. A film show, in Auschwitz? How strange that concept was. We crowded together, hungrily following the story on screen. It was a domestic love affair, full of careless living, good food, elegance, women and families. It felt like a mirage, a dream world, so remote from ours that if we looked any closer it would become obscure.

CHAPTER 13
THE WIND OF CHANGE

At long last, in late 1944, came the Allied bombers.* We hoped that was the first sign that the world around us was becoming aware of our suffering.†

Conscious of being a target, the SS garrison hastily prepared dugouts, painted the buildings with camouflage stripes and equipped themselves with helmets and gas masks.

On hearing the wail of the siren, a welcome signal that could be as frequent as three times a day, we immediately left work. We headed for our place of assembly, making sure that no one, especially the deaf or sleepers among us, was left behind to face punishment as a fugitive.

The hurried rollcall quickly over, we raced back to camp, keeping to a close formation. Our squad had been working the furthest distance away and therefore had the longest run back, but we didn't regret it despite our exhaustion and blisters. While we were running along the road, we had the satisfaction of seeing the hated SS scrambling for shelter.

The 'Master Race' anxiously scanned the skies from within their dugouts, afraid now, particularly as their rifles were useless against bombs. Then, less to our liking, the camp district became shrouded in a blanket of evil-smelling artificial fog released to confuse the enemy planes.

Crowded into the camp blocks we had no protection whatsoever against the falling bombs, but we were still happy about the raids. The buildings would shake from nearby explosions, the panes shattering into splinters, proof that damage was being done to our enemy.

---

* There were four bombing raids between August and December 1944.
† The Polish resistance had been active within Auschwitz and had let prisoners inside the camp know about the outside world, as well as informed the outside world about what was happening within camp.

With almost half of Poland having been liberated, the Nazis were becoming uneasy. Selections to pick out more death candidates for Birkenau abruptly stopped. A rumour that the gassings were to cease altogether proved to be false, however. Transports from south-east Europe, bringing new Jewish victims to the forest of death, kept on arriving.

The attitude of the authorities and the SS showed a marked change. Instead of suppressing the inferiors, they now imagined themselves to be protecting us from the invading hordes from the East. As a last effort, a propagandist picked from the Polish brand of fascists, visited our camp to enlist his countrymen into a National Defence Army that was to ward off the aggressors. His mission, futile though it seemed, nevertheless netted a handful of followers.

A newly founded bomb-disposal squad left the camp each day equipped with digging tools, long hooks and a trolley to tackle misfires. This was also supposed to consist of 'volunteers'. Members drawn from all nationalities had been attracted by the unambiguous and realistic bait of extra food allocations.

Around this time, we got news of the German inmates who had joined Hitler's army. Herded together and forbidden to abandon the battlefield, their company, all former prisoners, had been sent on a suicide mission and wiped out.

One autumn day in 1944, a motorcycle unexpectedly came rattling onto our building site. The rider, an anxious SS soldier, dismounted, called for the supervisor and exchanged a few hasty words with him.

'State of emergency. Send them back to camp, immediately. Report to barracks.'

Running at the double, we reached the camp gates to find that the guards were already wearing steel helmets. They had taken up positions in the air-raid dugouts and a strict curfew was swiftly being enforced.

'All the working squads have returned,' gasped our block-mates. 'Didn't you know? Birkenau is burning.'

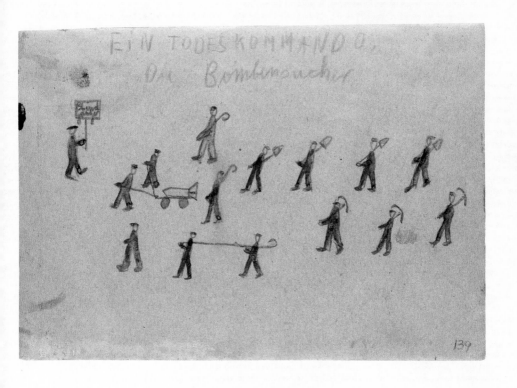

THE BOMB-DISPOSAL SQUAD
Another cruel exploitation of a prisoner's life.

Waiting for news, we nervously paced our room. In the afternoon, something unprecedented happened: we were issued our rations in advance – one and a half loaves of bread to last us for six days. Our fears intensified. Even influential prisoners who had 11 years of concentration camp life behind them seemed to be afraid. People became tense and irritable. As night came, we sat on our bunks, silent, restless and nervous. Straining our ears, we listened out for ominous sounds and rustles from beyond the fence.

By noon the next day, we'd returned to work. The imminent danger was over, but our fears had proved to be fully justified, for when the true story trickled through, the plot was more daring than we thought possible.

At Budy,* a working group of 100 Russians and Jews had overpowered their guards and escaped. At the same time, other prisoners set fire to one of Birkenau's crematoria, Krema IV, to create a diversion for other inmates to escape.

The Budy group that had escaped trudged through the woods and headed for the Carpathians, the partisan-held mountains a five-hour march away. Only a fortunate few, however, reached them. By the time they came to cross the last serious obstacle, the Vistula, it was already guarded by patrol boats. So was the Sola, the tributary parallel to the Vistula. At every crossroads and bridge there were heavily armed checkpoints.

Faced by a cordon of German military and police units, and pursued by ruthless SS soldiers with bloodhounds, the bulk of the brave rebels had no alternative but to surrender. Then they were massacred.

One crematorium at Birkenau burned down completely. Its work would be taken over by the other two. The revolt, although incredibly brave, had ultimately failed.

Later, the weapons with which the Budy squad had started their revolt were traced back to the Union plant, the munitions factory that employed prisoners. Three young girls who worked there had smuggled out a pistol and enough explosives to blow up all three

---

* Budy was an Auschwitz sub-camp at a farm set up on agricultural land covering Budy and Bór.

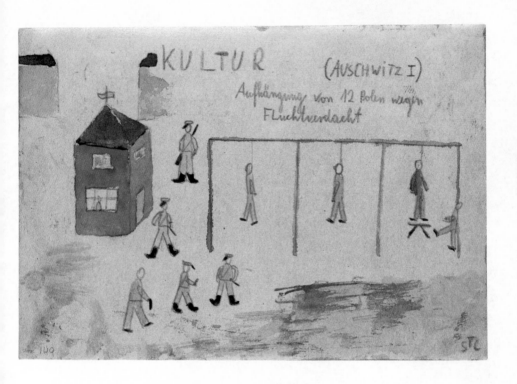

CULTURE
For the Third Reich, public hangings and
torture became part of their 'culture'.

crematoria. Unknown heroines, their fate was to be hanged. The executions took place at Birkenau women's camp.

Women inmates had to witness such a gruesome spectacle, some for the first time, and became highly emotional. Once ordinary housewives, they now faced the full and brutal reality of being caught trying to escape. Suspended from the gallows, 4 yards high, swung the lifeless bodies of three teenagers. They were lone casualties in the fight for liberation the world over. To their fellow women, to us youth and to all, they were an example of extreme courage, determination and honour.

At the men's camp, reprisal killings were frequent. Public hangings were staged once a month. When someone escaped, the first to suffer were his relatives, then his workmates. I saw it being enacted on a squad of bricklayers, neighbours of ours. One hundred of them were lined up, still uncertain of the reason why, and every fifth person was told to step forward. They were taken away as hostages and murdered.

There was a mass hanging of 12 Poles that was supposed to be a great spectacle of intimidation, but it failed. Instead, it developed into an unexpected show of defiance. When the rollcall was over, we were meant to march past the gallows. But we were hungry, tired and in no mood to cater to the Germans. It was already dusk when the first columns were ordered to turn left and march towards the kitchen square. However, to our surprise, they refused. The inmates assembled in the rear became restless and rushed for the safety of their blocks. When the others followed suit, the show was over, stolen, for the first time, by we prisoners.

I was transferred to a new squad engaged in building private air-raid shelters for SS officers living in Oświęcim.

Our daily trip to work, accompanied by six guards, took us past the outskirts of the camp and along 4 miles of country roads. Such journeys were always instructive, acquainting us with the nearby hamlets and the layouts of many SS encampments.

Our first shelter was for the commander of the Raisko farming region, an *Obersturmbannfuehrer* (a senior assault or unit leader). The preliminary stage for a brick-built, concrete-lined, underground hide-out that our German ruler would soon be forced to descend into was 100 cubic yards of excavation. The project had top priority, and as we had been picked as fast workers, this meant digging at speeds that were dangerously frantic.

Often the officer paid us visits to ensure that the necessary measures to guarantee his safety were being carried out properly. It was definitely not a fairy-tale, although he, the prince, arrived in a black carriage drawn by a couple of white horses. As he descended, he pulled at his grey uniform to straighten the silvery epaulettes and adjust his pristine white gloves before proceeding to inspect us, aided by a monocle – the symbol of Prussian precision. I was glad that manners forbade him to address us. Nor did he think our guards worthy of conversation. The next day he sent a note reminding those concerned 'that quick completion of the shelter was of the utmost urgency'.

Blue clinker bricks arrived to build the walls. Unloaded at record speeds, they were thrown down a chute, with me and some others at the receiving end 4 yards below.

Arriving like hard, sharp-cornered missiles, they bounced painfully into our bare hands. They came in their thousands and then had to be stacked. All we had to protect ourselves were hard-to-find scraps of paper, which were quickly worn through and woefully inadequate. To add to the misery, there was no time to look out for bricks that overturned, dropped off the chute and came hurtling down at us.

We desperately tried to keep up, despite our wounded bodies, bruised arms and bleeding hands, because when the days of unloading were over, things would become a lot easier.

During the midday break, we climbed out, got our litre of soup and sat on the grass, gazing around at our surroundings. A few yards away were two bungalows whose occupants, Polish civilians, dared not come out. But when our guards were busy eating their lunch, we sneaked away to the garden fence and waited for some of the inhabitants to notice us. Often, they gave us fruit and took letters for our families outside.

From time to time, a Polish girl, aged about 12, paid visits to sprawl on the flower-dotted grass and play with her big and cheerful dog. We could only stare at and envy her freedom, watching the carefree way that she moved.

My own existence in this world exceeded hers by a mere two years. Only a dozen yards of grassy field separated us. Yet our respective lives were worlds apart, divided by an imaginary line drawn by the Third Reich and the camp authorities. If we strayed beyond that invisible boundary marked by two large brown stones a foot high and 50 yards apart, we would be shot.

When, except for another two layers of bomb-protecting concrete roofing, the shelter was finished, we experienced our first air raid outside of camp. All 20 of us were herded into the dark, newly built vault, where we sat on its moist floor, leaning against the supports of the wooden framework. We waited.

From one of the houses, a radio blared out the raid report: 'Bomber formation heading for Blechhammer.' Blechhammer was an industrial district and another sweatshop that drew its cheap slaves from concentration camps. Shortly afterwards, the announcer bellowed: '*Die Amerikanischen Angreifer wurden siegreich zurückgeschlagen*' ('The Americans were victoriously beaten back'). The bombs had likely hit their intended target.

My workmates, all Russians and Poles, enticed me to find out whether the guards would let us rest until the all-clear signal was given. I groped my way to the shelter's entrance. The opening, sharply outlined by daylight from the stairwell, was blocked by a soldier reclining between the doorjambs.

'*Entschuldigen Sie bitte, ich möchte etwas fragen*' ('Excuse me please, I want to ask something').

Jerking to attention, the guard – who I noticed was wearing an ill-fitting SS uniform – grabbed his rifle and cocked it. Again, I proclaimed my intention, this time more gently.

'*Oh, Sie sprechen Deutsch?*' ('Oh, you speak German?') queried the surprised guard. Visibly relieved, he hurried up the stairs, looked out, returned and told me that his colleagues were out of sight. My interview was granted.

'We were frightened that you lot may try to escape,' he addressed me. 'I don't trust these Russians. One never knows what plots they are hatching, with these air raids tempting them. Four rifles handled by old men* for military service are no match for a bunch of sturdy lads. If we returned without you, one need not guess what our superiors would do, and don't forget we have families too.' He opened his breast pocket and pulled out a photo of his wife surrounded by three young children. 'They really hope to see me back. Actually, I am a newcomer; one of those who had no inkling of this place's vileness.' He sighed. 'It is a bad job, especially as it no longer protects us from air raids. Our situation is hardly better than yours.

'Why do you think they are making all these camp extensions? When they have finished with the Jews and the Gypsies, they will round up the Slavs. Next, they'll start picking inferiors from their own people, old people like me. A friend of mine who studies all these new books about race and destiny says that this is what they are aiming at.'

At this point, a long, penetrating wail interrupted him: the all-clear signal. Hurriedly, he resumed his position of authority.

'*Heraus! Schnell! Zur Arbeit!*' ('Quick, back to work!')

Perhaps there was some truth in what he believed about the plans of his leaders.

Our small construction squad moved on to a second shelter, and then to a third. The townspeople, still not daring to look at us in public, made detours around our working site. However, Oświęcim had become familiar to us and we grew accustomed to its streets. We knew the place by the prisoners' way, the exterior. Oświęcim's homes were a world apart. The inside of this town was happy, with red-brick houses appearing to me like hearts, while the bulbs from the bright lanterns above felt like eyes looking down on us.

The work was hard, and the long walk back to camp, tough. But, unlike the other prisoners, we had many opportunities to familiarise ourselves with our surroundings. All the checkpoints, administrative

---

* Wehrmacht and Luftwaffe soldiers who were too old for front-line service were often assigned to guard duty at Auschwitz.

centres, officers' villas, isolated farm buildings, SS camps and railway sidings had to be learned about.

Eager to prepare ourselves for emergencies, we memorised the area's layout and noted any changes. Almost daily we noticed something new. It made us happy, for we had become useful. We were confident now. Any scrap of information passed on to our campmates was more than merely valuable; it was ammunition in the fight against our cleverly enforced ignorance.

With only a few disheartened old men to guard us, it seemed easy to escape from the squad. But no one attempted to. Why should we endanger ourselves, now that it was our cause that was winning?

We went on mixing concrete. Attacking the huge heaps of sand and gravel as if they were our enemy. We savagely hit the piles with our shovels and flung them into the ever-rotating mixer. It did not occur to us that, unwillingly, we were continuing to help build the Nazi empire. It was only our youth that we were aware of and a dynamic urge for progress. Someone then told us that chunks of earth could ruin the concrete and had to be removed. We were determined to do the opposite. We fed the mixer with as much muck as possible. It was just what we had been looking for, a way to disrupt the enemy.

One day, on our way to work, we met a group of girl prisoners from Birkenau.

When they shouted slogans at us, we knew they were Russians. Our feelings were running high, and we replied with even greater vigour. They waved their kerchiefs, we waved our caps, for a moment united in our hopes.

Whether we had been born on the shores of the Atlantic or the plains of Mongolia, our fiery, unquenchable youth was the same. There were shouts of '*Da Zdravstvuyet!*' ('Long live!'), '*Krasnaya Armiya!*' ('Red Army!') and '*Za Stalina!*' ('For Stalin!') – was about all I could manage with my poor Russian.

The guards, despite only hearing an unintelligible noise, tried to stop us. It was useless. Neither they, nor their bosses, could turn back the tide of history. On the contrary, they were hastening it.

Then the girls took a road forking off into the valley and, separated by a shrub-covered embankment slowly rising in height, we parted.

I returned to the squad building the stables. Our job was to finish the interior, cover the floor with a herring-bone pattern of clinker bricks, then fix the fodder cribs, plaster the mangers and finally line the attic with panels of cemented wood shavings.

It was the nicest place of work I had known. Materials never arrived in time, so much of our day was spent waiting for them. The elderly foreman, who I spoke English with, had become a friend of mine.

'When after the last war I found myself on the German side of the border,' he told me, 'they used to look down on me as a *Wasserpollak*.'* 'When I returned to Poland, they snubbed me for being a German. In 1939, it suited the Nazis to make me a *Volksdeutsche*,† but they soon regretted it and put me in prison.'

'And now,' I interrupted, 'you are a Pole again.'

'Yes, a good one, and glad of it too.'

Half our workmates were now civilians, craftsmen from Poland and Czechoslovakia who had signed on for two years and more.

'Again, they have put sheep's fat on the sandwiches,' they would proclaim, abandoning their lunch on some windowsill where we could not help but notice it.

'Damn those kitchen people. Even rats wouldn't nibble at food like this.'

Except for these occasional, greatly appreciated gifts, the civilians did not dare show their sympathies openly.

Soon, though, we had unwelcome guests watching over us. The SS men in charge of the horses.

---

* A pejorative term for people speaking Silesian in the German/Polish border area.

† People in other countries whose language and culture had German origins but who did not hold German citizenship. They enjoyed certain privileges under Nazi rule.

Drunk, lazy and vulgar, they took over the two rooms at the far end of the barn. They came swooping down on us, trying hard to frighten us away. They detested having to live under the same roof as us, but their colleague, the building inspector, would not listen to them.

'The workers will stay until they have finished,' maintained our SS boss.

'If they do, we'll kill them, all the stinking lot of them,' cried the enraged stable boys. 'They make a mess of the place, steal turnips and frighten the horses, and you, you gullible ass, want them to go on with it.'

A few days later and drunk as usual, they came rushing in on us, cracking whips, fingering pistols and cursing both us and the civilians.

'We'll teach you to cheat us, you *Schweinehund!*'

Staring in my direction, one of them grabbed me by the neck and then shouted at me to continue my work. I raced off, climbing the ladder into the attic, glad to be out of his way. Below, the commotion went on. In a corner, leaning against the sloping roof, I met the foreman.

'Well,' he said, 'I expected it; they'll never recognise him.'

'Who?' I queried, taken by surprise.

'Didn't you know?' he grinned. 'One of our lads sold them brandy and, when they didn't pay up, he threatened to denounce them to their superiors.'

We had heard about the Warsaw uprising* being quashed when the prisoners – men, women and children, the population of whole streets – arrived at Birkenau. Polish inmates looked for acquaintances they knew and tried to find out more details.

Once again connected with the outside world, we pleaded with our civilian workmates to bring us the newspapers they wrapped their sandwiches in – the latest *Voelkischer Beobachter* or its Polish equivalent. The Allies, it seemed, were getting closer.

---

* The Warsaw uprising took place from August to October 1944. The Polish underground resistance led by the Armia Krajowa wanted to liberate Warsaw from German occupation. Stalin's nearby army did little to help, allowing previously stretched German resources to regroup and then defeat the Polish resistance.

Dressed in our blue-white uniforms, our bald heads covered by flat, round prison caps, we crouched over spreading heaps of moist building sand and drew maps of Europe, lining in the war fronts.

Considering that the Allied effort already had the blessing of nearly the whole world and that it had many powerful backers, the progress of the armies of liberation seemed disappointingly slow. With the Nazi extermination policies probably known by this time to our far-away friends, we had expected a 'Blitzkrieg' in reverse. By now we realised that the fascists and all they stood for had crumbled and were being driven far back by a well-equipped, determined army supported by the local populations. Having the Allies so nearby, we yearned for them to do more.

Grown-ups were preoccupied and worried about their overwhelming losses – families, homes and so much more. They longed for their pre-war lives when they had been able to enjoy pleasures such as female company and good food. By contrast, we youngsters rarely thought of the past. It was the present we were concerned with.

We were eager to understand our fellow prisoners, who had come from all over Europe, and to learn from them. They were likely to be frank with us; for, unversed in politics, we were unlikely to inform on them. Nor would we take offence as quickly as the more biased grown-ups.[*]

I enjoyed observing other people's attitudes and customs. No habit, however strange, was repulsive to me if no fellow human being was hurt by it. Only planned, premeditated evil deserved to be condemned.

For me, the thrice-weekly 1.5-ounce sticks of margarine were to be spread on bread, evenly and sparingly. To the Russian country lads, however, they were more like frankfurters – to be gobbled up on their own.

For me, hitting someone meant being angry with him, but with the Greek boys, it was a game. They called it *Klepsiklepsi* – a nickname given to stealing. The harder you slapped your blindfolded playmate's

---

[*] Thomas and other youngsters like him were trusted by other grown-ups from different countries to carry messages and transport important information around the camp.

face, the more fun it was watching him try to recognise you (once his eyes were uncovered) from among a crowd of grinning bystanders – all doing their best to look guilty. If he did, it was then your turn to cover your eyes and guess who was hitting you.

Then there was the Jewish boy from Belgium, a mere child in his outlook. Before he was sent to Auschwitz and became my neighbour, he had never made his bed, never washed his clothes and never sewn on buttons. In fact, he had done very little for himself; he also had never mended socks, cut bread or left home without asking for permission.

'At home,' he confided in me, 'I had a big head of hair and mother combed it for me every morning.'

After lights out, he used to cry, his small, feeble body rolled up in a pair of rough, flea-infested blankets. 'If you really want to help me,' he begged, after I tried to comfort him, 'please make my bed in the morning. I'll never manage it on my own and I truly dread being punished by everyone for being untidy.'

I did. Perhaps it would have been better to let him manage on his own, but I doubted whether the cruelties of Auschwitz would wait for him to become independent.

Maurice was another character. A young Greek Jew, a tall redhead, stringy, freckly and snub-nosed, he was the symbol of optimism. Instead of wasting his time looking for food and companions, Maurice was determined to learn and educate himself. While our crowd talked about camp news and the war, Maurice spent his evenings with a Polish friend of his, a professor, who in exchange for lessons in ancient Greek taught him Russian, Polish and Czech. I first got to know him when, trying to baffle us with a puzzling maths question, he was surprised to find an equal before him.

And then there was a former workmate of mine, an unusually well-educated Ukrainian. Despite grappling with our language difficulties, we talked about the things that worried us. My bitter criticism of his compatriots was quite a challenge to him.

'They are callous robbers,' I hissed, 'cads, hated and despised, bullies who do not even shrink at attacking the *Muselmann* weaklings.'

'Everyone does that,' he countered, 'and you certainly can't expect the peasant lads to be sensitive about it. Their stomachs are much bigger than yours and hunger teaches them to be ruthless.'

'Yes, I interrupted, 'I know, but they should concentrate on thieving from camp supplies and the stores like the rest of us, and not taking their neighbour's bread ration.'

'Ukrainians speak neither German nor Polish, so how do you expect them to be clever at scheming? Their only asset is their strength and muscles. Naturally, they use that to the full. Your compassion for those who save up their bread to trade it for things like tobacco is out of place, kid. They deserve no better. Anything they save up is surplus, so don't worry yourself if it goes to those who need it.'

Aghast at my acquaintance's attitude, I stubbornly maintained that stealing from fellow prisoners could be nothing else but 'a crime . . . a wicked crime'.

'No worse than those the others commit,' said my equally passionate opponent. 'It's an open secret that the German personnel take away part of our rations. The Gypsies having skilfully poked out half of the tobacco, sell cigarettes. The Jews will cheat you on anything and everything. That's ruthless, too. Or isn't it, because you do it more pleasantly? Our people are rough and outspoken; they do the same, only by force.'

I still had ammunition to reply with. 'You can't convince me,' I shot back. 'They are repulsive hooligans, nothing Russia can be proud of, a bad advertisement, indeed!' He came back with a quiet but sneering, 'Ask those lads about the Western world. Go on, tell them that what they have seen of it is civilised.'

The Ukrainian – a little unfairly, I thought – had cornered me with something I was too young to judge. Then, to my relief, he changed the subject.

'Next time you start arguing,' he broke off, 'remember that gentle cheating and open robbery smell the same to us.'

I talked to a fellow prisoner, a Pole who worked at the butcher's. 'It is nearly impossible now to get rich by smuggling out sausages,' he told me. 'All our "organising" methods have been found out and there are strict controls.'

One of the ways of 'organising', I learned, had been to block the drains and call in the sanitation squad, who had to poke out the muck with long cleaning rods. When the rods came wriggling through the inspection hole, all the partners on the inside had to do was to hook a few sausages onto them.

Much of the meat that found its way to the sausage factory had been condemned as unfit. 'Sometimes there are even worms in it,' said my contact, 'something really sickening to look at.'

On Thursdays, when we received our twice-weekly sausage allocation, a worker's ration of 100 grams, I struggled hard not to remind myself of its ingredients. Previously, the relative merits of spiced black pudding, liver sausage containing fish bones and jellied pork sausage – the three traditional camp varieties – had greatly interested me. Now I dared not pass opinions on them. Yet despite thinking of their repulsive origins, they were still a cherished luxury, a treat we counted down the days by.

Officially, the stables were complete now. Our little construction squad was disbanded, much to our despair. The autumn winds heralded another camp winter. Could we face a bigger, harder place of work where, as newcomers, we would be exploited to the full? We racked our brains trying to find an alternative.

A dozen of us, the remnants of the former New Stables squad, were assembled at the place where the unemployed gathered in order to be assigned to unload railway trucks – I had already once experienced the slavery of the materials yard. It was dawn, a few minutes past six. One by one, accompanied by metallic marching music, the working squads were marched out of camp. These were 'specialists' who left behind a dozen haggard, useless, unskilled workers like me. I felt as helpless as the day I arrived in Auschwitz.

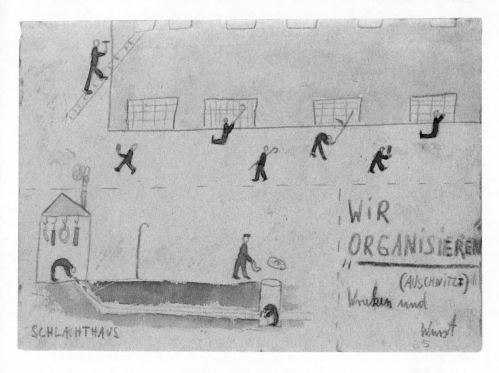

WE ARE 'ORGANISING'
A never-ending search for anything that was considered to be 'food' to manage one's never-ending hunger.

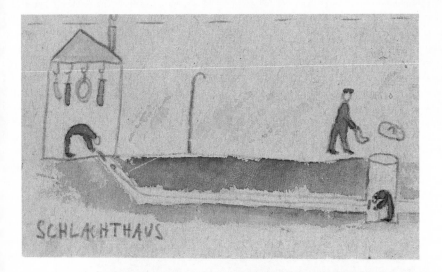

Then, completely unexpectedly, our foreman, the one that knew English, suggested that we, too, start marching out. He had a plan but would not reveal it.

'You leave that to me,' he said briskly, already jogging in front to lead us on. 'If we don't take the risk now, they'll send us off to become '*Muselmann*', by unloading bags of cement running at the double. Come on, lads, all I ask of you is to march smartly. Don't forget, hands and caps pressed to the seams of the trouser legs, short, quick steps!'

'*Kommando Aufraeumungsarbeiten Neue Pferdestaelle 12 Mann Voll*,' yelled our spokesman when we had reached the gate ('Cleaning-up squad, New Stables, 12 men, full'). The guard on duty scanned the list. He had never heard of such a squad and could find no record of it anywhere. Nor was there any, but our foreman soon accounted for it.

'Yes,' agreed the SS man, carefully adding our newly created squad to his checklist, 'if you have left a dirty mess at the place, you'll damn well have to clean it up yourselves.'

Our trick had worked. At noon, the foreman would look for our former SS supervisor, convince him, if necessary, and have our squad legalised. Work would not be lacking. We would tidy the stables: level the earth all around, fill in the cracks, touch up the whitewash and climb up the attic rafters to look for leaky roofing tiles. Any duty-conscious SS supervisor would be satisfied with that.

The 12 of us, now perhaps the smallest but most fortunate working squad in Auschwitz, were glad to be back at the stables. Warm horses, soft bales of straw, heaps of turnips, the penetrating smell of fodder and a roof over one's head all represented a pretty good place to spend the winter. We even felt attached to our stables. We had sweated blood and tears to build them, now we would try to enjoy them. Our foreman friend, too, was satisfied. He had been promoted to a sub-capo, and certainly deserved this honour for his ingenuity.

My second winter in camp seemed far more endurable than the first. I was less hungry and no longer afraid of the cruel world around me. It now lay before me like an open book, waiting for me to tear away the few pages that were spoiling it – to rebind it with a strong, unbreakable cover of equality and comradeship. To brighten it with the achievements of progress, to gild it with an unquenchable determination for justice.

Often, the room-elder sent me along to the kitchen compound, to act as the spokesman and persuade the head cook to allocate another vat of soup to us youngsters at Block 13a. Sometimes, drawing heavily on that part of my brain that stocked polite, German eloquence, I succeeded so that, much to the envy of the other blocks, we could feast on a noodle-with-milk diet of leftovers from the hospital.

People had begun favouring us young prisoners. Everyone was eager to show himself helpful, now that supplies were being bolstered by the provisions that the well-supplied Hungarian transports had brought along. A good name could be had for little sacrifice, and the adults around us were quick to grab the opportunity. In 1943, we were young, bewildered and on our own. Now, hardened and experienced, we scorned those who, at the time, had shrugged their shoulders at our sufferings – those who called themselves men. We no longer needed them.

Then there was Leo,[14] a Dutchman and a new friend of mine, who was much older than me. A lanky 6 foot, flat-footed and clad in grotesquely large shoes, Leo was the ideal figure to make fun of. He was frog-eyed and wore a tired pair of glasses that were held together by string, but he was full of gentle and pleasant memories of Scheveningen, his hometown. But jolly Leo did not mind the teasing; on the contrary, he took pride in being the object of laughter.

'All right, lads,' he would concede. 'You say I should sing something to you because I am called Voorzanger.'* And then, his shifting eyes full of glee as his big feet tapped out a jazz rhythm, he would continue, 'All right, here we go: Hey, baba ree bop . . .!'

At home Leo had played the saxophone, 'the shiny thing that comes second only to Holland and my wife', he told me. Leo was also an enthusiastic patriot, even though the Nazis had found out that the Voorzanger half of the family was Jewish.

I greatly liked easy-going Leo. He was a good friend who was frank and trustworthy. In addition, he knew a thing or two about cooking, which was handy now that I daily robbed the docile horses of turnips.

---

* Voorzanger, Leo's name, also means a *cantor*, someone who sings and leads prayers in a synagogue.

On Sunday evenings, when the lone stove in his room was not littered with toast, he would make soup that included a delicious brew of turnips, bread and an occasional onion.

Surrounded by cold, snow-covered fields, our lucky, secluded squad at the stables avoided the attention of the roaming SS supervisors, which afforded us independence. Of the 12 of us, one was a foreman, two were lookouts, and another two spent half their time plodding back and forth to the camp to fetch our soup.

Once, together with a young Polish Jew, it was my turn to get the soup. We were stamping along the icy road, pushing a wheelbarrow that had a thermos container strapped to it.

'What do we do when we arrive at the gate?' I asked my companion.

'Don't you worry. Leave that to me, and for heaven's sake don't do anything else. Just keep on pushing the barrow!' he said. 'It's not the first time I've gone for soup, so leave all the reporting and standing to attention to me.' Within sight of the camp, he again reminded me: 'Remember what I said, you go straight on!'

When we reached the checkpoint, I did, and marching neatly while at the same time carefully balancing the barrow, I passed the gate. But I did not get far. Someone shouted and grabbed me from behind, then a flurry of punches followed.

'You *Schweinehund*, how dare you ignore us?'

I was thrown onto the paving and kicked. The barrow overturned. Crouching on the ground, trying to ward off the blows, I perceived glimpses of running feet, jackbooted ones of more SS men rushing towards me not wanting to miss out on the fun.

'That'll teach you a lesson!' shouted the fierce grey figure above me.

Then an SS officer came and asked the guards what I had done. Someone said that I was only a harmless *Schweinehund*.

'Take your bloody barrow off the roadway,' shouted another.

'How dare you block the traffic!'

'Get away from here, you bastard!'

I got up and gladly did as I was told. My confused colleague, pale with fright, and myself red and bleeding, pushing the barrow

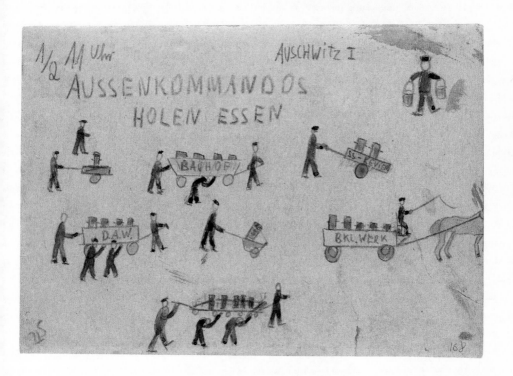

**FETCHING FOOD FOR OUTSIDE
WORKING SQUADS**
It was a long and sometimes dangerous journey
to camp and back with the precious food.

like drunkards, entered the camp. Our fellow prisoners stared at us. Silently, we made for the nearest washroom.

When I had cooled down and my anger had subsided, I asked what had happened. The SS man who had to check us in could not trace our little-known squad on his lists, so he had told my companion to stop. The Pole was supposed to have transmitted the order to me, but his nerves made him forget and I, 'unaware' of this, marched straight into camp without being registered. This, by the code of the SS, was an offence only exceeded in severity by leaving and not being registered. I got off lightly, I realised.

A few minutes later, there was another surprise. 'You nearly got us into trouble, this time,' mumbled my Polish companion, opening the container and extracting two packets of black-market butter from it.

'Didn't you rather?' I replied, now unpleasantly aware of what his nervous forgetfulness had been caused by. It taught me yet another lesson.

By permission of the SS, or perhaps by order, a colourfully decorated and sparkling Christmas tree was erected at the camp. With no blackout, it shone like a beacon of hope, but we could not bring ourselves to like it. There was too much irony and sadness about it.

Christmas Day 1944, unlike the previous year, was declared a holiday. We did not work, we received extra allocations of soup and bread, and, for once, we stopped worrying about being hungry.

Saucy Gert invited me to Block 5, where more than 100 people crowded into a little room to celebrate. In the far corner was a table with a small, poor-looking Christmas tree on it. Few of us still believed in religion, but it was comforting to know that, at this moment, people could concentrate on thinking about their fellow men.

Would those surrounded by their carol-singing children remember us? Would the devout who filled the silent churches remember us? We started singing solemnly and impressively. 'Silent night, holy night . . .' A German camp veteran next to me was weeping. It was the 12th time now he had heard this song battling against the cruel walls of a concentration camp.

Most of the assembled were Germans, all veterans. Saucy Gert's superior, the capo of Raisko's farming squad and a former German criminal, pushed himself through the crowd towards the table. As patron of the gathering, he wanted to say a few words to us.

'Comrades,' he addressed us, 'today, in the year 1944, it is Christmas again. We think of Jesus. We think about our families. We think of those who have left us. In our many years of trials and tribulations, we have often been on the brink of despair, but we kept on hoping, confident that one day the spirit of the Lord will prevail. Today, on this memorable day, we not only hope but know for certain that next year will bring us the decisive moment we have all so anxiously been waiting for. Let us spend this Christmas with the conviction that the forces of brotherhood, love and self-sacrifice will be victorious. Let us look forward to a world of equality and peace. When, God willing at Christmas 1945, we shall be free men again, however far-flung we may be, let us remember what we had wished for. Then, as now, may our conscience guide us . . .'

We had listened neither to a Christian nor to a German, but to the voice of a bitter, hardened concentration camp inmate. When his voice faded, we joined in to sing: '*Wir sind die Moorsoldaten*'.

After Christmas, our hopes were brighter than ever before. Only very few transports were arriving now, and the SS was unexpectedly quiet towards us. Again, there were chances of quick liberation, for the Soviet armies were expected to start their long-awaited winter attack within days.

On New Year's Eve, I had an invitation to Block 16a. When I arrived, the room was already filled with dense smoke from *ersatz* tobacco. The inmates were sitting on their bunks, feet dangling down to the wooden frames below, and tapping out rhythms on them. At the end of the gangway sat a band of three Dutch Jews with a drum, a violin and a saxophone that they had borrowed from the camp orchestra.

Towards midnight, the listeners climbed down from their beds and started to dance – waltzes, foxtrots and polkas, all within the bounds of the 3-yard-wide corridor between the bunks. A few busied themselves imitating women, others drew laughter by jerking the lower halves

of their bodies, sportively thrusting them back and forth. Everyone
– except myself, a non-dancer, watching attentively from the third,
upper tier of a bunk – was doing his best to be funny. Then, with the
three sweating musicians playing jazz, people danced lively solos. It
was now 1945.

A week later, rumour circulated that the camp was about to be evacuated
to the West, but no one seemed to know when and how. So we all went
on working, otherwise the whole district would become paralysed.
Without prisoners at the supply depots and without those manning the
various maintenance squads, Auschwitz would cease to exist.

Our little squad continued its work; trudging through the Polish
winter to the far-off stables, to enjoy the warmth of the horses, we
contemplated things to come, hidden among the bales of straw. While
other squads still numbered a few hundred, or even a few thousand,
ours had shrunk to six *Schutzhäftlingen* (protective custody
prisoners) as the authorities ironically chose to call us whom, to our
good fortune, no one bothered to supervise.

Some months ago, realising that their cause was lost, the Nazis had
ordered all major construction to be stopped. Every second building
littering the camp's working territory was unfinished. The bare walls
stuck out like ruins. Row after row of red bricks surrounded by a vast
sea of lifeless snow. Where there should have been roofs and windows
sat deep cushions of white snow, triumphant like conquerors. An icy
wind whistled through the empty shells. No one had been near them
for a long time. There was not even the faintest sign of footprints.

The incomplete structures were as grotesque as the ideas of those
who ordered them to be built. Like antiquities, they would soon be
relics of a culture that had killed itself; a way of living that was a path of
death; a system that failed. And we who built them had marked their
foundations with names and hidden messages to those who'd survive
us. One day the world would know.

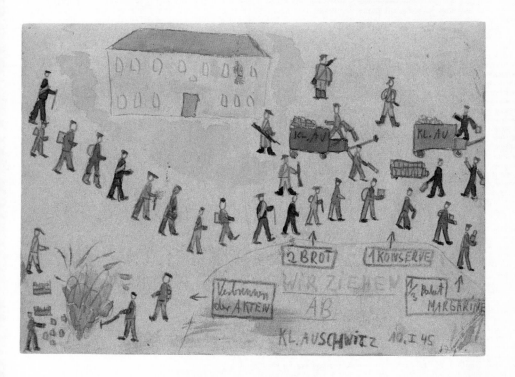

WE ARE MOVING OUT
Leaving Auschwitz for the last time and
marching towards the unknown.

Suddenly, it was the day of our departure. Early in the morning we joined the long queues of people, coiled around the blocks oblivious to where we were heading. Restless with nerves, we waited to leave the camp. The block personnel, under SS supervision, busied themselves burning index cards. Feeding the pyre came documents from the administration barracks.

First, we were led to the bathhouse at the vast, newly finished disinfection and laundry building just beyond the fence. At the still-incomplete delousing wing, we saw an array of heavy metal doors lying on the icy floor. Doors that would no longer be hung. Doors to gas chambers whose purpose would no longer be fulfilled. Instead, we would be marched to another place, and this would be left behind.

Our beds too, the only things that we could call our own, and that we had become so fond of, would also be left behind. Carved on their wooden posts and boards were our names and numbers. How often had I spent the evening lying on my sack of straw, reading the fading chronicles of people who had slept there before me. No more beds for us now; only two blankets, rolled up and slung diagonally over our shoulders, to take refuge in and dream on.

Then, I queued up again for hours. I had lost contact with my friends, the ones who I wanted to be together with. Near the gate, surrounded by guards with fixed bayonets, were cars full of provisions. Each of us received two loaves (the ration for eight days) and a tin of stewed steak. Every third person was given a 500-gram packet of margarine. They were supposed to share it, but most took this hallowed treasure and disappeared. Other prisoners wanting their fair share threatened those who had margarine and who looked likely to be intimidated.

It was already dark when I passed through Auschwitz's gates, as I had done some eight hundred times before, but now, in January 1945, it was for good. We passed a detachment of guards with heavy machine-guns; none looked sympathetic. I was marching out of the vast territory of Auschwitz for the last time.

Then, joining the long columns that moved slowly along the dark country road, came the women of Birkenau camp. Barely recognisable, they looked old. 'There you are,' said, someone. 'I told you so. We are not going to be led far. Otherwise, they would not drag along the old ones.'

'Probably they are marching us to another camp somewhere around here,' argued another. 'Who knows how many places like Auschwitz there are by now.'

The moon had come out. We were trekking along the road parallel to the Sola river. There were guards on the right, to the left, behind and in front.

Liberation had just been a dream. It would eventually come to Auschwitz, yes. But not for us.

PART 4

CHAPTER 14
RETREAT FROM LIBERTY

The column of prisoners seemed endless. As it crawled along the road, more and more joined from Auschwitz's subsidiary camps. At every crossing, there were new additions.

We moved without stopping, the fast ones in the front, the old and slow behind. When we first left Auschwitz, we marched in rows. Now we shuffled along like a herd of sorry-looking animals, weak and exhausted.

Lining the fields on either side of our column were lone heaps. I had noticed these ever-recurring landmarks previously, but only now, by the dim light of the risen moon, could I see what they were. A pitiful sight, lying on the snow in their blue-white prison coats were lifeless bodies. One of them had a ripped-open cardboard box next to him, empty except for a bundle of letters that fluttered in the icy breeze. Had the owner been too slow or too quick?

My head was humming with the words that once decorated the walls of Block 7a, 'There is but one road to freedom; its milestones are obedience, diligence . . .'. The guard, before pulling the trigger, must have heard the same words. How else could he have sworn blind obedience to those to whom humanity was nothing more than exploitable cattle?

I looked away from the heaps. Trying not to think at all, I staggered along in a shattered daze. All that mattered was for me and for us to reach our destination.

At dawn, we reached a road junction. Beyond lay hills, and to the left a village. To the right was an ice-covered field, littered with squatting and slumbering prisoners. On being told to join them, I sprawled onto the trampled snow and immediately fell asleep.

Loud shouts soon woke me up again. A messenger, sitting on a motorcycle, his legs apart, with one hand on the handlebar and the other gesticulating wildly, was arguing with some officers. He looked like a Wehrmacht soldier from the Front and had come to warn them of Russian observation planes.

The officers, on hearing this, shouted orders at the guards and we were shoved into the nearby farmyards. I squeezed into the warm barn, which was already crowded with men from other camps. Before they spotted my intrusion, I clambered up onto a haystack and fell fast asleep. Someone tapped my shoulder.

'Wake up, kid, the old woman at the farmhouse has just invited some of us in to have some food. You'd better hang around there in case she asks another group to join her.'

The Polish peasants, I reflected, were much more courageous than we had expected them to be. When we passed their villages, old women stood at the kerb handing out milk – even at night. They were beaten by the guards, who were infuriated at not receiving such favours for themselves, but that did not deter them. I did not care, however. Food or no food, kindness or not, I just wanted to sleep.

Barely four hours later, we were chased out onto the road again. Not wanting to burden myself with items that would not save me anyway, I left behind my blankets. Of the provisions that were to last a week, only one loaf of dark army-issue bread remained for the brutal journey ahead. It was tucked beneath my armpits, for my fingers were too numb from the cold.

The column was no longer continuous. In its place, plodding along the country road, were several independent groups, some quicker, others slower. If the guard was decent, he would allow the weak to wait for the column behind. But it was more likely that these stragglers would join the silent heaps at the side of the road.

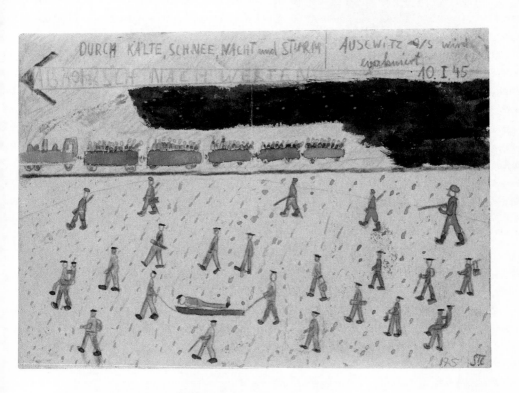

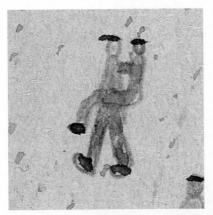

DEPARTURE TO THE WEST
Through the freezing cold and stormy night,
we kept on marching.

Everyone tried to walk near a 'good' guard. If the soldier really was good, he would shout, 'Keep on moving. It's only a few more miles now, and it sure isn't worthwhile giving up now. I'm tired too, but we have to make it.' They were all too few, however. Many guards, although they frequently rested and were equipped with plenty of marching provisions, felt sorry for themselves. Self-pity, it seemed, had become a virtue in Germany. To make it worse, they made us carry their backpacks.

'Come here, boy,' they demanded. 'Take my rucksack for a while; it's getting damned heavy for me.'

There were also the old and sick among us asking to be helped. My feet were blistered and aching, but I could not refuse to do my share. Having someone support himself against my shoulders became routine. Unfortunately, when I asked to be relieved of them, I never sounded imperious enough to have others share in my burden of supporting the weak.

As darkness fell on the second night of our long march, we ceased to be of any particular age, nationality or standing. We were just skeletal figures, trudging through the cold night.

Hail and snow drove into our faces. We were hungry, but our fingers were too numb to grip the cherished bread hidden in our pockets. Around midnight we passed a churchyard. I was not squeamish about cemeteries. Two years ago, when I was barely 13, I had dug graves and walked around tombstones after dark. Even this deserted little burial-place would not merit the attention of ghosts, I reasoned. If there were any such spirits, they were right among us. I looked ahead and behind me. I seemed to be surrounded by ghostly shadows, hundreds and thousands of them.

Then, something happened that shook me up. Suddenly, from the east, behind the woods, fiery trails started shooting into the sky, plenty of them. They rose and fell again. Someone shouted 'Katyushas'. We were later to discover that it was the beginning of the Russian offensive that ended with the encirclement of Breslau.

Katyusha, the Russian multiple rocket gun, was not new to me. We had heard it sung about so often that it had become synonymous with victory. Our lips were pressed closed to keep out the cold and retain some warmth, but again, I recalled the tunes we had sung – this time from that part of my being where hope was stored – 'We'll bring *Katyusha*; Good luck to you *Katyusha*!' It was a dream no longer. They were coming now.

Thirty minutes later, the sky to the left of us was still illuminated by rockets. They penetrated our hearts, turning them from despair to confidence. We found new strength.

'Come on, comrade, pull yourself together,' we encouraged each other, 'we might be liberated any hour now.'

A group of two dozen women prisoners and their guard were seen moving along a footpath obscured by shrubs to the woods beyond, where the rockets came from. A guard of ours, spotting them, shouted across the field: 'Hey, you, where are you taking your flowers to?'

'Don't worry, I know the district,' came the reply; 'we won't get lost. We are just taking a short cut to get there quicker.'

I never found out what he meant by 'there'. But, judging by the look of it, I wished them good luck for their adventure.

The attitude of the guards began to change dramatically. They now told us we would be marching on until rail transport could be found, and then we would be evacuated westwards.

On occasion, the sledges crammed with the luggage of the guards became resting places for the weak. Prisoners whose legs had failed them were laid on top of planks of wood and were pulled along the snow.

Finally, we reached a railway station. Dazzled by the bright lights illuminating the tracks, we slowly passed by a greasy black engine. It was standing near the road, blowing off steam. The driver leaned out of the cabin.

'Nothing doing any more,' he shouted at us in a strong Polish accent. 'Our line has been cut. The trains have been overdue for hours now.'

The *Katyushas*, it seemed, had been more than a nice firework display.

We marched on to the town of Pless, where my great-grandfather had lived. In the market square, we met a group of Birkenau women prisoners resting beside a fountain. We wanted to join them, but were forced to keep moving. The town's inhabitants were asleep, doors and windows covered with shutters. No one seemed to notice us as we shuffled along through the dark, narrow, cobblestoned streets. Only the howling dogs in the backyards took an interest in us.

The road rose into the wooded hills, turning and twisting, sapping our precious energy.

As we progressed, the landscape changed to coalmines and pitheads. We were in Upper Silesia.

Some of the mines worked night shifts. They stood out like beacons from the otherwise blacked-out countryside. Others seemed deserted. I remembered a time, six years earlier, when coalmines were my favourite playgrounds in which I tried to climb slag heaps and admired the elaborate railway engines. It was all so different now.

Adjoining one of the mines was a concentration camp. Both were deserted. I scanned the barracks. The windows were broken, and the walls were charred. The streets were littered with smouldering furniture, blankets and eating bowls. *Had the inmates been liquidated? Had the SS tried burning them alive? Had there been a revolt?*

The forest encircled us as we kept dragging ourselves along; our column had now rapidly dwindled to a mere thousand. We passed more railway tracks and links, but our destination remained uncertain.

My eyes grew dim, and I walked in a trance. I may have been determined, but my legs, sadly, were only those of a boy. The guards fired over our heads. I would not have noticed had they not used tracer bullets, which awoke me from my lethargy. Later, I was told that there were partisans in the forest. The shooting was probably meant to scare them away.

I no longer recognised what was going on. Silhouettes on the horizon seemed to be rows of tall buildings, but moments later they appeared to be outskirts of a forest; then again, I imagined we were in a town. I shuffled on.

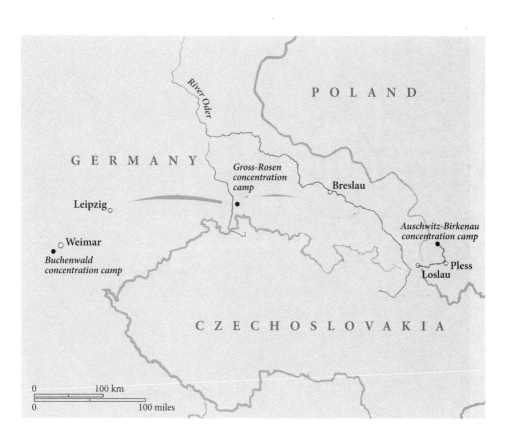

In January 1945, my fellow prisoners and I were evacuated from
Auschwitz, and force-marched by foot to Loslau. There we were put on
open goods train wagons, for the remainder of our journey west.

Finally, our column stopped. The shadows I had moved along with came back to life. It was dawn. Ahead of me was a sea of prisoners moving slowly towards a tunnel. From the far end of it rose ominous clouds of smoke. High-ranking SS officers moved about, taking a close look at us. Our guards had now left, telling us that this was the destination.

Some prisoners seeing the smoke tried to escape, but were ruthlessly shot down by soldiers, who lay camouflaged in the fields around us. One of the victims, still wearing his yellow armband, had been a capo. Once more, the snow was dotted with bodies, but this time their deaths seemed to have been violent. For the shapes, in their striped clothing, hugged the ground as if they had been wrestling with it. There was lots of blood.

Our morale reached its lowest ebb. The rumours flying around our bedraggled lot were terrifying. No one returned from the tunnel. We could not see the far end where the smoke was coming from, but could not help fearing the worst.

Jostled by the pushing crowd, I descended the funnel-like slope. The decisive moment had come, and I wanted to be prepared for it – to fight to the last. I dropped my precious loaf of bread, loosened my belt and flung away the useless metal mug that was tied to it. My hands were free, and I was ready now.

For once, though, my youthful imagination was wrong. At the far end of the tunnel was nothing more ominous than a railway station. The smoke had risen from an engine shed. We were at Loslau, the rail line to the West.*

Lit by the rays of the rising sun, I finally found some old friends of mine, who, also exhausted, had nonetheless held on to their precious luggage – blankets, shawls, bowls, mugs, loaves and, here and there, even carefully saved tins of meat.

'Where did they snatch your blankets, boy?' they asked me. 'At the farmyard when you were asleep? Eaten up your bread, too, eh?'

All I could answer was a meek, 'yes'. I was too ashamed to tell the truth.

---

* The prisoners were force-marched from Auschwitz along a route of roughly 65 kilometres until they reached Loslau (also known as Wodzislaw Slaski in Polish).

We were ordered into the open goods wagons that stood stationary along the platform. There appeared to be no more of us than two trainloads full. Arranging ourselves into neat rows, legs spread apart gripping the neighbour in front for warmth, we squatted on the dirty floorboards and fell asleep. When the train pulled out, we were jerked backwards and bumped together, but I barely noticed it. I was worn out. Over the last tortuous 50 hours, only four had been devoted to rest.

In the late afternoon, I summoned the energy to look over the wagon's sides. The district was familiar. Back in 1939, I had passed through it sitting in an express train munching sweets.

On the left, running parallel to us, was the Oder. I never tired of looking at it. I had known the Oder since birth – I had drunk it, dipped in it, and crossed it in a rowing boat with my Aunt Ruth. Even now it fascinated me.

Our hunger was unbearable. When we stopped at small country stations, we begged the railwaymen to fill our metal bowls with snow. The icy fluff, dirty or white, had become a delicacy, and the type of bystander willing to hand it to you a subject of study.

At some places, even workers with Nazi party emblems in their buttonholes were helpful. Mostly, however, our requests were ignored. To expect sympathy at the larger stations was folly. Platforms were crowded with suitcase-laden German civilians desperate to be evacuated westwards. When they learned that 'sub-humans' were being given preference, they threw us spiteful glances.

It must have hurt the pride of the many pompous, arrogant wearers of brown SA uniforms that dotted the impatient throngs to have fewer privileges than mere prisoners. *Will there still be time?* they must have asked themselves in despair. *Will there be enough wagons to take unproductive civilians?*

Now it was over, the murderers of yesterday were clamouring to be rescued, to be saved for the sake of all the virtues they themselves had never had the courage to show.

Now we became determined to stage a show of strength. Whenever we spotted fellow prisoners in the surrounding fields, we yelled greetings and wished them freedom. The guards, two to each wagon, were helpless. They neither risked provoking a revolt nor felt entitled to stop the train.

Near Breslau, we passed hundreds of prisoners slaving away on new embankments and extension lines to the railway. They were concentration camp inmates – POWs from Russia, Poland, France and Belgium, conscripted labourers from the Ukraine and Czechoslovakia – men and women.

As our wagon slowly passed a storage depot, we saw prisoners running at the double, unloading sacks of flour. Our defiance could be held in no longer. Someone started singing; not the camp tunes that once helped keep us alive but stirring songs and rousing anthems. We all joined in, wagon after wagon. So did our comrades at the depot, who had stopped work and lined the ramp to greet us.

'Arise, ye starvelings from your slumber . . .' We drowned the protests of our guards with the strains of the 'Internationale'. It was the only song known to all of us, the only hymn none of the bystanders would fail to recognise. It was not a particular favourite of ours, but it united us and gave us hope. At the far end of the storage depot, an irate SS man busied himself chasing his flock of prison-clothed beings back to their jobs.

Of Breslau, we only saw the shunting yards – the endless fields of rails, the criss-cross canopy of electric feeder cables. The overhead steel wires dangling down loosely, damaged from a recent air raid.

We arrived at a fenced-in barracks compound. On one side of the single railway track rose a wooden mountain slope, on the other the unmistakable site of a concentration camp. I felt glad. I could not have stood the journey much longer.

We had been exposed to the freezing cold for days, and our provisions that were supposed to have nourished us with 350 grams of bread a day had all been gobbled up. I could not remember when I had last nibbled a crumb of hard, frozen bread or swallowed a mouthful of snow.

The SS officer who came to meet our train shouted out in a manner typical of his kind. He barked at our head guard that they were full up and we should move on. Once more, the train jerked into motion and pulled out towards the main line.

When, after less than an hour, we reached a village, the guards opened the doors and shouted the familiar '*Raus!*' I jumped down onto the gravel below, my knees shaking with weakness, to join those who were waiting to be marched off. But others with whom I had shared the wagon stayed behind. Many who had been sitting on the floor for days no longer had the energy to raise themselves. Most of those seemingly sleeping quietly in the corner were dead.

We trudged through the village. On the left were old farmsteads, on the right rows of new bungalows, most of them unfinished. The road sign read: Gross-Rosen*.

At a bend, the road was blocked by a big horse-drawn cart full of hay. Manning the reins, we recognised French prisoners of war. They were talkative and quite unimpressed by our guards, shouting at them to get out of the way. I asked a colleague what they were saying.

'There is a concentration camp a few kilometres down the road, but they don't know how the prisoners are being treated,' someone translated for me.

'And what was that they were shouting?'

'They are wishing us good luck and say we should forget our troubles and be full of spirit like themselves.'

We reached the camp gate after passing large stone quarries and scurrying figures in blue-and-white prison clothing. From there, to vigorous commands of 'Left, right! Left, right!', we rigidly marched on to the vast *Appellplatz* for a rollcall; then finally along the road to the barracks.

On either side were large flowerbeds. The plants were immaculate, and yet they seemed ugly – mere dots in painstakingly symmetric patterns, implanted on square plots of earth, designed to divide off the SS buildings from the wretched prisoner shacks.

---

* Gross-Rosen was established in the summer of 1940 as a satellite labour camp of Sachsenhausen concentration camp.

On our right was the fenced-off women's camp, its ragged, haggard inmates also having arrived from the East, shouting messages at us in Hungarian. To our left, under curfew, the men's compound, rigidly supervised by guards and criminal block-elders. Ahead, at the end of the road, another gate, and beyond that our destination: some fifty widely spaced barracks embracing the rough hillside, 'the extension camp'. Next to it, the perilous threat of a crematorium.

CHAPTER 15
GROSS-ROSEN CAMP

I had been pushed into Block 40, a bare wooden floor surrounded by walls, enclosed by a roof and approached by a precariously supported ramp, 2 yards high and covered only by tree trunks 2 feet apart.

The ramp was dangerous, perhaps purposefully so, and accidents were a regular hazard. We slipped and fell on it, often right through it when being driven out for the long three daily rollcalls. One night the ramp collapsed at one of the blocks after the blind onrush of some one hundred freezing inmates.

Gross-Rosen, they called this camp. 'Great Roses', indeed. Here people were nervous, irritable and unwilling to cooperate.

In the evenings, after the noisy, troublesome issuing of blankets, we all had to look for a place to sleep. The floor never seemed big enough. At night we risked being shot at if we needed to go to the lavatory. Outside, we had to grope our way to the lone pit. On coming back, we would find our sleeping place occupied by someone else. Then, unless we felt strong enough to use force, we could only wait at the door until the next lavatory visitor had to give up his place.

Even those hugging their precarious part of the floor without ever budging from it had anything but a quiet night. There was not an inch of stepping space, and people trying to pass the mass of sleeping bodies rarely bothered to take off their shoes. If you slept near the door, you had to lie on your hands, otherwise they would be trodden upon.

In the distance we could hear gun battles, but even that failed to pacify the more hostile characters among us. Before their imprisonment, most had been respectable people; well-mannered family men who went to church or synagogue. But, forced to live under abnormal conditions among people of different tongues, intellects and ideas, their outlook had changed. God – the one they had built their hopes on and put their trust in – had shown no direct interest in their

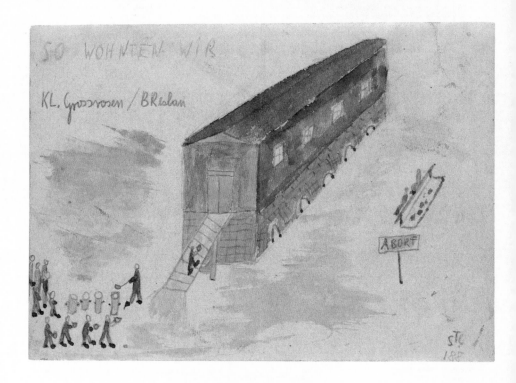

THE WAY WE LIVED
Gross-Rosen was a camp full of extreme
dangers and horrors.

suffering. So, no longer bound by scruples, the more disillusioned ones became violent. It was now 'every man for himself'. The rights and needs of their fellow men – for whom they had never truly cared – were ignored.

When you reprimanded someone for his vile behaviour, he would excuse himself by saying, 'Camp life is camp life. If you want to survive you do what you have to do, regardless of others. You must be ruthless.'

We youngsters knew the worst offenders, but we did not feel down as we wanted to look towards the future.

The camp kitchen was far too small to supply the 80,000 newcomers. So, we now lived on a daily ration of only 300 grams of bread and a spoonful of jam. Just three times a week we received half a litre of lukewarm soup – flavoured water whose main ingredient seemed to be salt.

Obtaining this pitiful measure of soup was quite a procedure, for it usually arrived without warning at night. The moment our block-elder was notified by the camp kitchen (which operated 24 hours a day) that our allocation was ready, he would start looking for volunteers to fetch it.

At first, conscious of the extra quarter-litre it earned, people had volunteered to help, but soon the incentive for trudging through the cold, slippery camp, laden with heavy vats, lost its appeal. It did not warrant giving up sleep and risking our health. Instead, we preferred to risk being picked by force, and then chased around the block by the infuriated block-elder, who kept shouting that if we didn't collect our soup the kitchen would stop supplying us altogether.

One night, when my dodging the block-elder had not been agile enough, I was sent to get the soup. *Was it to be as dreadful an ordeal as people said?* I did not trust rumours.

Twelve of us took the carrying battens, the U-shaped iron vat supports, and strolled dreamily through the sleeping camp. Instead of roads, there were steep, winding footpaths, slippery with slush and littered with boulders. On our left, in front of the crematoria, lay piles of frozen blue naked bodies. We looked away, scanning only the descending ground ahead lest we slipped.

Our destination, the gate leading to the main camp, was already blocked by 300 others who had arrived before us. Blinding searchlights looked down on the impatient and hungry throng hemmed in by the barbed-wire enclosure. More lights shone from the central tower beyond the main gate, an array of big projectors, eight in all – like an enormous chain of pearls.

At 2.30 a.m., after waiting for over an hour, the crowd arose from its slumber and started shouting. The soup vats had arrived.

One by one they called the numbers of the lucky blocks. But the frantic bystanders could not endure seeing food carried away for someone else. Like human hyenas they attacked the open vats of soup. Some tried to dip in their caps, others attempted to push their heads inside. Everywhere, we heard piercing yells, fierce and hysterical.

Finally, they called for Block 40. But once we had jostled ourselves to the gate and stood before the steaming vats, we were faced with another group claiming also to represent Block 40. It was an obvious scam, but by the time the kitchen people made up their minds, another 30 minutes had passed.

Eventually, we collected our precious soup, two to a vat, and made our way back to our block. We were led by a brawny Ukrainian, who threatened any potential thieves by swinging his spare carrying batten.

Careful not to spill the hot soup onto our feet, we climbed the dark, treacherous hillside, slowly and skilfully, step by step. On occasion, a desperate inmate would try to kick our legs away to make us fall. At times we slipped ourselves through sheer panic. I seemed far too weak for the heavy vat. My knees were trembling, but I had no choice. I was just a number no one cared about, a slave entitled to live only as long as I was useful.

Finally, we arrived. The block-elder was furious at us for spilling so much. Still shouting, he turned to the sleeping mass of inmates and woke them up for dinner.

As inmates of Block 40 and the latest newcomers, we were not working yet. Half our day was spent standing at seemingly endless rollcalls.

The rest was spent walking around the camp anxiously looking for a friendly companion to talk to.

Many of our fellow campmates were not accustomed to the premeditated and continual intimidation practised in concentration camps. Organised mass killings were new to them. Until now, they had only experienced life in labour camps. There, work may have been harder than at Auschwitz, but the surroundings were more civilised. There were no criminal or hardened prisoners among them, and they were grouped according to nationality. As a result, their outlook on life was different from ours. They lived and thought as secluded, unbalanced individuals, either helplessly lost or overly self-absorbed.

I saw few youngsters and knew none. Talking with adults was a hopeless cause, for they soon let you know how depressed they were. The tragedy of having lost their families was forever a shadow, too big to be ignored even for a few minutes. Whenever I dared to mention the future, they looked at me, aghast.

Long-term prisoners were different. Most of them were socialists, people whose positive beliefs were like the sun to them that nothing could overshadow. I knew them and they had often helped me and given me hope. Now that their sun was rising, they had all the more reason to support the young. Aware of this, I was determined to find some of them. But where were they? They had gone. They must have been sent 'elsewhere' or murdered.

Unable to find diversion among this crowd, I absorbed the details of the camp scenery, and with no one to talk to, I listened attentively to the thunder of the gun battles. The guns sounded nearer now and had become loud enough to disturb our sleep. Rumours said that we were to be evacuated again, but Gross-Rosen life went on as usual.

Working squads, driven on at a ferocious pace, still sweated away constructing new barracks. Hauled up the steep hillside by a noisy power winch, wheels squeaking, came trolleys laden with building materials. At one unfinished barrack stood a rapidly rotating concrete mixer. The floor was being laid. Five workers, stripped to their waists so that the wintry air could cool their sweat, shovelled away frantically at a heap of mortar. Those at the far end of the room, loudly clapping their trowels, shouted for the worn-out wheelbarrow pushers. Near the entrance stood a watchful capo, his left hand circling back and forth, reminding his fellow slaves to be quick, his right gripping a black whip.

Around us stretched mile after mile of lifeless, snowed-in barbed-wire ramparts, charged with deadly electricity and cordoned off by a wide, low belt of entanglements. Behind them paced threateningly grey-coated guards carrying their rifles, one for every 50 yards of silent snow. This was our only landscape.

Eleven years earlier, some lone prisoner had composed a song about it: the '*Moorsoldaten*'. By now, this moving, sentimental melody had become the concentration camp anthem and it gave us hope. Looking at the seemingly endless rows of fencing, I could not help but hum it:

> *Up and down the guards are pacing*
> *No one, no one can go through.*
> *Flight would mean a sure death facing;*
> *Guns and barbed wire greet our view.*

The hilly, stone-littered campsite, together with my youthful desire to explore it, had taken its toll. My left shoe, a precious companion that had served me for thousands of kilometres, was falling apart. The sole was hanging down and stubbornly refused to be fixed again. I tried mending it with rare bits of string, rusty iron ends and twisted remnants of nails. But it was useless, the shoe had come to its end. Clinging to my left foot was nothing but a dirty grey monster that gaped at me like the threatening snout of a crocodile.

Any hour now they would drive us out for the long-feared evacuation march. Despair and rage overcame me. Everything on earth and in heaven seemed wicked and vile. More than that: it begged to be punished for its own evil.

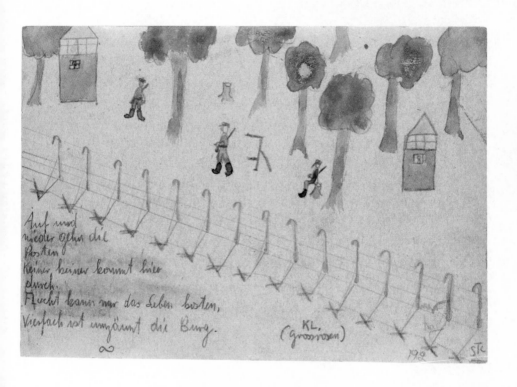

UP AND DOWN MARCH THE GUARDS
Our world of guns and barbed wire continued
at Gross-Rosen.

I limped through the frozen rubbish heaps, digging at them with my frozen fingers, hoping to find something resembling a shoe. Others, too, were searching the dumps. Torn prison clothes, broken spoons, leaking eating bowls, fragments of cement sacks, splintered spade handles – all of it could be useful to desperate camp inmates. With luck, there might even be tattered remnants of garments taken from the bodies of the dead. Finally, in the evening, I dug up what I was looking for: an oval object, flattened out by the weighty rubble above it, frozen together and encrusted with earth. It looked like a shoe, but before I could find out, someone shouted, '*Das gehoert mir!*' ('That belongs to me!')

A prisoner who had been lying on the other side of the dump crawled my way. He threw a stone at me and then followed that up by biting my wrist. His cruel teeth buried into my lean flesh were those of a madman, a human beast in search of prey, a wild animal. His jacket was crammed with amassed junk; everything from sticks and wires to paper.

Before the war he might have once been a university lecturer, but now he was a creature who, for the sake of a slice of bread, would have happily murdered me in my sleep. I hit back, kicking him in the stomach. The beast rolled back, defeated.

A few days after the shoe affair, I walked along the trolley tracks, over which rolled lorries full of sand.

Always on time, the lorries passed steadily through at five-minute intervals, a spectacle I could watch for hours to while away the time. It reminded me of home, the pit railways and coalmines.

Suddenly, my dreaming was interrupted. Someone had come up from behind and put his hands over my eyes. Helpless, I waited for my pockets to be searched. My attacker only laughed. Surely, he doesn't want to tease me, I thought. My campmates were all strangers, and the short, sausage-like fingers pressing onto my cheek felt far from friendly. He released his grip and patted my shoulders. There stood a squat Russian with a smile on his broad, round-featured face. Beside him were three other lads, the other lorry pushers.

'Don't you remember me?' he cried, hugging me like some old woman welcoming her long-lost son. 'It's me, Wajnka; Wajnka from the bricklaying school!'

I remembered now. It was one of the Wajnkas, the silent lad who had left a year ago. Both of us had changed. We were old friends now, veterans. There was much we would have liked to tell each other, but the lorry had to move on. I joined in pushing it.

'They, too, are coming,' stammered Wajnka in a mixture of Russian and broken German, pointing to where the guns were thundering. '*Etom nashe*' ('They are ours'). You – I – comrades!'

CHAPTER 16
EVACUATION

Evacuation was upon us again. It was the last week of January 1945. We were given tiny rations of bread and margarine, led off to the station, and herded into the cold but already familiar open goods wagons.

Minutes later, accompanied by the soothing click of the wheels, we pulled out, leaving the Breslau countryside to the east. The thunder of the guns, too, seemed to be moving with us. At some places, it was even louder than it had been at Gross-Rosen, and along the railway line, soldiers were digging in.

During the night, when the relentless cold and rushing air quickly penetrated our emaciated, thinly clad bodies, I woke up with a painful urge to relieve myself. Carefully stepping over my sleeping, curled-up wagon mates, I climbed down the wagon's walls, balanced myself on the buffer, pulled down my trousers and bent my knees. The next thing I remember was being in a different wagon where no one wanted to know me. I found neither my place nor my blankets. I wandered about tapping at the wrapped-up bodies and looking for someone familiar. They whispered to each other that I was mad. The less sleepy ones even kicked me.

'Get away with you, you loony ass.'

Finally, I squeezed in somewhere and fell asleep again. *Was it all a dream? Or was it a trance? Or had I returned to the wrong wagon?* I never found the answer.

By dawn, we reached Leipzig. It was badly damaged but alive. From within the cellars and beneath the ruins, children came out with shopping nets and buckets to join the early queues for bread and water.

We stopped at the terminal. The station hall was not only intact, but as busy as it would have been during the summer holidays in peacetime. Food buffets and newspaper stands were being wheeled around. Platforms were crowded with well-dressed, healthy-looking

German civilians. People strutted around in uniform or with swastika armbands. They all looked happy and used to seeing ragged and haggard prisoners.

Except for a few, who were whispering to their neighbours, none of the bystanders appeared to be interested in us. Some of our German comrades wanted to tell the onlookers who we were, but we proudly decided that it was not worth it.

A little pig tailed girl, her neatly ironed black skirt whirling over a pair of agile legs, came running towards the train, followed by her mother.

'Look, Mummy, so many faces,' she cried, pointing to our wagon. 'There is a young one. And over there another one.'

We youngsters felt proud. If the adults ignored us, the children still remained. Would the little girl remember us?

Opposite our wagons stood a modern hospital train, clearly well equipped with treasure from all over Europe. It was being received by a flower-bearing delegation of Red Cross sisters. We called to them, begging them for water to help the sick among us. But they too shut their eyes.

We slowly rolled towards a siding, some miles out of town. There again was an ambulance train; this time we were 3 yards away from it. From the kitchen wagon, delicious smells escaped. We saw the pots and pans, the luxurious compartments, the soft, white beds.

Limping along the strip of gravel came a soldier, his leg bandaged. Soon, more of them appeared. They wanted to know why honest-looking people like us wore prison clothing. We told our story and it was news to them.

'We at the front knew little of what really went on back in Germany,' said one.

'So that's what we have been fighting for,' mumbled another.

Our train started to move. The soldiers scrambled back to their compartments. They threw something out of the windows, and it fell into our wagon. It was sweets, boiled sweets wrapped in cellophane.

We arrived at Weimar, at the eastern end of the main goods station. It seemed that we were going to wait there. The engine had left and so had most of our guards.

I scanned the new surroundings, a vast railway yard on one side, beyond and behind, and on the other, a road. Along the road were gardens, but just opposite our wagon was an engineering college.

Through the large window, I could spot the students, lads of about 18 dressed in suits and neckties, sitting in front of a chalk-marked blackboard. A bell rang and they jumped up, raced down the stairs, laughing and shouting as they pulled out their sandwiches. They were in a world of their own, a universe of rules, books, traditions, regular meals and sound sleep. This at a time when, for five years, boys much younger than them were being killed on the front line and in concentration camps.

Then the air-raid siren started howling. Grouped into classes, the students marched in an orderly fashion to their shelters. High up, from the west, came rows of little silvery crosses, leaving long white trails in the blue sky. Allied bombers. A scout plane, flying low, drew a circle of vapour around us. I looked about me. There was silence. The trains were standing idle and people were hiding. In the distance, the bombers started to dive. The noise of the explosions was drowned out by a strong wind, but on the outskirts of the town rose dark clouds torn through with flying debris. More vapour trails appeared in the sky, this time heading towards the station.

We were rocked to our core by the explosions. The storage sheds were hit, wood splinters flying everywhere. Our guards ran for the shelters. We opened the wagon doors and rushed out, desperate to find some sort of cover. Some ran across the rails towards town, others crawled underneath the train. Only I remained in the open wagon.

I made a decision. To be crushed by derailed railway wagons or be buried among Nazis underneath an obliterated building was not worth running for. I took three round metal eating bowls left behind by my companions, stacked them on top of each other, placed them on my head and crouched into a tiny ball in the corner. My improvised red helmet must have looked strange, but there was no one there to find it funny. Bombs exploded all around my wagon. An extraordinary cacophony of noise that deafened me and left me terrified. Deadly rubble, shrapnel and metal rained everywhere.

When the bombers had passed, I carefully shook off the dust and looked out of my lone wagon. On a nearby rail, a train full of turnips was being pillaged by prisoners. Slowly, one by one, our brave guards returned. They shot at us to demonstrate their alertness. They seemed to have drunk some rum during the raid. The prisoners ran back to the wagons. There was more space now, as many had escaped and some had been killed.

As darkness descended, the train, attached to a little puffing steam engine, was pulled along a one-tracked branch line.

Kept awake by the moaning of the wounded and the dying, I stood in a corner of the wagon and watched out for any change of landscape. A trail of smoke hung over the wagons and blew into my face. It was black and dirty but warm. In less than an hour, we reached our destination. Those of us who still had enough energy jumped out, then tried to help those barely clinging to life, but there were just too many of them.

On the ramp waiting for us were men in blue uniforms, black berets and tidily polished jackboots. We thought they looked like the fire brigade. They ordered us into rows of five and marched us off. By the light of the streetlamp, I looked again at our new guardians. Their armbands read: *Lagershutz*. On their breasts were prison numbers like ours.

Beyond them we saw endless double rows of lamps, and the familiar charged mass of barbed-wire fencing. We passed what looked like the buildings of the camp's administration. In front of one of them stood a cannon, old fashioned, but a monster all the same. *Was it there merely to intimidate us?*

We reached the camp, and, as at Gross-Rosen, the entrance was through a passageway. Over it was the main watchtower. On either side spread wings that housed guard rooms, offices and prison cells. Then there was the large *Appellplatz*, the rollcall square.

'Jedem das Seine' ('To each what he deserves'), read the tablets bolted to the entrance. We had arrived at Buchenwald. I was entering my third concentration camp.

CHAPTER 17
BUCHENWALD CAMP

After a day's waiting in a huge tent, it was our turn to queue up for disinfection. I talked to a group of Gypsy prisoners beside us, who were current inmates of Buchenwald.

They were about to take their monthly bath and be deloused. Lice, it appeared, were plentiful in Buchenwald. One of the lads, who had been there since 1944, had also been at Auschwitz's bricklaying school.

'Don't ask me about the other Romany boys,' he sighed. 'It's such a long time ago. I don't know what happened to them. There are only four of us now.'

When we reached the disinfection block, we surrendered our clothing, shoes and whatever other possessions we had. Cherished bits of paper, pencil-ends, nails, strings, spoons and self-made knives – they all went. Then we were penned into a room with tiled walls. There, we waited.

We lay, sat and stood there for hours. It was hot. Our naked bodies stank and sweated. Those near the windows would not let us open them for fear of catching pneumonia. We were thirsty and cried out for water, but no one came. The door was locked.

Prisoners from the camp were forbidden to enter the disinfection compound. Those in charge of it were busy with earlier arrivals. Finally, we were let out again, after 10 hours of torture. Many had fainted and could no longer get up, some most likely died. Apparently, there had been a delay due to the air raids cutting off the water supply.

Our hair and bristles that for some had grown to a full proud inch was cut by irritable, overworked Frenchmen handling tools that badly needed cleaning, oiling and sharpening. Once scalped, we dived into a tank of sharp, biting disinfectant. It clung so obstinately to our burning skin that even the warm shower that followed failed to wash it off. In the next room, at a table, sat an SS doctor. His so-called medical examination consisted of us running past him at a distance of 4 yards.

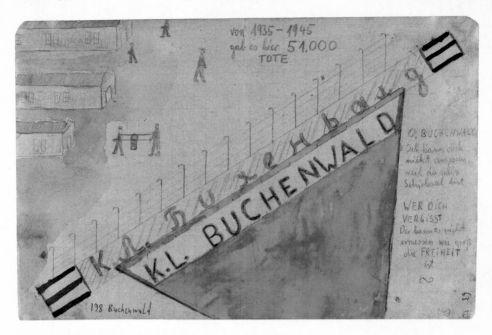

TOP: BUCHENWALD CONCENTRATION CAMP
From 1937 to 1945 tens of thousands of prisoners
died at Buchenwald.

BOTTOM: LAGERSCHUTZ
The camp police run by prisoners in Buchenwald could
be trusted to guard and protect us.

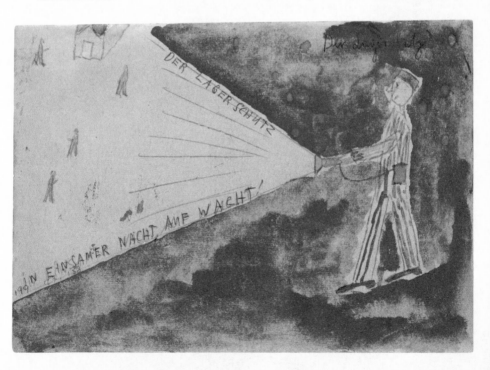

For the sake of the card index, someone also measured our height. I was handed a shirt, jacket, trousers, socks and shoes. There was no underwear.

Once dressed, I entered the registration room. A clerk in prison clothing pushed a form towards me. 'Fill it in yourself.'

The questionnaire seemed rather out of date. Eight years had passed since the first prisoners were registered. Not counting those prisoners who had taken over personal numbers from the dead, 127,157 of them had come before me. Most youngsters, fearing to be declared unfit for work, registered themselves as older, but I, besides having once been educated to be honest and upright, did not believe in cheating Fate. My age was 15, my profession was a bricklayer.

The clerk, a German political prisoner, checked my form.

'So, your father is fighting for the Allies?'

'Yes, I hope so,' I proudly replied.

'Don't ever think that no one cares about you here,' he went on like a hotel manager welcoming a guest. 'This is Buchenwald and here we feel like comrades to each other. We political prisoners have done all we can to improve conditions. One of our achievements is the *Lagerschutz*. Instead of SS guards, we have our own camp police, people we can put our trust in. We struggled to accomplish this and we need cooperation from you newcomers. I hope that you, too, will find your place among us.'

I told him that I was Jewish and would not enjoy any privileges. That did not seem to interest him.

'Here, we are all alike,' he continued. 'Do you really think that the few lousy privileges they allow us Germans make us any happier? They only embarrass us. Don't worry about how the SS classifies you. The will to cooperate among ourselves, so that we may survive, is stronger than the Nazis.'

Later that night, we trudged to a shed escorted by the camp's police. There we received a bowl of soup. We had not eaten for two days, but, occupied with the many new impressions around me, I had temporarily forgotten my hunger.

Afterwards, we went inside and sat on the floor, in rows, with legs clutched around our neighbours, the way one rides on a toboggan. That kept us warm. We had to, for the shed's windows had no panes and an icy wind blew through them.

At the door, watching us, sat a *Lagerschutz* (camp police) man. In other camps, his orders would have been to intimidate us, but here it seemed that he was told to help ensure that troublemakers cooperated. Perhaps, I reasoned, it was true that our new superiors could be trusted. My first impressions of them, even if contradictory, had been favourable. Shattered, I fell asleep.

In the morning we were taken to what was called the 'cinema' – a large hall filled with benches that, judging from the wall's fixtures, had been used for gymnastic displays and films. There, lying on the floor, crowded, cut off from the other prisoners by wire fences and the camp's guards, we spent our time in quarantine.

I was sent to the 'little camp', the new extension camp of Buchenwald built for newcomers from the East. It lay on a roughly cleared hillside below Buchenwald's main camp.

The little camp consisted of wooden barracks, similar to Birkenau, and was divided by wire fences into seven compounds. Three of the barracks were filled with the sick; three with invalids; the remaining 10 were crowded with those on the waiting list.

My new home was Block 62. At first, I slept on the cold, moist floor. Later, I was allocated a bunk. I already knew these square wooden contraptions called 'boxes' from Birkenau, but there they had been filled with sacks of straw, blankets, bugs, fleas, lice, mice and five inmates. Here they were mere trays of bare boarding, but they had to house 10 humans.

We had to lie on our sides like tinned sardines, without moving. Turning over or lying on your back was impossible. The width per person was less than a foot. On waking up, a distinctly unpleasant

moment in a prisoner's life, our hands and feet were numb and our
backs were sore. Where our thighs rubbed against the boards, obstinate
and persistent abscesses grew.

Our block-mates were mostly Ukrainians and Poles, who had been
evacuated from labour camps.

They were the opposite of righteous Buchenwald prisoners that
the office clerk had previously boasted about. Every night they staged
bitter fights. In the morning they would carry off the wounded,
battered and bleeding. People knifed each other over petty quarrels,
and there was no one to stop them. Even I had bought a knife. It was
not sharp enough to cut bread, but it was big and, if necessary, could
be used as a weapon to defend myself.

The block resembled a den of wild animals, predators that
howled, robbed and killed. They were primeval in the dark, relieving
themselves in the bowls they used for eating during the day. By
daylight, they stared at each other with eyes of hatred and suspicion.
They were decaying in mind and body. Some had already been certified
as mad and 'sent away'. We knew what that meant.

In the evenings, after the rollcalls, we were given food discs that
would allow us to collect our food rations for the next day. We held
them tight so that no one could snatch them. We hid them in the
seams of our clothing should any pickpockets try. They meant life or
death. After hours of queuing up in front of the cinema, we would
exchange them for 1 litre of watery soup and 300 grams of bread. Four
times a week there was 25 grams of margarine, twice a week a spoonful
of jam or white cheese and on Sundays a much-dreamt-about 50 grams
of sausage.*

As at Auschwitz, the sanctuary where we could smoke and
exchange the latest news was the lavatory, a hut with a large open tank.
We perched around its edge like birds on a telephone wire, carefully
balancing ourselves and looking out for any block-elders that were
likely to disturb us. Luckily, the lavatory was in our compound, and if

---

* Thomas's drawing 'What We Ate' (see page 82) compares the food rations in Auschwitz and Buchenwald.

we found our way across the stone-littered mud in the dark we could use it even at night. People in other compounds, however, had to wait for their fixed visiting hours.

The washroom was less popular; it was opened for 30 minutes in the morning, but the water was icy cold and there were no towels. All the same, every time any of us youngsters met there we would surprise and greet each other with a cold, generous splash.

'Wake up, boys,' we shouted, 'you want to be alive, don't you?'

One day, suddenly and unexpectedly, we were driven out to work. They took us to a field littered with stones.

We were told to pick them up and stack them on a heap some 500 yards away. The route to this pile was lined with guards. Naïvely, I thought at first they had come to take us back to camp again. That theory soon disappeared as I came to realise they were there for a reason.

They were divided into five distinctive groups. The first shouted at us to keep running. The second barked at us for taking stones that were not heavy enough. We were made to drop them and run back to fetch larger ones. The third group amused themselves by kicking and hitting out at us. The fourth thought up games. Activities like races, obstacle courses, making us run blindfolded and telling us to balance the stone blocks on our heads. The fifth group sat underneath the trees about a hundred yards away, clutching their rifles and looking on. They would shoot any of us, if we approached them.

That evening, on returning to my barracks, I was bruised, blistered, exhausted and distraught. But something kept me from utter despair.

I had seen the surroundings, the hidden, mysterious machinations encircling us, the 'unknown' that every newcomer was so afraid of. Now that I knew it, I could fight it. On the way to work, I memorised the layouts of the vast SS living quarters, the solid barracks and fashionable villas.

For every hut in this huge concentration camp, there seemed to be three buildings beyond the fence. The SS barracks could hold a

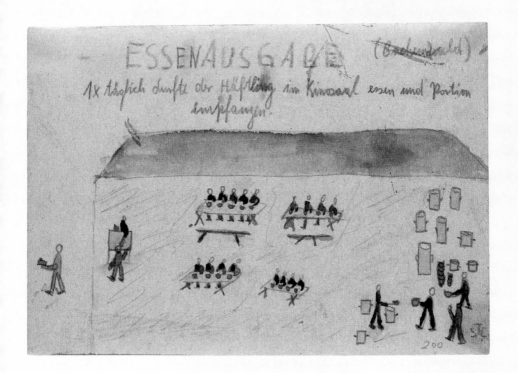

FOOD ISSUES
Once a day we ate our poor ration of watery
soup and bread. At night we dreamed of food
and sausages.

garrison of 15,000 men. But that was not all. Buchenwald seemed to be a country of its own. There were parks, stylish villages, a zoo, a bear pit, an aviary, a riding hall, a concert hall and more – all for the pleasure of the 'Master Race'.

For us, there was an abundance of ammunition plants, factories making parts for V-2 rockets and stone quarries.

They said that the authorities were aware that our long trek from the East had weakened us, and that our having to work was temporary. That was a lie – like the one about our being 'protective custody prisoners'.

We went on working, day after day and week after week. With work came more new experiences.

One day, we were sent to clean up a woodland area that looked as though a bomb had fallen on it. It was beyond the camp's working territory, so we had our own chain of guards. The SS men had ordered us to pick up all the stones and fallen twigs, and then left, hiding themselves somewhere among the trees.

I was alone, rummaging about on the forest floor. Lingering in my mind were stories of prisoners tricked into being 'shot while escaping'. For a guard would receive money and bonuses – five marks, a packet of tobacco, three days' leave – for killing an escaping prisoner.

I heard the shots. They did not surprise me. Frantically, I raced back to the assembly place, hurtling through the undergrowth, my heart thumping violently, my eyes looking only ahead, my ears straining for voices.

It was now March 1945. Our purpose in life seemed to be nothing but exasperating, tiresome waiting.

We waited for our litre of soup, for the rollcall, for a free place at the lavatory, for sleep, for the lukewarm rays of the sun and above all we waited for someone to defeat Hitler and for liberation.

Often, as a punishment for something trivial, we would have to wait to be let into our barrack of crowded sleeping bunks. After the rollcall, standing to attention, we would be left in the creeping cold of the evening. Then, all that we could do was dream of other things.

Longing to go to sleep, I thought of the moment when, stumbling over the mud littered with stones and rubbish, we would all rush impatiently towards the small barrack door, and the glad seconds when I would climb into my bed to lie on the planking and be pressed in by the warm bodies of my neighbours.

Hungry, I would appease my stomach by dreaming about food. Liver sausage, blood sausage, garlic sausage, Bologna sausage, frankfurters and salami. Above all, however, my mouth would water at the thought of Sunday, when, clutching 50 grams of camp sausage, we would enjoy a royal feast.

We were soon divided into groups to be sent away to Buchenwald's branch camps.

Speculating as to which of these new places were the worst, people tried evasion and trickery to avoid them. But it was useless, as conditions were bad at all of them.

The innumerable subsidiaries to Buchenwald stretching from Eisenach to Chemnitz, and from Coburg to Leipzig, were nothing more than large slave cages. At Dora, Ohrdruf and Plömnitz, prisoners dug tunnels for big underground factories that were producing V-2 rockets. These flying bombs represented Hitler's last trump card. With them, the blond, cultivated Germans would kill thousands of equally blond and cultivated Anglo-Saxons. It was irrelevant, then, if they also cost the lives of a few thousand scrawny half-dead humans reared in forests, caravans and ghettos.

When it was my turn to be sent off, I trudged to the hospital compound to face the selection board. I must have been little more than a mere skeleton, but to my surprise, they decided that I would stay in Buchenwald. This time, quite unexpectedly, my weakness had become my strength.

Excited by my luck, I ran back to pick up my clothes from where we had undressed. My cap and shoes had been stolen. All that could be done was to take somebody else's. The only cap left was a green one. I pondered whether this colour would match the rest of my random garb. To be strikingly dressed meant attracting attention, and I could not afford to be picked out by the SS guards. I had no choice, so I grabbed the green beret, put it on and ran to our block. I was alone, hoping to remain unknown and unnoticed.

One day I saw a boy of four, the saddest character I had ever come across, abnormal in his physique, behaviour and speech. He staggered along like some weak, wounded animal and uttered cries in German-Polish-Yiddish gibberish.

'That', I was told, 'is the child they keep hiding from the SS. His father brought him here in a rucksack. Every time there is an inspection, they gag the poor devil and tuck him away underneath the floorboards. What a life!'

I asked whether there were other children.

'Yes, there is another one at the main camp, at Block 8, the children's block. All the other boys are at least twelve.'

About a hundred youngsters lived at Block 8, mostly Poles and Russians aged between 14 and 16. Several of them were attached to influential camp personages and quite openly their 'girlfriends'.

'There also is a youth block at the "little camp", I was advised. 'If I were you, I would try getting transferred to it.'

At long last, I was sent to Block 66, the home of some three to four hundred youngsters. The block-elder, a blond Polish Jew with years of German concentration camps behind him, regaled us with a noble introductory speech.

He seemed concerned for his protégées and repeated what I had already been told at the registration office. The block-elder of 7a at Auschwitz also had good intentions, but had bawled at us like a dictator. His equivalent at Buchenwald, however, appeared more friendly.

I was happy to be back among youngsters. It was the nicest block I had ever been to. Even the SS man who came to receive the rollcall did not bother us, as somehow our block-elder had succeeded in being on good terms with him.

Most of my block-mates had come from labour camps and were Jews. In my room, they hailed mainly from Poland; in the other, from Hungary. Those of my bed-mates who had lived in secluded ghettos since 1939 knew little of the world around them. Their lot had been much harder than mine and they had witnessed horrific tragedies. They had been too young, too ignorant to truly grasp the situation. They had reacted by retreating into their shells, a mental barrier that kept them isolated. To the ghetto youngsters, 'the unknown' was something they could not or would not think of. Suspicious of foreigners, some of them even suggested that I might be a German spy.

There were also two German Jews. Friendly, educated chaps, they would have made ideal companions. But I avoided them. Their pride in being 'Germans' and 'Westerners' repulsed me. Nor did anyone else like them. All they earned for their stubborn arrogance was contempt and general ridicule.

Our various backgrounds led to several differences between us, but our quarrels remained petty ones. We were teenagers and were still trying to understand ourselves and each other. At the worst, we would feel sorry for one another not having grown up yet.

During the day we perched ourselves on projecting rocks and tree-stumps and tried to catch as many life-giving sun rays as possible. A tough, perilous concentration camp winter had now surrendered to a spring of hope. Days were becoming warmer now. Soon things would be different.

Once, we youngsters at Block 66 even received Red Cross parcels – gifts from abroad addressed to French and Dutch prisoners who were no longer alive to enjoy them. Their arrival meant fervent excitement.

We loudly argued about the supposed contents and worked out how these treasures would be divided, hopefully imagining that the lettering on the tins was French for a meat delicacy. With our mouths watering, we dipped our spoons into the sandy mud to polish them and clutched our eating bowls.

We waited impatiently for the moment of the food's distribution. Those who had received grain searched for twigs and implored the block-elder to lend them his cherished cooking pot.

My own luck in the lottery was a tin of sardines without a tin-opener. This had to be divided between five of us.

Then there was the hobby of our block-elder. A choir – something he had thought about, founded and made a success.

If one wanted to be among his favourites and be given preference when his friends at the main camp allocated us an extra vat of soup, we had to sing for it.

The choir met after bedtime, so their new songs would remain a secret to us. Once, however, I had a chance to eavesdrop. It was close to midnight as I groped my way to the urinal. The washroom next to it was locked, illuminated and emitting a catchy tune – a fascinating chord repeated again and again as on some broken gramophone record. They certainly worked hard in there. I sneaked to the door so that I might also hear the words, but someone must have seen my shadow.

'Get back to bed, spoilsport,' they cried.

That was the end of the concert for me. Back in my bunk, however, I meditated, for the tunes had so impressed me that I could not sleep. *I must have misjudged my roommates.* They seemed to have emerged from their shell of isolation and now appeared to me like young people everywhere. More than simply that, they sang with such vigour and conviction that others would be encouraged by them.

I felt extremely happy. For the first time in years, there were friends around me, true friends. The chords I had been listening to were far from being part of a missed concert. No. What I had sneaked in on had merely been a preview of the beginning – a glimpse of the glorious symphony of youth.

Finally, the long-awaited moment had come. There was to be an evening of entertainment for the choir's debut. Even the SS had been invited, to legitimise the venture.

Restlessly sitting on improvised benches of borrowed bunk planks, we waited for the guests. Our room, hardly 8 yards by 10, was filled with hundreds of spectators. Each one craned his neck to see the door and stage, supported on soup vats. It looked promising.

The VIPs arrived from the main camp – friends of our block-elder, half a dozen SS men and a few officers. They sat down in the front row, which was reserved for them. The show began – a programme of songs, sketches, acrobatics and solo dances. Each nationality was represented.

First came the Polish youngsters with a song about what life would be like in the new, rebuilt Warsaw. Our applause was wildly enthusiastic. We clapped our hands rhythmically in unison. There were calls and whistles. More likely than not, this would be a farewell party, and we knew it. No one would stop us saying what we wanted. The SS visitors understood little of what we were singing about. Oddly enough, however, they were cheering us.

Next, the Russian boys trooped onto the stage showing off their muscles and their traditional choral singing. There were only a handful of them, but their voices were strong, praising Stalin, the Red Army and the Soviet Union. Any of the SS officers present who believed Hitler had re-educated these vigorous and determined youngsters must have been greatly surprised. I knew these lads from when, nearly two years previously, they had arrived at Auschwitz. Then, they were far from certain about the cause of their motherland; some even despaired of it. Now they praised it. Their confidence was stronger than ever before, their zeal and loyalty unquenchable.

The last but biggest group of performers were the Polish Jewish boys. To begin with they chanted about ghetto life, mothers, rabbis and learning the Bible – a moving portrayal of the Yiddish-speaking people. Next, we heard the sad laments of those being led to their death, a story of helplessness and despair. It was a picture of dismal self-pity that only a Jew could draw. Suddenly, however, the singers changed their tone and we were jolted into a mood of hope and determination.

They started to sing melodies about the future, songs they were proud of, their own songs. The stirring tunes I'd listened in to during my secret nightly tour burst into the open. The muffled words whispered in that cold washroom were verses written by fellow prisoners. They were clear and powerful now. 'Oh, how they will suffer for having laughed at us', proclaimed one of the songs. Others told of the time when all men will be free and equal. 'Then our children, living in a better world that is sure to come, will find it hard to believe what their fathers tell of the past.'

Our SS visitors sat perplexed. It had all come so unexpectedly to them. They had not prepared themselves for being ridiculed. They had wanted to laugh.

I scanned them to see their reactions. Their skull-and-crossbones-decorated uniforms seemed less threatening, less polished now. Some nervously scratched their heads. One officer started to wipe his glasses. They must have understood a few of the Yiddish words. And the performers were far from what the Nazis would want them to be. There were no 'stupid Polish peasants', 'Russian barbarians' or 'timid, side-locked, Bible-chanting Jews' on our stage. Only dynamic and defiant youngsters, seeing the future and wanting to build it.

The show was over. Prisoners and SS men rose, stretched their limbs and left. It was as though we all lived in a dream.

April arrived, and with it the thunder of the Allied guns. Our compound, at the exposed lower fringe of the camp, had become a gathering place for eager watchers, prisoners who would spend their day anxiously looking down onto the vast plain below for any signs of the approaching liberators.

Among them were prominent people from the main camp, armed with concealed binoculars. They had little to be afraid of, for by now the SS seldom entered the camp without us being aware of them. The end, good or bad, was near. It would only be a matter of days. Someone shouted that there were tanks in the distant fields.

'I can't spot them yet,' replied one of the visitors, fiddling about with precious binoculars.

'Let us have a look, then,' we cried.

One by one we were honoured with a magic glimpse of the silent, distant and miracle-hiding countryside, but our efforts were in vain. When my time came, I painstakingly scanned the valley, the stretch of a grey country road, the fields, the hedges. The only thing resembling tanks – or anything else that may have heralded our liberation – was a line of haystacks.

Later, after rumours that the camp was to be evacuated, the SS authorities issued a declaration. 'The inmates of Buchenwald will remain in their camp . . . it will be in your own interests to be disciplined and to obey orders . . . With the arrival of the American army, you will be handed over peacefully and in an orderly fashion.'

It seemed reassuring and we felt happy.

One night, when I was returning from the lavatory (an unpleasant 200-yard walk across the rugged, pitch-black hillside), I heard strange voices in the block-elder's room.

Although it was well after midnight, he seemed to be entertaining visitors. They talked about Poland and their hometowns. One of them appeared to be speaking English. This attracted me. I pressed my ear to the wall and listened. His voice was very weak. It crackled and was disturbed by whistles. I was so excited. I was listening to a hidden radio set.

All that apparent interest in remote Polish villages seemed clear to me now. It was a gathering of senior camp inmates who had come to hear the news. While they talked to drown out the radio noise, someone was scanning the airwaves for details of Allied successes. They used our block because it was the furthest away from the SS barracks, remote and inhabited by prisoners who were too young to be informers.

I strained my ears for local town names, proud to be among the privileged listeners.

Before long, however, I was joined by other lavatory-goers. They asked me to translate what I had heard, so they could discuss it, loudly and excitedly. But the block-elder opened the door and persuaded us to return to our bunks.

After that, I listened in night after night. Leaning against the wall with the voices of the Allies behind it, I tried to grasp the news. Before long, our quiet waiting came to an abrupt end. The loudspeaker from the main camp repeated an order over and over again. 'All Jews to the gate.'

We fell immediately into despair and fear. It was well known what had happened in some of the Eastern concentration camps shortly before liberation. We sent a scout to report back to us. When he reached the rollcall square, he found it to be empty. The order had been disobeyed.

That afternoon, the SS declared a curfew and staged round-ups. SS search parties were seen roaming the main and little camps. They came as far as our lavatory, but no further. It was dusk. For today they were satisfied. '*Das Hauptlager ist judenrein*' ('The main camp is clean of Jews') blared the loudspeakers.

All the Jews from the main camp, together with most of their brethren from the little camp, had been led off to a separate compound.

Next morning, we again had an unexpected surprise. Our block-elder received a parcel of red-, black- and green-coloured cloth triangles, and in a matter of minutes, all the Jewish lads were adorned with new identification cloths. The boys from the ghettos became Poles and Russians – political, unsocial or criminal ones. I became a German political prisoner. Now, too, our block was '*judenrein*' ('Jew-free').

The familiar Yiddish vanished. My roommates now only spoke Polish and Russian. Their knowledge of these newly acquired mother tongues was fair at best, but Buchenwald's SS guards would never notice it. Anyhow, the standard answer to all questions being asked would be the good old '*Nix verstehen, Deutsch*' ('No understand German').

I, however, was the odd man out. My new role as an 'Aryan' was far from easy. German prisoners, as a rule, were well dressed, looked healthy and lived in a different block from other inmates. I would be asked about looking different to the others and my explanations would need to be accurate, natural and convincing.

That evening, I was mercilessly teased.

'Come on,' shouted my roommates. 'Let's see you playing the bully. Don't forget you are German now and if you aren't rude, we'll lose all respect for you.'

'The Führer will be sorry to see you here among all these foreigners.'

In their eyes, a German and a criminal were the same. The lads wanted a good laugh and I wasn't going to refuse them.

'*Reichdeutscher politischer Schutzhaeftling Nummer 127158*', I bellowed, 'wishes to complain about these dirty Pollaks for mocking our fatherland. Number 127158* begs to be transferred to more civilised surroundings, where German is spoken.'

We greatly enjoyed ourselves and went to bed in better spirits. Someone patted my shoulder.

'And don't forget to snore like a German!'

Contrary to what we had been led to believe, Buchenwald was being evacuated. The first to go were the Jews from the tents. Then came the Czechs from the main camp. Some transports left by rail and others by foot. Their destination was said to be either Dachau or Mauthausen, concentration camps in the south, where the Allies had not yet reached.

For a whole week, those who were still to leave had been fed nothing but bread and artificial honey. Each day we became weaker and hungrier.

In a desperate search for food, I managed to smuggle myself into the main camp. Sadly, many blocks were already empty. The few confused inmates that scurried about the camp seemed busy trying to find ways to avoid evacuation.

The streets were littered with the belongings of those who had left – cardboard boxes, parcel wrappings, old newspapers, photographs and letters. These cherished and smuggled possessions that would have meant so much to the prisoners lay thrown onto heaps of junk.

With a stick I searched through the rubbish, hoping that something

---

* This was the prisoner number that Thomas received in Buchenwald.

was edible in there. There was nothing. There was only paper – paper everywhere, fluttering in the breeze. There were stacks of hoarded camp money, useless blue-mark bills and equally useless red two-mark bills; a card covered with clumsy handwriting, red censorship marks and a postmark giving the name of some obscure Polish village; scraps of dirty, stained paper with old-style German letters carefully drawn.

My rummaging proved useless, so I returned to the relative safety of our block.

Next morning, I was out again, this time to the vegetable gardens. There was a large, barbed-wire-surrounded plot neighbouring our compound, which supplied the SS with vegetables and flowers. A daring dozen starvelings, I among them, had cut an opening in the fence and quickly started plucking spinach leaves.

Bent over, I tugged away at the stems and greedily collected what I expected would make a grand salad into a cardboard box. Occasionally I looked up. The distant woods were being attacked by American dive-bombers and I could see columns of dense black smoke. I grew so enthusiastic about this that I thought of nothing but Americans and spinach leaves, spinach leaves and Americans.

Then, still absorbed in my dreams, I suddenly heard shots. Running across the field came a pistol-waving SS officer. Panic-stricken, we sprinted over stubble and ditches towards the opening in the fence. But I was weak. My ill-fitting shoes hurt my toes; I hobbled and could not run fast enough.

As a last resort, I dropped the cardboard box with my precious collection of spinach leaves. But that was to no avail. The SS officer was upon me; a wooden club came scything down. Instinctively, I ducked my head and absorbed the blow with my left forearm.

'Stay where you are, you ass face, or I'll shoot you,' shouted the officer as he made for his next victim.

But as he turned, I bent my back to make myself a harder target to hit and ran towards the fence.

Back at the block, I nursed my bruised and swollen arm. I had escaped but felt like an utterly defeated fool. After all these years of trial, I had risked my life for a bunch of spinach leaves. My escape had been a lucky one and I had lost both my salad and my cherished cardboard box.

The next day, 10 April, our compound was to be evacuated. We hid wherever we could. In the cavity between the boarding and lining of the hut's walls. In the dark, musty and narrow space below the floorboards, underneath and inside our stuffy sacks of straw or huddled up in some stinking vermin-infested manhole. We refused to leave our block.

The block was cordoned off by the camp's police and SS guards came thundering into our room with whips and revolvers. Our resistance was quashed and we trudged up the slope towards the camp's gates.

In Buchenwald's main camp, I desperately tried to evade the cordon of camp police.

'Be sensible, kid,' they warned me, 'most of the other inmates have left already. We ourselves are also leaving today. By eight o'clock this evening, the camp will be empty. Only those at the hospital will stay behind. Besides, are you all that sure that the last transports to leave Buchenwald will be the safest? Go on, kid, join the rest.'

They persuaded me to join the group waiting near the rollcall square between Blocks 3 and 9. As I squatted on the pavement, contemplating things to come, long columns of silent, worried-looking campmates passed by us heading to the front gate. They knew that beyond it was the unknown.

We stayed behind and kept on waiting.

'There aren't enough guards,' said one of the camp's police. 'Your turn will come when the contingent that led off the preceding column comes back to take another one.'

Then the air-raid siren started howling. It was glad tidings for us. Road and rail traffic would stop. The evacuation would be delayed. Overhead buzzed a small American reconnaissance plane. German

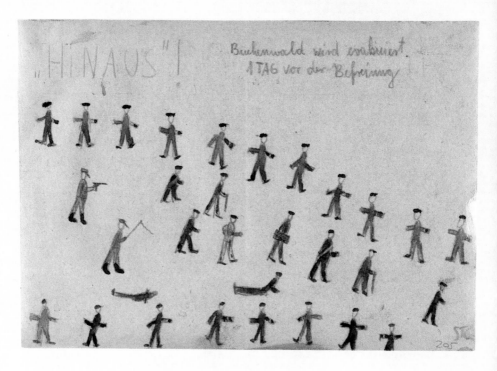

OUT!
The days before liberation thousands were
evacuated to the unknown.

anti-aircraft guns had long ago ceased to exist, so it came down low enough for us to see the head of the pilot. We half expected him to drop something – weapons, food or at least leaflets. But he did not. All he brought was more suspense and expectation.

Afterwards came hours of silence. People sat on what had once been garden plots, in the shade of adjoining blocks. All movement ceased. None of the guards had returned yet. By evening there was still no news. The all-clear had not been sounded. When it was dark, we slowly trickled back to our blocks. Less than half of my roommates had managed to return.

Everyone was confused. We knew only that this night was to be decisive. For a whole week now, we had said so. Evening after evening we hoped to wake up and be liberated. But now it seemed final. Whether there was to be a future or not, the decision about our fate was imminent.

As we lived on the fringe of the camp with the open plain below us, there was much argument about us being vulnerable. The thin wooden boarding of our block afforded no protection at all. The few hiding places behind solid concrete walls were too small for all of us. We stayed awake and speculated about stray rifle shots, bombs and shells until early in the morning. Then I dozed off.

When we awoke, things had not changed. There was a curfew and a troubling stillness. What went on at Buchenwald's gates was hidden from us by the sea of barracks making up the main camp. For the last 20 hours, we had had no news. It was two days since we had been issued our last 300 grams of bread with the spoonful of artificial honey.

At noon, we heard a howling we had never heard before. The Germans called it the tank-alarm siren. The moment of truth had come. We scanned the valley below us. At the outskirts of the wood, we saw a rapid moving file of steel-helmeted SS soldiers retreating with ammunition boxes and machine-guns. Sometime later we spotted more of them, in an even greater hurry now, just armed with rifles. Then the landscape was quiet again, and the uncertainty continued.

I put my trust in my comrades, who were said to be 'on the alert even if one never notices it'. Should there be an attempt to annihilate us, they would act. Their numbers would be inadequate, I feared, but their resistance fierce.

We were not defenceless. We would fight.

It was 11 April 1945 between three and four o'clock in the afternoon. We waited in suspense, everyone tense. No one talked any more. Some lads lay on the bunks and stared at the ceiling. Others gazed through cracks in the wall, onto the valley. Suddenly, there were shouts, from the main camp. They became louder and louder. Our compound was lifeless as we rushed out to investigate.

'Look at the gate!' shouted someone.

I lifted my eyes and searched for the pyramid roof of Buchenwald's head watchtower. The crooked cross of Fascism had gone.

Fluttering from the symbolic flagpole was something white. The moment we had so anxiously been longing for had come. The cherished moment of victory, for which we had all been waiting for countless days and nights, was here at last.

There were tears of joy and jubilation from everyone. We half-dead prisoners were now free. The moments after this momentous scene were a blur. Many just stood in shock, shaking, tears of relief running freely down their gaunt cheeks. A white flag now flew over Buchenwald. It was not a flag of surrender; it was the flag of victory. It was not a victory for an army from over the ocean, but a self-fought victory. Nor was it a mere military one. It was a far-reaching victory – our victory.

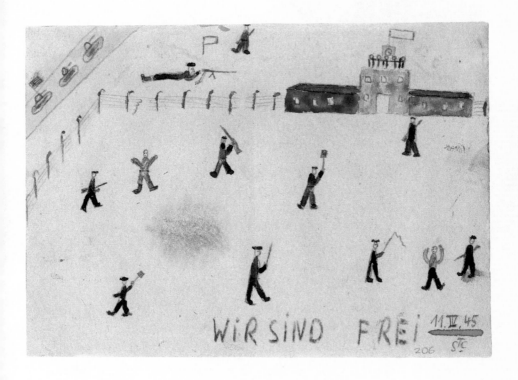

WE ARE FREE
Free at last! Liberation came on 11 April 1945.

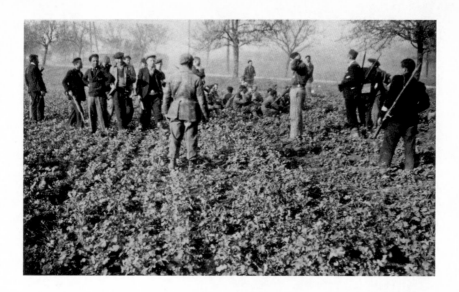

TOP: Captured SS guards just a few hours after the camp's liberation.

BOTTOM: THEY GO INTO CAPTIVITY
The hunters became the hunted.

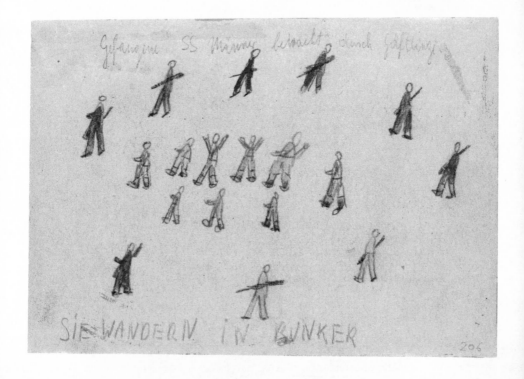

CHAPTER 18
FREE AT LAST

Buchenwald was free. Proudly flying over the main gate was a bedsheet from the camp hospital. As soon as we saw the American tanks, we seized the watchtowers and liberated ourselves.

The Allies, in hot pursuit of what remained of the Wehrmacht, had bypassed us, but we had been ready. While we in our secluded compound had waited and anxiously counted down the minutes of fear and uncertainty, others had cut through the fence. First to bravely break out into freedom had been those with guns in their hands, who fanned out to seek the enemy.

When the few of us who the day before had so narrowly escaped being evacuated lay down to sleep that evening, we did so in the comforting luxury of security. The time of being helpless victims of reprisals had passed. We took no chances in guarding our liberty. There were armed comrades in the streets, the watchtowers, the dugouts, the former SS barracks and the surrounding woods.

In the morning, as we woke up to freedom, it was as though we were reborn. I had never experienced this feeling of independence before. Nor had I ever known about being free. For us youngsters it was the beginning of something new: a new life, a new world, a new era.

The old chains had been broken. Sooner or later we would have to cope with the loss of our families, to grow up and become good citizens. The tasks facing us would need to be carried out with the same determination that had helped us to survive.

Our Polish, Russian and Czech comrades would go back home to prove that if there can be war, there can also be reconstruction. Many of the Jewish youngsters would make for their ancient homeland in Palestine, where they would have to show that deserts can be made habitable.

'The world cannot supply food, shelter and happiness to all its ever-growing population,' I had once been told at school. But the past and all it stood for had crumbled ignominiously. Together with youth everywhere we would help to disprove the theory. To achieve this, we would have to cooperate and remember our common sufferings. After all, we had not lingered in concentration camps simply as individuals, but as youngsters unwanted and forgotten.

Millions of our Jewish comrades and many others too had not even been allowed to join this bitter struggle for survival that was now over. They had been murdered, monstrously and mercilessly before even having had a chance to realise what was happening. Thousands of boys who had been our campmates, block-mates, roommates and bed-mates had perished, regretting ever having been born, with disappointment and anger in their hearts. They hailed from all over Europe – some even from Asia – and their beliefs and emotions were different and many, but they had become part of us. In our memories, they lived on, and what they had wanted to say we would have to say.

The sun was high on the horizon. I had slept through. I had thought enough about my future. I now had to focus on the present. My legs were weak, but I dragged myself out into the camp. The elderly say that old age creeps up on them. In my case, I felt the reverse. Weakness and frailty were creeping out. Soon I would be agile and young again.

Buchenwald was as busy as an ant-heap. Everyone wanted to see everyone and everything. Groups of proud ex-prisoners with newly issued rifles were doing drill. It was our self-equipped, self-planned and self-organised army, all clad in blue-white prison garb.

By afternoon a reconnaissance plane hovered over our compound. It had American markings but we, nevertheless, regarded it with suspicion. We knew enough about Nazi trickery. The guards loaded their guns and pointed them skywards. Then the pilot dipped his wings.

'He's saluting us,' cried someone with wild enthusiasm.

'It's an American, a real American!'

In the evening a contingent of American infantry arrived at the gate. The first GI to enter was carried shoulder-high throughout the camp. People yelled, sang and shouted. Precariously, I pushed myself through the crowd. From beyond, among a sea of blue-and-white-

striped prison caps, bobbed an egg-shaped brown helmet and a brown
pair of marching boots. The American! At last, I had spotted him. I
also shouted and so did he. Perhaps they were hurting him or maybe
he was dizzy. But he was ours now; we were glad that he was yelling.

As the days passed, the food became more and more plentiful. The
changeover from 300 grams of dry bread to unlimited quantities
of goulash soup was too quick. It gave us diarrhoea, uncontrollable
diarrhoea. The stagnant brown pond in the lavatory pit threatened to
overflow. Everything around it, together with the footpaths leading
to the blocks, was contaminated and sticky from the bowels of our
stomachs that were not used to food.

Lavatory attendants, whose job had once earned them a much
sought-after extra litre of watery camp soup, no longer showed the
slightest interest in their profession. Nor was there anyone to cart the
stinking mud to its former use, manure, where vegetables grew and
were gobbled up by Aryan SS supermen. All we could do now was ask
for volunteers, who did eventually come forward, and the first problem
of freedom was solved.

Those who felt strong enough for it explored the countryside. After
a few days' relaxation, I dragged myself up early in the morning to join
the wanderers. The dusty path to a village nearby was thronged with
groups of shuffling ex-prisoners. Our spirits were high and the air was
filled with the smell of spring. There was much I wanted to do, but I
was still too weak. I hobbled along like some aged pilgrim.

Upon reaching the village square, we made for the water pump.
We put our heads under it and doused ourselves. Some, amid peals of
applause, stripped naked and dipped into the pond.

Then, for want of a suitable companion or any other youngsters for
that matter, I strolled along on my own. Observing things and being
inquisitive were hobbies of mine, and now that we had been liberated
I could concentrate on them without fear or disturbance.

We discovered that the town's population was frightened. They
moaned about being maltreated by us. If in their eyes the confiscation

of eggs, milk, butter and potatoes represented rough treatment, they were right. To feed the many sick among us, Buchenwald's kitchen badly needed fresh farm produce. We had to get it, even if it meant using threats.

There was certainly some truth in the fact that excessive force had been used against the German population around us, but I had never heard of murder. Bodies could only be seen at Buchenwald. So many survivors were dying of disease, exhaustion and malnutrition.

Down one of the deserted village paths came an old, sour-faced woman carrying a pail of water that was far too heavy for her. I was determined to exploit this opportunity to take my own revenge.

'Tell me,' I somewhat naïvely enquired, 'where does one get eggs around here?'

'*Da Kommen Sie zu Spaet, die sind alle schon weggestohlen. Mit Ihnen kann man ja reden, Sie sind ja selbst Deutscher*' ('You're too late; they are all stolen. With you, I can talk, you are German').

Her unexpectedly frank reply so astonished me that I completely forgot my desire for eggs. *Sie*, she had said to me. When I left Germany for the world of barbed wire, I had been a mere *Du*, a child. Now I was a *Sie*, a man. Moreover, she had put her trust in me because she saw me as a fellow countryman.

'No,' I said determinedly, 'I am no German; I am from Buchenwald.'

'*Ja, Sie sehen aber vertauenstwuerdig aus*' ('Yes, but you look trustworthy'). Tell me, why do they treat us so terribly? What have we simple countryfolk done to deserve that?'

'Nothing. You have not done anything. For eight years you have lived next to Buchenwald and merely looked on.'

'The SS, the Americans and your people have all plundered us.'

Complaints about anything and everything rained down upon me. I had to stop her.

'All right,' I interrupted. 'I am in a hurry. Give me that bucket; I'll carry it home for you.'

'*Danke, danke, Sie sind sehr anstaendig*' ('Thank you, thank you, you're very decent'). Following my encounter with the old lady it came to me that after all these years of hatred and oppression it was for me to decide what kind of man I would grow to be. Being a gentleman that day made me feel strong and proud. However, I had seen enough of the villagers.

Later, I met a German ex-prisoner who was also looking for food.

'It's disgusting,' he said. 'The whole village is besieging me with complaints. They said I should intervene for them. They all forget that, as a German, I know much more about Buchenwald than those foreign "comrades" they are complaining about. It was Buchenwald. They did know about it, those bastards.'

In a field on my way back to camp, I spotted a group of excited Russians and Poles. Curious, I joined them.

'What's going on here?'

Lying on the ground between them was a man dressed in a bedraggled uniform. '*Dolmetsch* (interpret), come on kid, translate for us.'

The huddled-up, filthy man was shaking with fear and whimpering: '*Italiano, Italiano kaput, kaput!*' He pretended not to know any German, but on hearing that I did, he tugged at his breast pocket and screamed, '*documento, documento*'.

A stained, sweat-drenched army paybook was pushed into my hands. It was from a German auxiliary unit; his nationality was given as *Italiener*. I told him that he was in the Buchenwald district, a territory that we ourselves administered prior to the American army taking over, and that he was under arrest. He must have understood little of my explanations.

When we arrived at the camp, he nearly fainted as he was led away by two armed escorts in prison garb. He might have deserved to be gored like any other fascist pig. But we were the proud victors now, and the young armed guards possessed soldierly discipline. He was taken to the barbed-wire cage to join officers, SS soldiers and Nazi officials who had been caught in hiding during the skirmishes or while still unaware of their defeat.

Our French comrades, whose government were sending transport to get them, had already started to leave for home. The rest of us were either transferred to the former SS barracks or to Buchenwald's main camp.

I was allocated to Block 29, the block of 'German Politicals'. One of the camp's oldest barracks, it had become a kind of 'hotel'. Its occupants, all veterans, some camp personages and other well-known personalities from pre-1933 days, were away a lot, either at the administration offices or on outside missions.

Newly acquired comforts included cupboards, clean blankets, books, stacks of news sheets from SHAEF (the Supreme Headquarters Allied Expeditionary Force) and useful 100-watt light bulbs.

When my block-mates came in for supper, they did so mainly to talk among themselves. It was only natural that they liked to hear their free voices after years of fear and suppression. They revealed many interesting things to me.

I discovered that the brains behind Buchenwald's resistance efforts had been a so-called International Camp Committee. Its pre-liberation members were mainly German and French left-wingers experienced in organising underground tactics. They had a secret arsenal of rifles, pistols, gas masks and binoculars. At the same moment that the famous white flag was hoisted, our force was equipped with machine-guns and mortars that had been previously stowed away, awaiting liberation. For years, the camp's resistance had stored weapons in preparation for an opportunity to fight back.

Now the committee was the supreme camp authority. Its heads represented all the various nationalities. The number of its armed guards ran into hundreds. We patrolled the countryside to round up former SS men and discover hidden Nazi stores. Trucks in search of supplies for the camp kitchen travelled as far as Erfurt and Jena.

The local population weren't eager to reveal their carefully concealed emergency stores. However, we searched woods and cellars until we found them. There was a whole chain of underground stores. One hide-out was a cave containing wine stolen from France. Another was stacked with tinned Hungarian chicken.

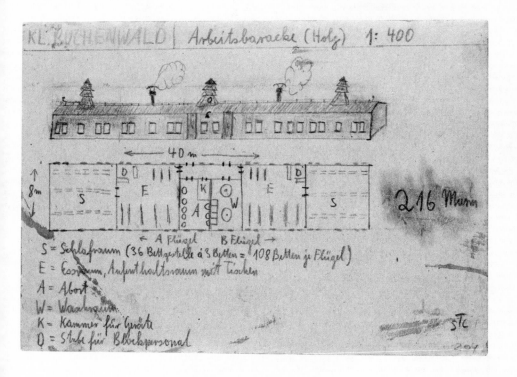

A BUCHENWALD WORKING BARRACK
After liberation I stayed in Block 29, a smaller
block of 216 men in the old camp.

We had heard that the hospital compound, which had now been taken over by Americans, was issuing noodle soup with milk. I liked milk and sweet things. Seeing soldiers from over the ocean greatly fascinated me. So, early the next day for fear of missing anything, I walked down to the sick blocks. I became aware of my improving walking pace, which was a sign of my returning health and strength. I eagerly joined the already-growing queue at the hospital kitchen and sat on the pavement to wait.

'You are early,' wisecracked someone from among the few in front of me. 'They don't come to work till eight, don't bring the milk till eight-thirty and don't start cooking till nine-thirty. If they get finished by ten, we'll be lucky. I know from experience.'

'But never mind, kid, it's worthwhile,' said another. 'It's made with butter, you know. And it's only supposed to be for the sick.'

Bored with waiting, I glanced over at the hospital gate, hoping to catch sight of something to stop the current boredom. I studied the lone American sentry as if I were his commanding officer – his high-laced boots, his tucked-in trouser legs, his slightly off-level ammunition belt, his fluttering brown tunic, his jolly face and his egg-shaped helmet. Then I heard the noise of engines. Racing down the roadway from the camp, chased by clouds of dust, came a few army ambulances.

'There they come,' cried the one who had seen it all before; 'it's eight now. In half an hour they'll bring the milk cans.'

The previously bored guard jumped to attention and saluted. The hospital yard was getting busy.

Time moved on in Buchenwald. The district administration had been taken over by the Americans, and the Buchenwald army disarmed.

Several Allied missions arrived to study the horrors of German concentration camps. They inspected the crematoria; saw the stacks of bluish emaciated bodies; visited laboratories where prisoners had been scalped to provide lampshades and beheaded to make shrunken miniatures. They learned about the mechanism of gas chambers, and

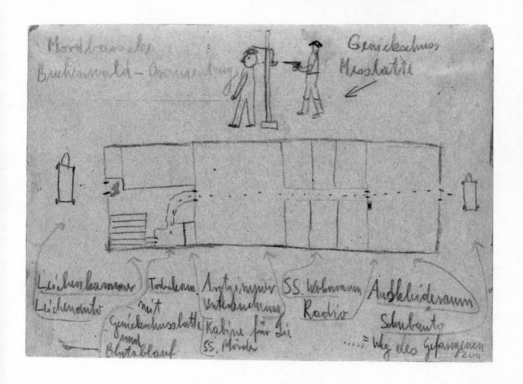

MURDER BARRACK
The Nazis had deceptive and disguised
mechanisms of murder.

were shown a height-measuring device with an adjustable hole in it for shooting unsuspecting prisoners through the head during a medical inspection.

The visiting delegations were shocked. Their conscience must have been shaken by these discoveries. They visited when the battle was over and won. Now their whole concept of Western civilisation was being challenged.

Where had all these eager humanitarians been in 1937 when Buchenwald was inaugurated? Even during our final struggle, eight years later, no effective aid had been given to us.

It had taken them 12 years to grasp the stark reality of the concentration camps, and four years to realise that Hitler's genocide against the Jews and many other 'inferior' races was genuine.

The Americans brought in the local German population to visit us.*
They were rounded up in Weimar and other towns, loaded onto trucks and assembled on the former rollcall square. They were addressed by an officer speaking through a loudspeaker.

Then they followed the loudspeaker van through Buchenwald and trudged past our shabby barracks as if on some pilgrimage or funeral. Some even looked as if it were a pleasant day out in the countryside for them.

A few girls, dressed in short skirts, giggled. They were too young to be vicious, I thought; they only lacked tact. What annoyed me were the Hitler-era police and railway officials' uniforms I saw. If their wearers had really felt ashamed of the Nazis, they would have discarded them. As it was, they had not even bothered to obliterate all the swastika markings.

We didn't like these guided sightseeing tours, and when some of us who thought them an insult threatened to attack them, they stopped.

Our nicest visitors were the American soldiers on leave. They arrived in hordes – young, happy and talkative. Above all, their pockets were bulging with goodies. The tall Yanks were loaded with chewing

---

* Historically, the Americans, who were deeply shocked at the horror of what they saw when they entered the camps, decided to bring the local population to see for themselves what had happened. It was to open their eyes to the atrocities.

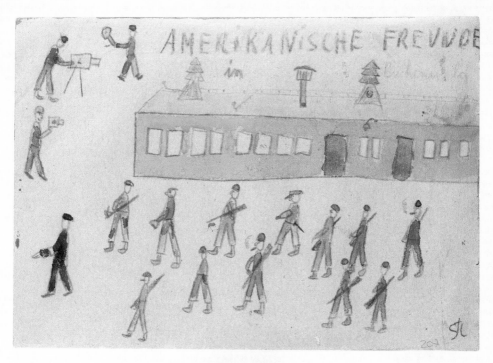

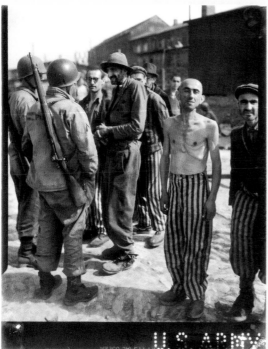

TOP: AMERICAN FRIENDS
The American GIs were generous and fascinating to us youngsters.

BOTTOM: Liberated prisoners from Buchenwald's 'little camp' talking to American soldiers.

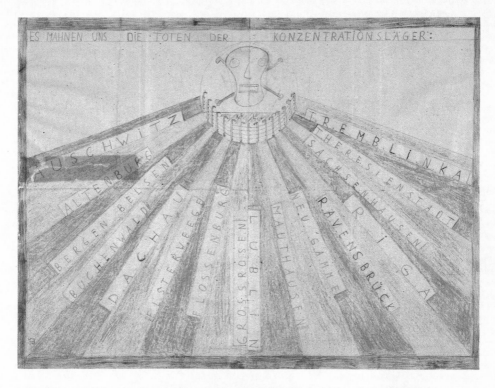

TOP: REMEMBER THE DEAD IN THE CONCENTRATION CAMPS Concentration and extermination camps, fuelled by hatred, where millions of people were systematically murdered.
BOTTOM: Citizens from Weimar are crowded around Buchenwald's crematorium courtyard. US soldiers confront them with the dead bodies piled up there. This was the first photo of Buchenwald to be published.

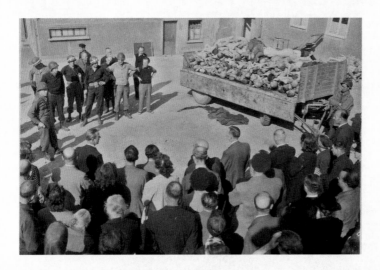

gum, chocolate, cigars, cigarettes, cameras and flashlights. They made
no secret of being generous. Eagerly clutching their cameras, they
invaded our sleeping quarters.

'Do you mind, chums? Just a little snapshot for the folks back
home.'

'With pleasure!' We lined up arm in arm and smiled. The room was
buzzing with talk about the front line, homes beyond the ocean, the
Allies, the Nazis and concentration camps.

'We've got to move on now,' called a soldier who had a peculiar
combination of sloping and curved stripes on his shirt sleeve. 'Who's
responsible for this room here?'

'I am,' said a worn-looking German intellectual, whose eagerness
to sit in a corner and absorb long-missed books had recently caused
him to be named room guardian entrusted with ladling out soup and
sweeping the floor.

'Okay, boys, empty them out.'

Onto the table dropped bars of chocolate, strips of chewing gum
and packets of cigarettes. They pushed some cigars into our room
steward's breast pocket.

'That's for you personally, for seeing that everyone gets his share.'

Once unknown and forgotten, Buchenwald seemed now to have
become the hub of the world. It was our world, a new world. That time
proved so interesting that the days ended far too quickly for us. We
prepared to return home. Overhead, day and night, hastening the end
of Hitler's Germany, hummed long trains of American supply planes.

In our block sat camp veterans drawing up reports on Nazi war crimes.

I discovered that the population of Buchenwald had once been
bigger than that of Weimar. The survivors amounted to 20,000.
Since 1937, 51,000 people* had died in Buchenwald. Another 15,000
comrades had perished in its subsidiary camps. The many thousands
who were put into the transports that left the day before liberation –

---

* At the time of liberation, this was the officially recorded number. Over the years since liberation, official
numbers have grown considerably.

which we had escaped from – had been stoned, shot and massacred.

After we occupied the administration offices, there had been a phone call from Weimar for the SS Commander. 'The requested platoon of flame throwers has arrived,' it said, 'and is awaiting transportation.'

We did not want to forget. On the contrary, we felt an urge to document what we had witnessed, set it down on paper and to tell people about it. If we who had experienced it, I reasoned, did not reveal the bitter truth, people simply would not believe the extent of the Nazis' evil. I wanted to share, not just the horrors but our lives, the day-to-day events and our struggle to survive.

Less than a week after Buchenwald was liberated, my roommates brought in documentary material found from the abandoned SS offices and officers' barracks. From these valuable documents I could now copy plans, maps and lists.* Too weak to wander around on my own, I asked my grown-up colleagues to find some paper and pencils for me. Armed with a stack of postcard-sized swastika-imprinted questionnaires of the Nazi party and 7 short coloured pencils, I embarked on sketching camp life.

I recalled my time in Auschwitz where I first had the urge to record camp life. There, using torn-off scraps from paper sacks,† bits of charcoal and a pencil that I had found, I started to make lists and draw. Anxious that these rough black-and-white sketches would survive, I hid them in my straw sleeping sack. When we were hastily evacuated from Auschwitz, I had to leave them behind. But these images stuck in my mind. And now finally, as a free man, I started to recreate them.

Over the proceeding days and weeks, I drew and drew. I started by outlining each drawing with my pencils and later on added water colours that I received from one of the American soldiers who took an interest in my work.

I added writings, maps and lists. Scenes of days gone by became vivid again – the arrival, the selection, the punishments, the food, the

---

* One of the people who helped Thomas document life in the camp was the Austrian journalist and historian Eugen Kogon.[15] Kogon was busy collecting and documenting camp information – he shared some of these findings with Thomas.

† Fifty-kilogram cement sacks that were made from seven layers of paper.

diseases, the endless rows of fencing, the work, the rollcalls, the winter, the revolts, the gallows, the evacuation, the *Katyushas* and so much more. The experience of 22 months of my life in three concentration camps was just waiting to burst out from my restless brain.

Depicting the dark, sad, colourless life in the camps in all the seven colours of the rainbow made my heart rejoice and spurred me on. Those creations, in honour and memory of my friends and comrades, became another precious victory.

Buchenwald's cinema hall held crowds again. Usually, they came to see glamorous American Technicolor films, but one day they congregated for something entirely different. A Jewish remembrance service was held. An American army chaplain, a rabbi reared in far-away Brooklyn, issued small pocket-size prayer books. On either side of the improvised altar stood tall, white candles, behind them brown-uniformed Jewish-American servicemen. Filing into the hall, thoughtful and heavy-hearted, came the survivors of Europe's Jewry. Many had nearly forgotten their historic heritage. But this was a day of remembrance. We all wanted to greet and thank those who had fought to liberate us. We all had lost families to pray for.

It was 1 May 1945. Former inmates who had settled in surrounding towns and villages returned to celebrate with us. Our dirty, old barracks were covered in a sea of fresh white slogans.

The Russian compound looked like a fairground. Its streets were hung with garlands and blocks vied with each other for the best hand-painted picture of Stalin. The prize-winning portrait measured 2 metres square and hung above the Russians' reading room flanked by flowers, a bald Lenin and a bearded Marx.

German blocks displayed the proud notice 'We Are Coming Back' and pictures of Breitscheid and Thaelmann.* Other banners read: 'We

---

* One was the leader of the Social Democrats, the other of the Communists; they both perished in Buchenwald.

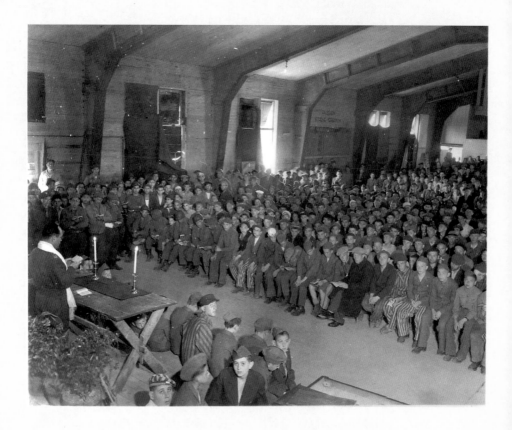

A Jewish memorial service was held in
the cinema barrack for the survivors of
Buchenwald concentration camp.

Remember Our 51,000 Dead'; 'We Thank Our Allies'; and the short but forceful 'Nevermore!'

Our Spanish comrades hardly had enough room around their sole block for all they wanted to say. 'You are going home, what about us?' they painted on its wall. 'Fascism is Not Dead Yet, Franco Lives!' 'Now Franco is Enemy Number One!' 'We shall not give up!' *No pasaran!* ('They shall not pass!')

My roommates hoped I would join them for the May Day Parade. They showed me a stack of boards painted with the names of small German provinces.

'There are no survivors from these provinces, so someone else will have to carry them. What about you? You are tall and would look impressive marching on your own.'

I grabbed one of the boards with the name of a province and was guided to my place in the marching column.

Then we marched off towards the gate.

We assembled on the camp square, each column behind the flag of its homeland – Poles, Czechs, Russians, Dutch and Spaniards as well as many more. In front of us, near the fence, was a huge stage, marked 1 May 1945. On it stood a boarded trapezium painted with the colours of England, Russia and America, and decorated with diagonally spaced portraits of Churchill, Stalin and Roosevelt. From high-up poles, gently stroking the liberated clear blue sky, fluttered all the colourful flags of Europe.

To begin with, we saw a symbolic play about Buchenwald, including its dark past and liberation. Afterwards, the platform was filled with guests from abroad and we listened to speeches. We paid tribute to our dead, thanked the Allies and affirmed our solidarity. We also pledged ourselves never to forget our common suffering. 'The remnants of our suppressors and their supporters must be brought to justice.' Our applause was powerful and enthusiastic.

Then the band started playing and, one by one, the columns marched past the saluting base. This square, that had for eight years of daily rollcalls been filled with helpless prisoners with the Nazi flag towering over the entrance gate, now held triumphant crowds parading with the proud banners of their homelands. Its vast expanse of asphalt, which had once heard the moans of thousands and thousands trudging to their deaths, now resounded with the victorious marching steps of the survivors. Countless striped blue-white trouser legs flapped in unison. The band struck up anthem after anthem. Hundreds of red May Day banners were raised.

Finally, it was our turn. The big red flag in front of me that had been making a nuisance of itself by incessantly tickling me on the neck was lifted up at last.

There were wide empty spaces between the marchers, to represent those who had not survived to join us. Someone intoned '*Brueder, zur Sonne, zur Freiheit*' ('Brothers, to the sun, to freedom'). My little neighbour wiped his eyes.

Soon we would all be heading home, I thought. If we had no home, we would be looking for a new one. Some of us would become ordinary working people, whose past no one cared about. Others would return to become members of parliament or even ministers. That impressive May Day at Buchenwald, however, would turn into a cherished memory – something we would be reminded of year after year.

Our column approached the guest platform. We marched neatly and stiffly. To my left, on the flag-surrounded platform, I spotted a row of army officers – Americans, Russians, French, English and others. When we drew near, they saluted. I, the haggard, shabby bearer of a little painted board with the name of some obscure province on it, I, the forgotten youngster who for years had starved in concentration camps, was being saluted! My cheeks flushed with excitement. Then a newsreel camera was turned on me.

I had stopped travelling to Weimar and instead I walked about the camp. I liked listening to the radio, looking at books and newspapers, and trying to impress the Americans with my English.

One day on one of my trips around camp, I was passing the elderly inmates who spent their time sitting and talking to each other, when I noticed someone young among them. He sat in the sun daydreaming.

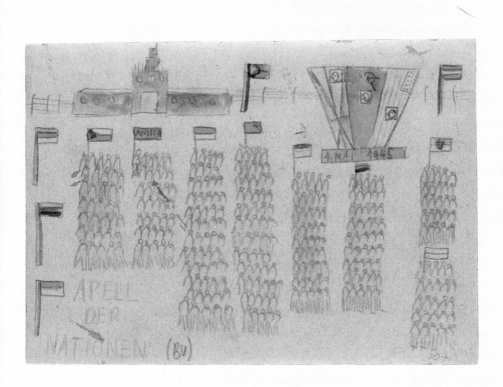

THE ROLLCALL OF THE NATIONS
1 May 1945 heralded the start of a new life
for me.

I bent down to see his face. It was long, angular and scarily thin. His sharp, prominent nose looked familiar.

I woke him up and we recognised each other and shook hands warmly. It was Gert, the dark one, a bricklaying school friend from nearly two years ago. He had just been released from hospital. I was so glad to see him. I needed suitable companions and Gert was more than merely an old friend.

Buchenwald had become a much happier place. In the evening, we all got together to dance, drink and mingle until the early morning.

The final collapse of Nazism was expected any hour now.
The week after May Day was crowded with farewell celebrations. One by one, the different nationalities took leave of their camp comrades and left for home.

A friend invited me to come to Block 45, for the Austrian farewell party. 'It's just going to be a social affair,' he said, 'without speeches, without pledges, but with plenty of fun.' I had no idea how to dance, but I went, mainly because I found out that there would be cakes. It was a room up on the second floor, complete with fiddlers, a jazz band, beer, Chinese lanterns, leather-trousered mountaineers, and Americans.

As it grew late, people partied hard and started to dance. I sipped some beer and contemplated heading to bed, before hearing shouts of 'Bravo, bravo!'

They cleared the floor and onto it stepped two Gypsy girls who had been persuaded to dance. I jerked myself up and watched. These two young girls turned and twisted to the heady strains of Gypsy music. I was transfixed.

Deep in thought, I continued to watch them. Someone crossed the floor towards the stack of beer bottles. It was a boy wearing a suit that was too big on him. How funny, I thought.

Then it suddenly dawned on me that he seemed familiar. I recognised and called out to him. *Had I drunk too much?* No, he also appeared to know me. He came over to shake my hand. It was Berger, 'Little Berger', our favourite Gypsy youngster from the bricklaying school. He told me that his fellow Austrians were looking after him and were willing to take him to their hometown.

It was late already, and I left. I was still thinking of Little Berger. *Would his friends really take care of him? Would he get the future we had always so anxiously wished for him?*

Our Russian campmates gave their farewell performance in the huge former SS theatre. When they all started singing, the hall vibrated with the songs of the Red Army – the song about the cavalry, the air force, the *Katyushas* and the partisans. I too vibrated. Wandering through my mind came all those Russian youngsters with whom we had been secretly singing these same songs in Block 7a. What had happened to all those lads who, while these tunes struggled against the dark, silent Auschwitz nights, had lain on their bunks dreaming of liberation?

My former companions of Block 66, the Jewish youngsters from Poland, also arranged an artistic evening. It was in Yiddish. Stealing the show, however, was the 'Dance of the Machines'. It showed shadows of working youngsters against the background of a red screen. The shadows toiled in unison, then sang, 'But machines have no hearts, know no pain and understand no jokes.'

Those who watched could not help being impressed. It was plain to see that these youngsters were striving for a future of freedom and security. Never again would they agree to being neglected and kept in ignorance. A new world was in the making, and these lads had broken with the old one.

It was 8 May 1945; Armistice with Germany. The war in Europe was over. Fascism and all it stood for had surrendered.

Someone turned the radio set on to search for news. It was filled with the peals of victory. There was jubilation everywhere: London giving the V sign; the singing of the rousing Marseillaise; the chimes of the Kremlin; Berliners rising from the ruins to celebrate.

As for me, I turned about on my pillow and contemplated. It was peace. What would we make of it? Soon I would be 16. Before long I, too, would have my say. Then I dozed off, dreaming about the future.

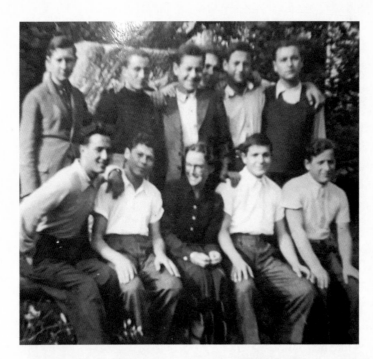

TOP: Recovering in Zug, Switzerland, with my fellow concentration camp survivors during the summer of 1945. I am standing second from the right.
BOTTOM: October 1945 in Zug, Switzerland. Turning 16 and soon to be reunited with Father in London.

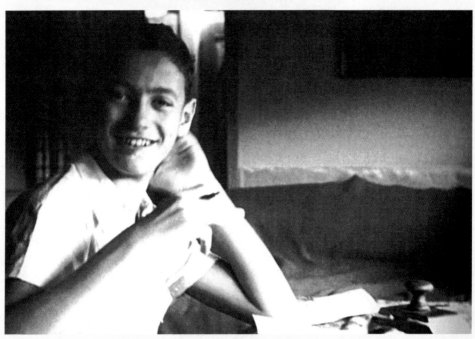

EPILOGUE

After Buchenwald was liberated, I spent another two months in the camp, recovering my health, working on my drawing project and enjoying my newly found freedom.

The huge undertaking to repatriate thousands and thousands of people from many different countries had started and the time had come to make decisions about my own future.

Various options were open to me. Along with 400 other teenage boys, all concentration camp survivors, I chose to accept the invitation of the Swiss government to spend a period of six months in their country. Switzerland, with its beautiful alpine countryside and history of keeping its freedom during war time, greatly appealed to me.

The summer of 1945, on the beautiful Zugerberg Mountain above Zug, was like heaven on earth to me, and it offered me a precious time of quiet, blessed recuperation. There I found kindness that I had never thought possible. Switzerland and her people looked after me extremely well. The Liebetraus, the kindest family in Rheinfelden, were my foster family during my stay, and their son, Hans-Rüdi, became a close friend.

While I was regaining my strength, a dream came true. With the help of the Red Cross, my father and I managed to find each other.

On 17 November 1945, I flew to England, thrilled by my first ever aeroplane ride, and excited by the longed-for meeting with my father in London.

Six long years of separation and war had changed us so much that it took both of us a moment to recognise each other. Papa's hair had gone grey, and I was no longer the little nine-year-old boy he had kissed goodbye at Berlin's Potsdamer railway station in the summer of 1939. Now, as we hugged each other at last, it occurred to me that I was recovering a part of myself that I hadn't really expected to regain. All I wanted was for those cherished moments, in that warm embrace, to stay with me for ever.

As one fervent dream came true, my most precious one was shattered. Mother was never found. She had perished in Auschwitz in summer 1944, sometime after I had got her last note.

Now it was time to reclaim my youth and gradually become a man in the new world that had endless options waiting to be chosen. I lived in England for the next four years and during that time I gained an education, graduated from high school and obtained a college degree in engineering.

Father remarried and three months after my 20th birthday I got the most surprising and wonderful present of my life: a baby sister! Dear little Judith made me a proud and happy big brother – a treasured title I could not have even imagined in my wildest dreams.

Time marched on and big decisions were on the horizon. Across the ocean a new country was born, fighting for her very existence. A deep-seated desire that had first taken root way back when I was a prisoner in Auschwitz singing the patriotic 'Song of the Valley' along with my Jewish comrades now became stronger than ever.

I felt it was my turn and duty to take part in the rebuilding of the only home we Jewish people had ever had, the one we had been dreaming about for 2,000 years. Although leaving my family and England was one of the hardest decisions of my life, I felt passionately that my destiny and future lay in Israel.

In July 1950, I arrived on the shores of Haifa and Israel became my home. Soon afterwards, I started to work as a building engineer and architect, and for the next 60 years I took part in building houses and settlements, and multiple construction projects around the country. The very same skills I had learned as a young boy in the bricklaying school at Auschwitz, which had been aimed at turning me into a builder of the Third Reich's empire of death, now served to help in the rebuilding of the new Jewish state. That was my private little revenge and another victory.

Like all other Israeli young men, I took my share in its defence and served as an officer in the Engineering Corps. One night I was sent to command a group of soldiers on guard duty in 'the valley' – the very one we had sung about in the concentration camps. When lying exhausted, barely alive on the bunks of Auschwitz, singing about the brave guard of the valley, I could never have imagined the day would come when I would be that guard. I lived, and that song became real. The heart of that young boy from Auschwitz, still a vivid part of me, swelled with pride.

An unexpected surprise in 1981 changed my life. Since 1958, my written testimony of the Holocaust had made its own very modest way into the world through a pocketbook, *Youth in Chains*, published under a pseudonym.

I went on with my life. Although I had the tattoo on my arm, its meaning clear, most people around me did not know about my book and had not seen my drawings. But attending the first Survivors' Convention that took place in Jerusalem that year changed things. As I arrived, I looked through the list of participants and found a familiar name. It was Gert Beigel! 'Saucy Gert', my good and loyal friend from 'Little Berlin' – he was alive! Our meeting was more than exciting, and no eye was left dry around us that day. I gave him the book. The next morning, Gert came to me and said, 'I read the book all night from cover to cover. Every word you wrote is true.' Having found dear Gert alive after all those years, and getting his confirmation that it really was the true story of us all, inspired me to become an active Holocaust witness. That became my main mission in life.

Since then my testimony has been published in various ways and languages. Up to the present day, I talk to audiences from around the world, answering endless questions about our life in the concentration camps and the Second World War. My family, another sweet victory of mine, have become actively involved in passing on the story and I hope future generations will continue to do so too.

My drawings are in safekeeping at the Yad Vashem museum

in Jerusalem and, together with my books and films, they mean a great deal to me. They hold the images and stories of my long-lost comrades, giving them the recognition they deserve and preserving their individual identities.

My testimony reveals a cruel and vicious world that had been planned to stay hidden – but history's justice exposed it all.

However, more than that, it tells about *life* in the camps. The way we prisoners stayed alive and kept our spirits going, grasping every possible piece of humanity and kindness within ourselves and others in the midst of such brutality.

Among all of this was the unique story of us – youth – we who had to grow up in the camps, shaping our identities, cherishing the power of unity, friendship and hope.

It became my role to tell the story and I am fulfilling it in memory of my comrades. Their stories are mine. My victories are theirs.

This testimony wishes to tell coming generations about the past so that they will know exactly what happened and comprehend the deep meaning of it. Mindful of this, hopefully people will make wise decisions and create a better life and future for everyone, everywhere.

That was our dream. That can be our legacy.

Thomas Geve, 2020

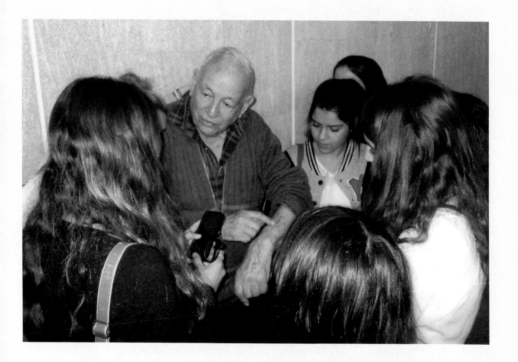

'It became my role to tell the story' – at a school
tour connecting with the young generation.

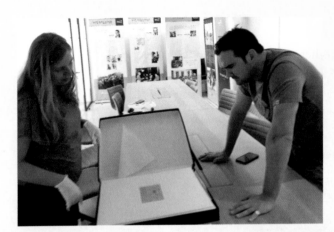

TOP: I had the privilege of seeing Thomas' original drawings at the Yad Vashem museum in Jerusalem. His attention to detail with only the size of a postcard to draw on is remarkable.
BOTTOM: Thomas and I discussing his experiences of life in the camps, Herzliya, July 2019.

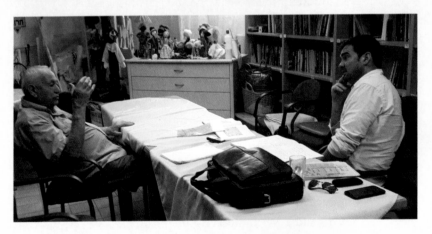

NOTE FROM
CHARLES INGLEFIELD

I live in Zug, a small town on the outskirts of Zurich, Switzerland. Not a lot happens here other than the activities of a busy business community and weekend escapes into the beautiful Alpine countryside. In March 2019, a client handed me a flyer on an exhibition at the Burg Museum. This exhibition was called the 'The Children of Buchenwald'.

This was where I first heard the name of Thomas Geve. On top of Zugerberg Mountain, the Felsenegg Youth Home housed 107 children liberated from the concentration camps, and Thomas was one of them. During the summer of 1945, in these beautiful surroundings, children could convalesce and start the long road back to recovery. Intrigued, I went onto Google and found numerous references to Thomas, but also his unique drawings. With the Zug connection, I wanted to learn more about this man and his sketches.

Yifat, Thomas's daughter, replied to my introductory email and, in July 2019, I had the honour of meeting both Thomas and Yifat in Herzliya. We discussed his drawings and what compelled him to put pencil to paper. I learned about his remarkable story of surviving 22 months across three concentrations camps before being liberated, aged 15, from Buchenwald. I saw his drawings, kept under lock and key in Jerusalem's Yad Vashem museum, and heard his testimony, which he still gives to audiences from around the world.

Thomas had already published two editions of his testimony in the 1950s and 1980s. They are both excellent reads, and therefore taking on the task of updating his book was a huge challenge. When I watched events around the 75th anniversary of the liberation of Auschwitz in January 2020, the significance of Thomas's testimony as a survivor really hit home to me. I read the second edition, *Guns and Barbed Wire*, many times and had countless conversations with the family before coming up with a direction that would keep his story the same and also keep Thomas' unique descriptions, style and 75-year testimony intact. My role was to transition Thomas' testimony to today's readers. The language and the structure were revised but it was Thomas's provision of new information that really helped shape this edition. We had more relevant detail to insert into the text and to add as footnotes, as well as the opportunity to include more of his drawings.

What became familiar to me was the positivity and 'good' that Thomas found on the frequent occasions where his life and those of others were threatened. Thomas and his companions faced constant and extreme adversity, yet, each time, a kind intervention from someone or something pulled him through. No matter how desperate the situation was for him and his fellow inmates, Thomas still found a way out. This helped me to portray Thomas's story as more than a book focused solely on the horrors of the Holocaust. Of course, we have to tell Thomas's account of what he saw and experienced. There were many dreadful scenarios, and issues of life and death were a reality on a daily basis. But there is also so much hope, positivity and *identifying* with kindness that shines through in Thomas's story. He goes to the very bottom of what a human being – and Thomas was barely a teenager when he first arrived at Auschwitz-Birkenau – endured. Time and again I found myself being pushed and pulled emotionally when reading through his account of facing up to near-death experiences but somehow getting through. Despite all of this, he still believed in the *good* of people. Criminals, communists, fascists, Gypsy and Romany cultures all showed him a path through kindness and support – people who he would have likely ignored or avoided.

You have read his story and seen his drawings; now you will have to make up your own mind on what you take from this. This is an eye-witness account of historic events. It is also rare to have both text and drawing to illustrate this notorious event in world history.

Thomas's drawings have, for the 75 years following liberation, become a powerful and very accessible means of engaging in the truth about not only Auschwitz-Birkenau but also Gross-Rosen and Buchenwald. I have often thought about why these drawings affect people, including me, so strongly. Perhaps it is that they were drawn by a young boy, simply recounting what he saw, without an adult's political agenda. Historians and experts have commented on the accuracy of them. For me, it is the level of detail. The drawings are small and at first glance so simple, and yet their message is frank, brutal and enormous. Many of these drawings are presented in this book.

The Boy Who Drew Auschwitz represents Thomas's words and it has been my life's privilege to be involved with Thomas, his family and his story.

Charles Inglefield, June 2020

BIOGRAPHICAL NOTES

Please note that the information on the names below is based on primary sources of Holocaust facts and information. These records may be further updated in the future.

1. Berta Cohn, née Goetze (Thomas's mother), was born in 1906. She arrived at Auschwitz together with Thomas on 29 June 1943. Her prisoner number was 47542. As a prisoner she worked for some time at the Union factory. Berta helped the underground organisation as a translator. Thomas last heard from her in June 1944. She perished in the Holocaust.

2. Dr Erich Cohn (Thomas's father) was born in 1896. He found refuge in England in August 1939. During the years of war, he served as a doctor to the British Navy. He died in London in 1951.

3. Dr Julius Goetze and Hulda Goetze (Berta's parents). Julius died in March 1942 in Berlin. Hulda was deported from Berlin on Transport 1/90 from Berlin to Theresienstadt ghetto on 18 March 1943 and perished there in June 1944.

4. Ruth Seidler, née Goetze (Berta's sister), born in 1912. She married Alfred Seidler (who also perished in the Holocaust) and was deported on Transport 36 from Berlin to Auschwitz-Birkenau on 12 March 1943. She perished in the Holocaust.

5. Irma Cohn (Erich's sister), born in 1894, was deported from Beuthen to Auschwitz on 20 May 1942 together with Magda Breit (housekeeper). Irma perished in the Holocaust.

6. Magda Breit, born in 1878 in Breslau. She took care of Thomas's grandfather Josef Cohn and stayed on as the housekeeper when he died. Magda was deported from Beuthen to Auschwitz on 20 May 1942 together with Irma Cohn. Magda perished in the Holocaust.

7. Wolfgang Kopper was sent to the notorious Hadamar Psychiatric Hospital known as the 'House of Shutters' located in Hessen. Thousands of children were murdered as part of the T-4 euthanasia programme. He was one of them.

8. Werner Jacobsohn survived the Holocaust and later emigrated to America. Thomas reconnected with him and they were in touch for many years. Werner died in 2019.

9. Eva-Ruth Lohde, born in 1929, was first sent to Theresienstadt ghetto on 30 June 1943 and then from there to Auschwitz on 15 May 1944. She was murdered on the same day.

10. Lotte (Charlotte) Lohde, née Veile, Eva-Ruth's mother, was sent together with Eva-Ruth to Theresienstadt ghetto on 30 June 1943 and from there to Auschwitz on 15 May 1944. She perished in the Holocaust.

11. Sally Klapper perished in Auschwitz-Birkenau.

12. Gert Beigel survived the Holocaust. He and Thomas met up at a survivors' conference held in Jerusalem in 1981 and kept in touch (see Epilogue).

13. One of the members of the underground who helped the connection between Thomas and his mother, Berta – at great personal risk – was Józef Cyrankiewicz, who later became Poland's prime minister.

14. Leo Jacob Voorzanger was born in Amsterdam, the Netherlands, in 1911. He was transported to Dachau and murdered on 1 March 1945.

15. Eugen Kogon was imprisoned for six years in Buchenwald and survived. Years later he wrote one of the most important books on concentration camps, *Der SS-Staat*.

ACKNOWLEDGEMENTS

We, Thomas Geve and Charles Inglefield, would like to thank the following for their valuable contributions to this book:

Yad Vashem World Holocaust Remembrance Center (Jerusalem, Israel)
Eliad Moreh-Rosenberg (Curator & Art Department Director Museums Division)
Michal Feiner-Rosental (Collection Supervisor)

Arolsen Archives (Bad Arolsen, Germany)
Martin Kriwet (Reference Services)

The State Museum Auschwitz-Birkenau (Oświęcim, Poland)
Dr Wojciech Płosa (Head of Archives)

Buchenwald and Mittelbau-Dora Memorials Foundation (Buchenwald, Germany)
Sabine Stein (Head of Archives, Memorial Foundation)
Rikola-Gunnar Lüttgenau (Head of Strategic Communications and PR)
Holm Kirsten (Head of Museology and Historical Collection)

Stephen D. Smith PhD
Finci-Viterbi Executive Director Chair USC Shoah Foundation and UNESCO Chair on Genocide Education

HarperCollins Publishers (London, England)
With special thanks to Ed Faulkner, Kelly Ellis and Sarah Hammond for their support, belief and guidance in taking this book from concept through to delivery; James Empringham for his design; Sarah Burke and Monica Green in Production; Sarah Davies and the Rights team; everyone in Sales, Marketing and Publicity for their support. Thanks also to Nick Fawcett, our copyeditor, for his observant eye.

I, Thomas, would also like to give my sincere thanks to:

Charles, for his unique partnership and special role. My heartfelt gratitude goes to him for his unstinting enthusiasm, vision and tremendous dedication, which touched my heart and made this new edition come true.

Yifat, my daughter, and Judith, my sister, for taking good care of my words and drawings with love and devotion.

Let me also take this opportunity to say a big thank you to all the people who actively supported and helped me bring out my testimony in various ways throughout the years. With special thanks to:

> The helpers at The Art Department, Europe Department and others at Yad Vashem World Holocaust Remembrance Center, Jerusalem, Israel
>
> The helpers at Buchenwald Memorial Site, Germany
>
> Dr Wilhelm Roesing, the producer of the film *Nothing but life*, and the Roesing family, Germany
>
> Agnès Triebel, France
>
> Elisabeth Marquart, Germany
>
> Lior Ziv, my legal adviser and nephew, Israel
>
> My dear supportive family

I, Charles, would also like to thank the following:

James Heffron for his invaluable support and expertise throughout this project.

My wife, Jen, and to Molly and Max, for your amazing support and patience.

Matilda and her team at Kahawa café in Zug.

Finally, Thomas and Yifat: what a journey it has been and what a privilege for me to be involved. Thank you.

INDEX